I0130607

"This excellent, multi-authored guide to group therapy is written in a clear, accessible and singular voice. Focused on enhancing the capacity of frontline practitioners to use group therapy effectively in a range of clinical settings, the book offers much to those who are beginning to work with therapy groups, and it is also a comprehensive resource for those with more substantial experience. This book meets a very important need in our field, promoting the delivery of high-quality care."

– Molyn Leszcz, MD, FRCPC, CGP, DFAGPA; President, The American Group Psychotherapy Assn; and Professor of Psychiatry, University of Toronto

"Great on theory and how-to for group leaders. Drawing from Swedish group analysts as well as Yalom and Agazarian, the authors' integrative approach is essential reading for new and experienced group leaders."

– Susan Gantt, Chair, Systems-Centered Training and Research Institute

"This will become a first-reference book at all levels of training. Practitioners will be grateful across the field and in many parts of the world. Written by a team of eight experienced clinicians, it is fluent, accessible and applied. It provides a thorough and lucid guide for practitioners in a characteristic Scandinavian voice – temperate and inclusive – that assembles the contesting factions of a wide field and their histories in a measured, authoritative, focussed, coherent text. Their account of Focussed Group Therapy is an original contribution that will be of value to all practitioners."

– John Schlapobersky, Institute of Group Analysis, London

Why Group Therapy Works and How to Do It

This book describes how group treatment offers a unique opportunity for group members to learn and to change as they interact with other group members.

The group structure presents a social microcosm of relationships that people who seek psychotherapeutic treatment find problematic in their private and public lives. In groups, the participants can observe each other, provide feedback to each other, and practice change strategies. In short, group treatment has a powerful healing and supportive function. Based on the authors' many years of education and experience in academia, the private and public sectors, specific guidance is offered to group leaders on participation, organization, and communication in group treatment. The authors describe the history and characteristics of group treatment, how to organize a treatment group, the roles and responsibilities of the group leader, methods of group treatment, and typical responses of participants. Given its purpose and methodology, this book takes an original perspective on group treatment aimed ultimately at improving healing processes in healthcare and social care.

This book will provide a helpful introduction and guide for a range of professionals who work in primary healthcare, company healthcare, somatic care, psychiatric and social care, and the non-profit sector.

Christer Sandahl is a licensed psychologist, licensed psychotherapist, and professor of Social and Behavioural Science at the Medical Management Centre, Karolinska Institutet, Stockholm, Sweden.

Hjördis Nilsson Ahlin is an occupational therapist, a licensed psychotherapist, a group analyst, and a supervisor of psychiatric groups.

Catharina Asklin-Westerdahl is a licensed clinical psychologist, licensed psychotherapist, group analyst, and team and organizational consultant.

Mats Björling, BSc, is a licensed psychotherapist, group psychotherapist, and supervisor in private practice.

Anna Malmquist Saracino, BSW, is a licensed psychotherapist, group analyst, and psychotherapy supervisor.

Lena Wennlund, BSW, is a licensed psychotherapist, group analyst, and psychotherapy supervisor.

Ulf Åkerström is a licensed psychologist, licensed psychotherapist, and specialist in clinical psychology.

Ann Örhammar is a registered nurse, licensed psychotherapist, group analyst, and psychotherapy supervisor.

The New International Library of Group Analysis (NILGA)
Series Editor: Earl Hopper

Drawing on the seminal ideas of British, European and American group analysts, psychoanalysts, social psychologists and social scientists, the books in this series focus on the study of small and large groups, organisations and other social systems, and on the study of the transpersonal and transgenerational sociality of human nature. NILGA books will be required reading for the members of professional organisations in the field of group analysis, psychoanalysis and related social sciences. They will be indispensable for the "formation" of students of psychotherapy, whether they are mainly interested in clinical work with patients or in consultancy to teams and organisational clients within the private and public sectors.

Recent titles in the series include:

Why Group Therapy Works and How to Do It
A Guide for Health and Social Care Professionals
By Christer Sandahl, Hjördis Nilsson Ahlin, Catharina Asklin-Westerdahl, Mats Björling, Anna Malmquist Saracino, Lena Wennlund, Ulf Åkerström and Ann Örhammar

The Art and Science of Working Together
Practising Group Analysis in Teams and Organisations
Edited by Christine Thornton

Dream Telling, Relations, and Large Groups
New Developments in Group Analysis
By Robi Friedman

Group Analysis
Working with Staff, Teams and Organizations
Edited by David Vincent and Aleksandra Novakovic

Why Group Therapy Works and How to Do It

A Guide for Health and Social Care Professionals

Christer Sandahl, Hjördis Nilsson Ahlin, Catharina Asklin-Westerdahl, Mats Björling, Anna Malmquist Saracino, Lena Wennlund, Ulf Åkerström and Ann Örhammar

Routledge
Taylor & Francis Group

NEW YORK AND LONDON

First published 2021
by Routledge
2 Park Square, Milton Park, Abingdon, Oxon OX14 4RN

and by Routledge
52 Vanderbilt Avenue, New York, NY 10017

Routledge is an imprint of the Taylor & Francis Group, an informa business

© 2021 Christer Sandahl, Hjördis Nilsson Ahlin, Catharina Asklin-Westerdahl, Mats Björling, Anna Malmquist Saracino, Lena Wennlund, Ulf Åkerström and Ann Örhammar

The right of Christer Sandahl, Hjördis Nilsson Ahlin, Catharina Asklin-Westerdahl, Mats Björling, Anna Malmquist Saracino, Lena Wennlund, Ulf Åkerström and Ann Örhammar to be identified as authors of this work has been asserted by them in accordance with sections 77 and 78 of the Copyright, Designs and Patents Act 1988.

All rights reserved. No part of this book may be reprinted or reproduced or utilised in any form or by any electronic, mechanical, or other means, now known or hereafter invented, including photocopying and recording, or in any information storage or retrieval system, without permission in writing from the publishers.

Trademark notice: Product or corporate names may be trademarks or registered trademarks, and are used only for identification and explanation without intent to infringe.

British Library Cataloguing-in-Publication Data
A catalogue record for this book is available from the British Library

Library of Congress Cataloging-in-Publication Data
A catalog record has been requested for this book

ISBN: 9780367531904 (hbk)
ISBN: 9780367439682 (pbk)
ISBN: 9781003080848 (ebk)

Typeset in Times New Roman
by Swales & Willis Ltd, Exeter, Devon, UK

In memory of Susanna Bergom Larsson, Olov Dahlin and Torsten Sjövall

Translation from the Swedish edition (*Gruppens potential. Att leda och utveckla gruppbehandling*, Stockholm: Natur och Kultur, 2014): Marcia Halvorsen

Contents

Authors

Ulf Åkerström is a licensed psychologist, licensed psychotherapist, and specialist in clinical psychology. Ulf works with leaders and managers with a focus on work and leadership teams, and with education and organizational development. He has also worked as a clinical psychologist in psychiatric and social services, and as a manager for family counselling and child and adolescent psychiatry. Ulf has also conducted research in the field of work psychology.

Catharina Asklin-Westerdahl is a licensed clinical psychologist, a licensed psychotherapist, a group psychotherapist, and an organizational consultant. Catharina has worked for many years with individuals, families, and groups in the areas of social welfare, education, healthcare, and psychiatry in Sweden and in England. As an organizational health consultant, she has worked with groups, managers, and their change processes at various organizations in the private and public sectors, including government entities, various institutions, and the Swedish Church. In her current private practice, she consults with groups on issues related to psychotherapy, supervision, and education.

Mats Björling is a psychotherapist, group psychotherapist, and supervisor. Mats began his professional career as a social worker advising drug abusers in Stockholm, Sweden. For a number of years, he was the director of an outpatient substance abuse clinic in Stockholm, Sweden. Mats was also an assistant investigator for a significant investigation into substance abuse and treatment that the Swedish Social Service System conducted in cooperation with the City of Stockholm. Currently, Mats is in private practice as a psychotherapist and supervisor in the areas of substance addiction and crisis/trauma processing.

Anna Malmquist Saracino is a licensed psychotherapist, group psychotherapist, and psychotherapist supervisor. Anna has developed a group-based, integrative relationship treatment for infants and parents with attachment difficulties within the Child and Adolescent Psychiatry Service in Stockholm, Sweden. She is a member of an infant and early childhood psychiatry team. In private practice Anna works with psychotherapy, education, and supervision. She is a specialist in infant, early childhood, and parenthood psychiatry. Currently she is studying the infant-to-infant interaction in infant–parent groups.

Hjördis Nilsson Ahlin is an occupational therapist, a licensed psychotherapist, a group psychotherapist, and a psychotherapy supervisor. Hjördis has many years of experience working with psychiatric therapy groups. She has also supervised and trained teams and various professional groups that conduct group activities and provide group psychotherapy. As an organizational consultant, Hjördis has worked with team and management development programmes in the public and private sectors. Currently, she works in private practice as a psychotherapist and supervisor.

Ann Örhammar is a registered nurse, licensed psychotherapist, group psychotherapist, and psychotherapy supervisor. Ann has previously worked in somatic care, occupational health, and correctional care. For many years she was active in the National Health Services in Stockholm, where she helped found and build a psychotherapy unit. Currently, she has a private practice in which she conducts individual and group psychotherapy. In addition, she supervises teams engaged in various treatment activities in which group psychotherapy is practised.

Christer Sandahl is a licensed psychologist, licensed psychotherapist, and professor of Social and Behavioural Science at the Medical Management Centre, Karolinska Institutet, Stockholm, Sweden. Christer has extensive experience as a practitioner in clinical psychology and organizational psychology. In 1985, he and his wife, Patricia Tudor-Sandahl, founded Sandahl Partners, which is a consulting company specializing in organizational psychology. For the past 20 years, as a full-time researcher Christer has studied group psychology with applications to psychotherapy and to team development in the healthcare and academic sectors. He was the president of the International Association for Group Psychotherapy and Group Processes (IAGP) from 2003–2006.

Lena Wennlund is a licensed psychotherapist, group psychotherapist, and psychotherapy supervisor. Lena works part-time in a psychotherapy unit at the Centre for Dependency Disorders that is administered by Stockholm County Council. She also maintains a private practice that serves clients in the areas of psychotherapy, affect phobia psychotherapy, and mentalization-based treatment. She also works with supervision, education, and organizational development. She is particularly interested in stress-related illnesses that exhibit symptoms of fatigue and depression.

Figures

Foreword by Dr Earl Hopper

William James "Count" Basie, the post-World War II African-American jazz bandleader, often instructed his musicians: "One more time ... one more, once". In an attempt to follow the music of our profession, I will state yet again that Group Analysis, with its three pillars of psychoanalysis, sociology, and systems thinking, is a very broad church. S.H. Foulkes, who is widely regarded as the founder of Group Analysis, often said to us that although he preferred his own formulations and perspectives, Group Analysis was at an early stage of development, and would become deformed if we ignored and insulated ourselves from a variety of theoretical and clinical developments throughout the world. Although this was easier for him to say than to do, he acknowledged the value of family therapy along group analytic lines, and recognised the importance of the work of diverse colleagues ranging from de Maré to Bion, Fairbairn to Klein, and from Winnicott to A. Freud. He would have appreciated the formation of the European Group Analytic Training Institutes Network and the Group Analytic Society International, but would have been sceptical of current calls for the purification of our professional identity and for the formulation of ideology masquerading as theory. It is in this context that I particularly welcome this contribution from Christer Sandahl and his team of contemporary group analytic psychotherapists from Sweden.

One of the distinguishing qualities of this well-translated book of contributions is its respect for empirical research concerning the efficacy of various parameters of our work. Moreover, the authors draw on the perspectives of various group psychotherapists from outside of Europe, including Yvonne Agazarian and Irvin Yalom, thus introducing us to thinking about living human systems and introducing existentialist questions and interpersonal orientations. In fact, these contributions are absolutely central to modern Group Analysis.

It is important to recognise that in each country and region of the world the development of Group Analysis has been influenced by its own founders who were inevitably both loyal and in polemic against their own intellectual and cultural traditions. These founders personified these configurations in their own approaches to clinical work in groups. Nonetheless, their work seems always to have had a radical and innovative edge. Torsten Sjövall (1913–1998) was a founder of group therapy in Sweden, and I well remember Olov Dahlin (1935–2009), whose pipe was always lit. Of course, other psychiatrists, psychoanalysts, and psychologists have taken important roles in this development. I have worked with many of them in the context of the International Association for Group Psychotherapy, of which Christer is a former president.

The emphasis in Sweden on empirical data and the use of what is taken to be the scientific method in the study of depth psychology and group process has shaped the continuing development of Group Analysis in Sweden and in other Nordic countries. However, this book is likely to contribute to the continuing development of Group Analysis, which does not recognise national borders. Ironically, it will help readers in other parts of Europe to learn more about work in the United States.

I will allow myself the luxury of what might well be a stereotyped metaphor of Swedes and Sweden: the Saab, with its superb design, was known as the car for an efficient engineer; the Volvo, with its record for safety and reliability, as the car for the family man; and IKEA, with its well-known sensitivity to the mind of the consumer market throughout the world, as a very effective and efficient organisation. I wonder if the determination to realise such values are not relevant to the development of Focussed Group Therapy (FGT), which the authors of this addition to the New International Library of Group Analysis have developed and so clearly elucidated. FGT is a significant development in our field, especially for work in the public sector. This book will serve many of the needs of our students, but will also stimulate and refresh the work of the more seasoned group analyst.

Earl Hopper, PhD
Series Editor

Chapter I

Introduction

Why a book on group therapy?

Given the considerable evidence on the value of group therapy, it is difficult to understand why its full potential is not made use of in practice. Although group therapy for healthcare and social care is found in most Western countries, it is the rule rather than the exception that such care is provided and supported by people who often have minimal education and experience in group processes. The unfortunate result of such lack of preparedness is that the true potential of group therapy is rarely realized. Group leaders who lack proper understanding and knowledge of group processes must deal with poor group cohesion as well as group members' silences, absences, and general disinterest in the treatment.

Much research exists on individual and group therapy in healthcare and social care. In comparisons between the two psychotherapeutic approaches, various researchers have been unable to identify significant difference between them as far as providing relief of symptoms. Unfortunately, some clinicians recognize only two benefits for group members from group therapy: the opportunity to share information about symptoms, and the communication of information on healthy lifestyles. This excludes the complex relational, interpersonal, and intrapersonal aspects of group therapy. The implication of this evaluation of group therapy is that it is a second-best alternative to individual treatment.

We challenge this view of group therapy. Man's basic need to relate and communicate also includes the fundamental need for a group to belong to, to be included in and protected by. In this book we describe how group therapy offers a unique opportunity for group members to learn and to change as they interact with other group members. The group structure presents a social microcosm of the kind of relationships that people who seek psychotherapeutic treatment find problematic in their private and public lives. In groups, the members can observe each other, provide feedback to each other, explore the relationships that develop, and practice change strategies. In short, group therapy has a powerful healing and supportive function.

This chapter contains	
Why a book on group therapy?	I

The number of patients and clients with psychiatric and psychological disorders is steadily increasing in many countries. The cost of their treatment is rising even more rapidly. The unavoidable reality is that healthcare and social care systems find this cost unsustainable. The authors of this book are convinced that group therapy, when provided as an alternative to individual treatment, can significantly reduce total treatment cost, perhaps by as much as one-third or one-half (Piper, 2008). Most research within this field is done on time-limited group therapy; i.e., 10–30 weekly sessions. When applied in healthcare or social care, the short-term format we focus on in this book is cost-effective and relatively easy to implement.

This book is intended for professionals in the private or public sectors who work with treatment and prevention in healthcare and with social care. Possible readers include nurses, physiotherapists, occupational therapists, social workers, teachers, psychologists, psychiatrists, psychotherapists, and general practitioners. The book may also be of value to any reader with general health and social care education who is interested in forming or supporting a therapy group that has clearly defined and limited goals. For professionals with more advanced education and training in psychotherapy, the book may inspire them to start and/or lead a therapy group that has psychotherapeutic goals.

Many therapists lack the training, experience, and courage to attempt group therapy. For example, they may fear that group members will offer negative criticism and pose difficult challenges. They may fear loss of control over the group, especially when certain members dominate the interaction and others decline to contribute. In short, they do not feel safe in the role of group therapy leader. The aim of this book is to help such group leaders overcome these fears by supporting and guiding them as they introduce and apply psychotherapeutic group methods in their work.

The authors of this book belong to the second and third generations of group psychotherapists in Sweden. As early as 1949, the psychiatrist and psychoanalyst Torsten Sjövall (1913–1998) went to Boston on a two-year Rockefeller grant. He worked at an outpatient psychiatric clinic at the Beth Israel Hospital. There he discovered American group psychotherapy in discussions with his supervisor Grete Bibring (1899–1977). In the 1960s and 1970s, a group of Swedish professionals interested in group dynamics travelled to England and the United States to study group psychotherapy. The first Swedish association for group psychotherapy was founded in 1962 by, among others, Torsten Sjövall. The Stockholm Group Analytic Institute (GAI) was founded in 1981 on the initiative of the psychologist and group analyst Lars Lorentzon and the psychiatrist, psychoanalyst, and group analyst Olov Dahlin. It was hoped that GAI would be able to develop a Swedish version of group analysis, based on the work of Siegmund Heinrich Foulkes and his co-workers. Compared to many other European countries, group therapy in Sweden developed relatively independently in relation to the London-based group analysis, at the same time as there has been a close relationship and exchanges with group analytic colleagues in the United Kingdom and the rest of Europe.

We, the authors, are experienced group analytic psychotherapists, while at the same time building on the work of the founders of group psychotherapy in Sweden. The first group psychotherapy training was undertaken during the 1960s at Stockholm University with psychologists Siv Boalt Boethius and Bo Sigrell as course leaders. The group analytic tradition was introduced in the 1970s through qualifying training programs under the leadership of psychologists Hans Gordon, Lars Lorentzon, and Eric Steadman. The culture of this training programme was indirectly influenced by Eric Steadman, who did not wish to teach but who brought his experience of the therapeutic community at the UK's Henderson Hospital and as a student of Foulkes. Later the psychiatrist and group analyst Göran Ahlin was for many years in charge of a three-year group analytic training program in Stockholm. All these colleagues have contributed to our understanding of group psychotherapy and indirectly inspired us to write this book.

However, we are also inspired by other group therapy traditions, not least the one represented by the North American existential psychiatrist Irvin Yalom (Yalom & Leszcz, 2020). For one of us (Christer Sandahl) it was a liberating experience 40 years ago to have the privilege of observing Yalom's work with an inpatient group and then to have the opportunity to discuss it with him after each session.

Another important teacher, mentor, and colleague was the British-American psychologist Yvonne Agazarian (1929–2017), who developed systems-centred therapy (SCT; Agazarian, 2006), a particular form of group therapy based on the Theory of Living Human Systems. This theory postulates that living human systems survive, develop, and transform from simple to more complex through discriminating and integrating differences. Implementing this idea is challenging for all human beings as integrating differences requires shifting from what we know to a difference; that means tolerating the unknown. Though the SCT approach as a whole is more complex than this introductory text can present, the heart of SCT work is its method of functional subgrouping which helps groups integrate differences. SCT's functional subgrouping teaches groups to join around similarities instead of reacting with differences. Simply put, changing from "yes, but" to "yes, and" opens the pathway for integrating small differences in a climate of similarity. Establishing this kind of group norm makes it less likely that groups will scapegoat differences or create identified patients. Our approach to the interpersonal work, the group leader role, and the implementation in different kinds of organizations is influenced and inspired by Yvonne Agazarian's work.

The book was created within the context of the relatively independent Swedish group therapy tradition, on the periphery of the mainstream discourse within group analysis. It is also the result of a creative group process in which we reviewed and discussed all chapters in joint writing seminars. The book is the outcome of a creative and rewarding group process. Our aim was to write an introductory book with wide applications, primarily in different forms of time-limited group therapy, and at the same time being deeply rooted in the group analytic tradition.

In several chapters of this book, we refer to Foulkes, the British psychiatrist and psychoanalyst who became the father of group analysis. Foulkes declined to use the term "group leader" in his work and writings. As a Jewish refugee from Germany, he was very sensitive to the idea of the "Führer", although the word "leader" had an entirely different connotation in his profession. He preferred the word "conductor". Using "conductor" to describe the group leader role in group therapy, Foulkes emphasized the idea of "musicality" – that is, interpreting the message behind what one hears in words. According to Foulkes, people should also listen to the undertones, nuances, rhythms, and silences in human conversation. He claimed that this skill is best acquired and developed in conversations that are characterized by sharing, openness, and feedback. In these conversations, people learn to reflect on their lives and to explore alternative ways of being.

We, however, prefer the term "group leader". In contemporary times – far distant from Nazi Germany – "leader" rarely evokes the negative connotation that it did for Foulkes. Rather, "leader" today has a positive connotation. We often think of the modern leader as a respectful and trusted individual who listens and responds to others. Group leaders take responsibility for group members. The individual who aspires to be a group leader requires the kind of formal theoretical knowledge that this book presents. However, theoretical knowledge alone is not enough. In any new activity – such as sailing, skiing, playing the violin, painting watercolours, etc. – people require practice and experience.

We have identified a clear need for more extensive training in group therapy for clinicians and social workers. To that end, based on our many years of teaching and experience in academia and in the private and public sectors, we offer specific guidance to group leaders on participation, organization, and communication in group therapy. In the chapters of this book, we describe among other things the history and characteristics of group therapy, how to organize a therapy group, the roles and responsibilities of the group leader, and methods of group therapy. Given its purpose and methodology, this book's key message is that group therapy supports and advances the healing processes in healthcare and social care.

The next four chapters provide the theoretical background to the more practice-oriented parts that will follow. Based on our conviction that it is essential for group leaders to understand the significance of groups in our lives, Chapter 2, "The significance of the group", begins with a discussion of human beings as social animals, like other herd animals, who thrive in groups. It has been our biological heritage to seek the safety of the group since we first descended from the treetops to the dangers of the plains. With this discussion as its starting point, the chapter continues with a description of the child's family and other group relationships and of the related psychological theories on human behaviour: for example, attachment, bonding, companionship, social cognitive theories, and group analysis. The chapter explains how the clinical use of these scientifically based theories has developed. It concludes with a commentary on how group therapy presents a golden opportunity for participants to develop new experiences in safe environments.

Chapter 3, "What is a group – really?", begins with a discussion of how the following concepts – the group, the individual, and the person – have been interpreted in various contexts. This analysis leads to the researchers' comparison of the group to an orchestra, a choir, or a jazz group in which the unique individuals act as a whole. Thus, the group is a phenomenon in which the whole is more than the sum of its members. In exploring the group phenomenon, the chapter also analyses group coercion (i.e., groupthink) that can elicit both positive responses/actions and negative responses/actions among group members. In the latter situation, the chapter emphasizes the importance of group leadership in counteracting destructive group behaviour.

Chapter 4, "The group as a learning and healing environment", begins with a summary history of group therapy with a focus on the contributions of pioneers such as Adler, Burrow, Lewin, Foulkes, and others. The chapter then reviews the numerous trends in group therapy from the twentieth century to the present. It continues with a discussion and analysis of its main focus: members' interactions (conversation and reflection) in groups, which is described as the central psychotherapeutic factor in group therapy. It is in such interactions that group members learn to explore their own and others' experiences, emotions, ideas, and motivations. Although groups can exert a destructive force at times ("the anti-group" phenomenon), the chapter emphasizes that the group can be an environment where we learn, heal, and grow.

Chapter 5, "Group therapy", introduces group therapy by giving a general description of therapy groups with emphasis on their varying aims, their different venues, and their different structures. In this chapter (and book), the focus in on the time-limited therapy group. This is a kind of group therapy that has a fixed schedule of meeting times and places with the same members and leader. Within this framework, the chapter examines various therapeutic group characteristics: focus, processes, boundaries, conditions, and structure. It also offers specific guidance for group leaders in their role as therapists and includes advice regarding how to match patients to suitable group treatments. Leaders should set reasonable expectations; not all patients/clients benefit from the same group model.

Chapter 6, "Starting a therapy group", takes a very practice-oriented approach to group treatment that derives from the authors' clinical experience. The chapter offers a practical, specific "hands-on" guide that organizers and leaders of group treatment will find useful. Initial comments on the importance of context and environment for group therapy are the lead-in to the guide on how to start a therapy group. This guide provides clear and specific advice on how to form and organize therapy groups, how to choose group participants, how to recruit suitable group leaders, how to prepare participants for group treatment sessions, how to establish group rules and a group framework, and much more. The chapter concludes with some recommendations on how to evaluate therapy groups.

Chapter 7, "Conducting a therapy group", begins with a general discussion on the role of the leader. Although leaders have different backgrounds, different views and opinions, and different personalities, they have the same position:

the central figure in a group. The chapter then narrows its scope to the role of therapeutic group leaders: their functions, tasks, and responsibilities. Therapeutic group leaders should clearly set out the group's purpose, goals, and framework; establish an accepting, reflective group culture; and provide support in various ways. Leaders who are new to the role in particular require sensitive supervision and collegial support. The chapter deals specifically with the leader's use of verbal or non-verbal interventions and also addresses the advantages of group treatment in which there is dual leadership.

Chapter 8, "Engagement and differentiation", and Chapter 9, "Interpersonal work and termination", discuss the development trajectories of various group types that group leaders need to understand so they can successfully lead group stages. The group stages are in some sense analogous to the identity development stages people pass through. Each group has its own mood, participant relationships, and themes. The chapters analyse the four characteristic group development stages: engagement, differentiation, interpersonal work, and termination. The leader's role and responsibility in each stage is described and exemplified. The chapter also suggests ways that leaders can handle difficult situations in groups when conflicts or other problems arise in the context of closed, open, and slow-open groups.

Chapter 10, "Slow-open groups", describes the advantages of such groups, the different developments in them, and how to deal with issues on boundaries, time limitations, and rules. The role of the group leader in such groups and how to start and end participation in slow-open groups are discussed.

Chapter 11, "Group therapy with pre-planned content structure", highlights the importance of group processes in cognitive behavioural therapy (CBT) and in psycho-educational groups. The aim of this chapter is to summarize some general group dynamic principles that are relevant in the use of CBT and psycho-education in groups. It describes how group CBT can offer participants a unique opportunity to observe cognitive and behavioural problems in others that they can then discover in themselves. This is an opportunity not available in individual therapy. Another aspect addressed is the role of the leader in group CBT as the individual who maintains group structure by balancing techniques and processes. It also describes group treatment in which pedagogical and psychological support is provided to the group participants who have sought help because of difficult and challenging life situations. The chapter describes their complementary role in other care treatments and their emphasis on participants' exchange of experiences and reflections.

Chapter 12, "Focused group therapy (FGT)", explains a type of group therapy that the authors developed, beginning in the year 2000. The method was developed in a research project on stress and burnout with patients on long-term sick leave. The authors have considerable experience with FGT in their clinical work with patients and have successfully trained many therapists in the use of FGT. The method is recommended, for example, for those who are unable to cope with the stress of everyday life; those with exhaustion syndrome, chronic pain, moderate anxiety, or depression; young adults with identity problems; complicated grief; women at risk of abuse; male loneliness; or eating disorders. The starting point in the therapy is what functions well in a person's life, with a focus on experienced obstacles to coping and solving problems in relations to others. The chapter presents the FGT framework and guidelines that therapists can use, explains which patients are likely to benefit from FGT and which are unsuited for FGT, and recommends procedures for the use of FGT. The description of FGT binds the book together in that the approach is based on the assumptions presented in the first few chapters.

The book concludes with some reflections regarding the process of creating enough safety for the group members to become fully engaged in the therapeutic work from the beginning. The approach described in this book is based on group therapy research and conclusions from evolutionary psychology of human beings as social animals. Based on this we developed FGT, which is not a new method but rather the expression of a way of thinking which requires some modifications of time-limited group therapy as it has been described in the literature. Finally, some recommendations for new group leaders are given, including a call to participate in international networks.

Chapter 2

The significance of the group

Man is a social being who has always lived in groups with others. The group has been a place to seek protection and community, to solve common tasks, and to discuss common interests. Today, we still lead our lives in groups: in the family, at school, in our leisure activities, with our peers, and at work. Many of the groups we belong to have been formed by others, and often our membership is the result of other people's decisions and not the outcome of an active personal choice. While there are certainly many people who prefer solitude, it is unusual that someone wants to be on his or her own all the time. Needing and wanting to belong to one or several groups is the typical human reaction. In fact, most of us spend a great deal of time and energy manoeuvring our position in a group's complex, and sometimes conflicted, context. To a large extent, the groups we belong to define our very being. Our social and participative connections create meaning in our lives.

Human beings differ from other animals in their ability to change and transform their natural surroundings. With language, imagination, and a capacity to mentally connect to the past, the present, and the future, people can step outside themselves, create survival mechanisms, and change their world. They can envisage an alternative reality that allows them to re-experience the past and to imagine the future. The dog lying quietly beside fire probably experiences only the warmth of the present, while its owner may foresee a future catastrophe or remember a cherished moment.

We humans are relational, sense-making creatures. We struggle to find meaning in our existence so that we can cope as well as understand and manage our relationships and our experiences in the larger social context. We create meaning through our relationships with others. The capacity to deal with personal relations also determines how our drive for closeness to others and our need for autonomy can be satisfied.

The human flock on the savannah

Man is, by nature, a flock animal. From an evolutionary perspective, man adapted to the hunter-gatherer life on the African savannah where survival was only possible via group cohesion and cooperation. Because we have to care for others in our group (i.e., our flock), one can argue that, of necessity, we are altruistic (Sloan Wilson, 2015).

When the early human species *homo erectus* (upright man) climbed down from the trees and stood on two legs, enormous changes took place in how people came to form their lives. This was especially true for their offspring when they left the protective shelter of the treetops. When parents had to guard them from the predators prowling the forest floor, the infants had to remain in close proximity to larger, stronger, and wiser kin who could care for them.

So that parents would assume this responsibility for the very long period required for a young person to learn to cope alone, the infants needed to develop attachment behaviours that made adults commit emotionally to them and to respond to their needs. Child attachment behaviours include smiling, screaming, crying, seeking eye contact, stretching out for, and clinging. In response, parents developed bonding behaviours within the caregiving system: for example, adjusting tempo, holding and rocking the child, changing voice tone, and facial mimicry. Such parent bonding behaviours require putting the child's need for nurture, protection, and social interaction before the adult's needs (Bowlby, 1999/1969; McClusky, 2005).

On a biological level, our bonding behaviour, important for creating interpersonal relations, is to a large degree related to the hormone oxytocin. This is the hormone best known for its role as a stimulant for milk production in breastfeeding. Oxytocin is also secreted when people touch each other, move and sleep, eat, and talk with good friends. As an initiator of the "peace and calm" system in people, oxytocin provokes a feeling of well-being. Therefore, one can say our bodies are "hard-wired" for social fellowship (Cambell, 2009; Uvnäs Moberg, 2003; 2005). The capacity for human empathy has its physical source in the brain's mirror neurons. An example of the strong influence of the mirror neurons is the physical shock we experience when we see someone slip and fall (Keysers, 2012).

Modern man spends much time in groups in conversation with others – at meals, at work, and in many other places. Language is our main tool for creating closeness, building on similarities, and establishing community. Before verbal language appeared, people developed non-verbal communications such as rhythmic songs and movement to seek and express fellowship. By dancing, singing, and playing in groups, our ancestors' experience of belonging was strengthened (Laland et al., 2016). Even if language, as verbal communication, is the dominant form of expression in modern society, many people can experience a deep and

primordial feeling of community by dancing and singing in groups. Common rec-
reational activities (e.g., choral singing, gymnastics, yoga, dance, and sports) are
our contemporary versions of non-verbal group interaction.

Lone wolves live dangerously

What connects human nomadic life on the African savannah and communication
and relationship development in group therapy today? Our clinical experience
and research on the effects of group therapy reveal that group members insist
it is crucially important that they know they are not alone and that others have
similar problems, thoughts, and emotions. This group support relieves the burden
of shame and guilt people have when they think both that something is basically
wrong with them and that they alone are responsible for their condition. If others have the same condition, perhaps their case is not hopeless. Perhaps they can
develop satisfactory relationships with others. Recognizing oneself in others is a
deep-seated human need that is entirely consistent with the evolutionary impera-
tive to preserve the species.

Based on this historical perspective, we can summarize the fundamental
requirements needed for development and survival as an individual living with
others:

> Avoid loneliness, connect with others, dance and sing, work cooperatively,
> experience others' emotions, mirror, and reflect!

The expression "Be strong alone" is somewhat paradoxical. For our ancestors,
being left alone could well be fatal. Even today, loneliness can have severe consequences, such as mental and physical illnesses, some of which may be life-
threatening. The quest for peace and solitude is understandable, but the fact of
abandonment and rejection is completely different. The latter arouses intense feelings of shame and anxiety that emanate from our innermost core at a primary,
biological level.

The family – our first group

The family is the first group for most people. We do not choose this group; we
are born into it. Our physical and mental health depends on how sensitively we
are cared for, how we are listened to, and how we learn to manage our emotions.
The roles and interaction patterns that are characteristic of our primary family are
imprinted in us. They become the basis for interpreting and understanding relationships in life outside the family.

S.H. Foulkes, the group analyst who fled Germany and worked in England during and after the Second World War, paraphrased and developed the well-known
statement by his contemporary British colleague, paediatrician and psychotherapist Donald W. Winnicott: "There is no such thing as an infant." Foulkes argued

that a man cannot be conceived without another man as little as an infant can be conceived of without motherly care. His view was that the individual, like the psyche, arises through others and develops and exists through others (Foulkes, 1984).

The contemporary influential theorists – Ronald Fairbairn, D.W. Winnicott, and Foulkes – and the British child psychiatrist and psychoanalyst John Bowlby, agreed in their resistance to the then prevailing one-person perspective and argued that the environment, the family, the group, and the relational perspective motivate human psychological development.

After the Second World War, Bowlby, as head of the children's ward at the well-known Tavistock Clinic in London, immediately renamed the ward as the Unit for Children and Parents. This name change indicated a shift to the relationship and family perspective. In the 1950s and 1960s, Bowlby developed *attachment theory*, which links human biological development and psychological development (Bowlby, 1999/1969, 1988).

The psychoanalytical establishment at the time was critical of Bowlby's views on the necessity of the interdisciplinary approach in which the child's biological and psychological needs are closely linked. It is difficult today to understand why his views were controversial. However, in the 1950s and 1960s the controversy was significant enough that Bowlby was ostracized by the British Psychoanalytic Association. In the last three decades, the intersubjective, two-person psychology that Bowlby supported has gradually replaced the one-person perspective within developmental psychology.

Foulkes's radical view that *there is no such thing as an individual* was before its time. The idea that humans are dependent on and interconnected with each other is probably still somewhat controversial in today's individualistic culture. However, in modern psychology the relational perspective is supported (Leman et al., 2019). This view is based on attachment psychology that assumes individuals throughout life chisel out their identity from the group and contexts in which they participate.

The significance of attachment

Different, inherited relational need systems, each with its own function, are necessary for survival. The *theory of attachment* relates to children's need for security, for connection, and for curious exploration and differentiation; the *theory of bonding* relates to parents' emotional ties to their children.

Children develop *internal working models* of themselves and of others that are based on their history of relational experiences with their primary attachment figures. These models, or schemes, which reflect actual experiences rather than inner fantasies, form the basis for how children and adults relate to others throughout life. Daniel Stern (1985) describes this as *inner representation of being with the other which has been generalized or, more simply, as ways of being with the other.* The members in group therapy bring their internal working models and schemes to the group interaction.

Attachment relations (theory of attachment) to the primary caregivers do not organize all the infant's interaction contacts, but contribute together with other kinds of relationships that the child develops, such as peer-learning, and companion relationships (*theory of companionship*) to the child's socio-emotional maturity. The infant's capacity for interaction develops in parallel – each with its special characteristics and functions (Malmquist Saracino, 2011; Selby & Bradley, 2003; Trevarthen, 2003, 2006).

It is important to emphasize that attachment to primary caregivers is fundamental. However, attachment relationships do not exist in a vacuum. From the very beginning of each person's life, such relationships are part of their larger social context. The proverb "It takes a village to raise a child" reflects a universal experience and implies that the child and the family are part of and dependent on the entire community.

As the scientific basis for attachment theory has developed, the clinical use of the theory has increased rapidly. Research on adult attachment in a transgenerational perspective has shown, among other things, that the inability to regulate severe emotional states passes from generation to generation (Fonagy et al., 1991, 2004; Fraiberg et al., 1975; Main & Hesse, 1990, Main et al., 2005; Stern, 1985, 1995; van Ijzendoorn, 1995, 1999). This research has been of importance in the development of group therapy methods for young children, teenagers, and parents (e.g., infant groups, toddler groups, groups for children who have witnessed violence, and groups for children with mentally ill parents). The research reveals that while attachment patterns are stable over time, maladaptive and destructive relational patterns can be broken and changed. Such adaptation can occur through life itself and in socialization with others and in psychotherapeutic treatment of various kinds.

Researchers have also demonstrated and substantiated the linkage between secure attachment and mentalization (i.e., the ability to reflect on emotions, thoughts, and intentions and to recognize and understand others' perspectives and behaviours) (Allen et al., 2008; Fonagy et al., 1991, 2004; Lyons-Ruth & Jacobvitz, 2008). Typically, the child has fully developed this ability by around four years of age. Security in attachment relationships provides good conditions for intersubjective learning, while insecurity and trauma in such relationships undermine the development of this mentalization ability. The efforts people make to interpret and understand their own and others' behaviours that arise from inner mental states reflect mankind's incessant struggle to understand human thoughts, emotions, and behaviours. It is an ongoing survival process.

Attachment behaviours and bonding behaviours as well as affects and emotions are culturally and hierarchically neutral. Thus, new-born infants all over the world exhibit similar behaviours with their caregivers and have the same set of affects. A similar correspondence applies to caregivers' bonding behaviours and emotions.

Infants have an inherent ability from the very beginning to relate flexibly to others. Mothers, fathers, and perhaps siblings are usually their first attachment figures. As early as the first year of life, infants at the same time need to interact with a wider circle of people of all ages (e.g., playmates, relatives, and teachers).

Social learning

People of all ages learn all through life by imitating and observing others' lives. In the second half of the twentieth century, Albert Bandura, a professor of Psychology and the Social Sciences at Stanford University, began developing a social psychological learning theory that he referred to as *imitation learning, observation learning*, and *model learning*. Bandura thought that people learn from one another by imitation, observation, and modelling. In their interactions, people influence behaviours and the environment (Bandura, 1977). An everyday example of his theory is the following: parents influence children more by their actions than by their warnings and advice; it is the opposite of the maxim "Do as I say, not as I do." Children observe not only how their parents (and other people) use objects and tools but also how they communicate, handle difficult situations, and negotiate and solve conflicts.

Modern developmental psychology also emphasizes the importance of imitation for human learning. In the 1990s, behavioural imitation learning began to be viewed as a fundamental way of communicating. This ability in infants is now considered the basis of their future verbal exchanges and comradeship with older children (Bråten, 1998; Delafield-Butt & Trevarthen, 2013; Fiamenghi, 1997; Trevarthen et al., 1999).

Already by the 1930s, before attachment theory developed, an international research field existed on how infants interact with each other, *infant peer interaction* (Bridges, 1932; Parten, 1932). An extensive body of literature is available today that deals with infants' interactions with other infants and with their early, non-verbal ability to develop meaningful relationships without the presence of adults. In the continual process of learning to adapt to a society in which they will live and work with their fellow beings, children are every day and increasingly members of formal and informal peer groups.

In her doctoral dissertation (2004) and subsequent book of the same title, *Kamratsamspel på småbarnsavdelningar* (in English, *Comradeship in Small Children's Pre-Schools*; 2005), the psychologist Elin Michélsen studied how small children (1–2 years of age) act in free-play groups. She saw that positive situations dominated over negative, conflictual situations. She also found that the emotions these children exhibited most with their peers were interest, enthusiasm, and curiosity. She observed the children seemed most joyful when they played together in physical games with gross body movement. She qualified her findings with reference to the small-group setting of her research and the presence of responsive adults. Based on these observations of children's interactions, Michélsen coined the concept of *sense of self as a friend*.

All learning related to necessary abilities useful to the culture involves communicating with other people of all ages. We can learn new skills and handle different challenges that occur in situations with others who are not necessarily our attachment figures. In these learning processes, children and adults develop the emotions of pride or shame – pride in one's own and others' recognition that you can do or know something and be seen as capable; shame in others' recognition that you are untrustworthy, ignorant, unskilled, or incompetent. Just as in the family, members in peer groups are important for confirming or negating self-image and self-esteem.

The group provides experiences of relationships

With its diversity of relationships, the group has decisive importance in people's lives, beginning with their very early experiences. Therefore, in times of trouble, trauma, or crisis, treatment and psychotherapy in groups provides healing opportunities that are similar to those in our growth conditions. In such groups, attachment patterns, internal working models, and habitual attachment behaviours are activated. A golden opportunity arises when we enter relationships with others and try out useful approaches and solutions to painful or stressful situations. To be effective, groups must provide a sufficiently secure social context for all members. Man is a relational creature who oscillates between approaching and distancing in fellowship with others. Closeness and autonomy are the two existential power fields for our basic needs. Navigating this dynamic area and striking a balance between the need for independence and the capacity to have fulfilling relationships is a constant challenge to human existence.

Summary

In this chapter we describe the group's fundamental importance for man. Human beings, as "flock animals", need groups to survive and develop. In groups, we create our identity as we receive support, comfort, and encouragement. At the same time, we are also challenged and questioned.

Chapter 3

What is a group – really?

Imagine you observe eight people in a room. Four people are intensely discussing some topic, two people are chatting about some other topic, and two people are sitting quietly and watching the others. Eight people in the same room. Are they a group? Three small groups? Or maybe four groups – one whole group and three small sub-groups?

"Group" is a relatively new word for an ancient phenomenon. In the Baroque Period, beginning in the early seventeenth century, *the group* referred to massive sculptures of figures who had something in common and were presented as a tableau (e.g., as in many Roman fountains). At the beginning of the twentieth century, *the group* began to be used to complement the concept of the individual. *The group* was used as background and an environment that featured the individual. A sculptural example is the Orpheus Fountain by the Swedish sculptor Carl Milles, which is located in front of the Stockholm Concert Hall. This bronze fountain features Orpheus (the individual) lifting his lyre above a circle of eight figures (the group members) who reach upward to the music of the lyre (https://sv.wikipedia.org/wiki/Orfeusgruppen; Widlund, 1995). Prior to the twentieth century, no general concept was used to reference groups of people. A collection of individuals was described in different contexts based on their place and function in the social order. The context could be the immediate family, the extended family, a parish, a guild, or a congregation.

When is a collection of people a group? For example, are the people waiting at a bus stop a group? It seems unlikely unless they have met at the bus stop each workday morning for some years and have begun to share experiences.

The group emerges when we need others

Kurt Lewin (1890–1947), a pioneer in modern social

psychology, proposed that a group emerges when its members become mutually dependent; for example, when they must jointly solve a task (Lewin, 1935, 1936, 1948, 1951). Thus, the crucial factor is whether the members are interdependent as they try to achieve some task, not whether they meet at the same place at the same time. According to Lewin, a group emerges when group members determine their mutual "fate".

It is useful in analysing Lewin's ideas to address the concept of "person". By most definitions, *person* refers to a conscious, self-reflective, and verbal being who exists and acts in a specific context. The concept of *person* derives from the Greek word "persona", which means "face mask". The derivation is apt: we often wear a social mask suited to our role in a specific setting (Goffman, 1959). Yet there is a deeper connotation. Behind the social mask is the naked face – the individual perhaps we alone know. The concept of *person* presents a dilemma. Which is the real face? Who is the real person behind the social mask? Being "personal" implies that parts of the naked face peek through the mask. Most people are familiar with the experience of oscillating between presenting oneself in a role and trying to be oneself as a person. As a group leader one must both find and take the professional role and at the same time be oneself as a person.

Usually, one assumes that experiencing one's own self as a person involves experiencing others as objects that interact with that self. As a person, I represent others, I know that I affect them, and I recognize how they affect me. Foulkes viewed a group member as a nodal point of a network of communication and dependencies (Foulkes, 1984). He used the word "matrix" for the core of the group dynamics, in the sense of womb or mould, to describe this network that has an outer, social side and an inner, intrapsychic side. If we return to our room with eight people, we can say that, in reality, these eight people as persons form eight groups. Each person has a unique inner image of the group. In sum, the sociological reality is the "outer" group of eight people; the psychological reality is the eight "inner" groups.

A social-psychology perspective

The group, as a phenomenon, became the subject of scientific interest and research with the birth of social psychology in the late 1800s and early 1900s. This research contributed to the modern understanding of groups. The American sociologist Charles Horton Cooley (1864–1929) was an important figure in this movement. Cooley created the concept of "the looking-glass self", which describes how we create our "I" based on how we perceive others think we behave and expect us to behave. George Herbert Mead (1863–1931), who was inspired by Cooley and the sociologist Émile Durkheim (1858–1917), was another pioneer in this movement. Durkheim claimed, among other things, that interpersonal factors, not intrapsychic factors, cause suicides. In his investigation of the individual's consciousness of self, Mead argued that self-awareness occurs when people mirror themselves in others. Furthermore, assumptions about the ego are not static; group experiences shape the ego.

As noted above, Kurt Lewin was a very influential figure in social psychology. He was born into a Jewish family in Germany and was educated in Germany. He immigrated to the United States in 1933 because of the political and social situation in Germany. His research focused on group dynamics and group processes, including how the group influences people's attitudes.

In a famous study, Lewin researched American eating habits with groups of American housewives as research participants. The study was conducted during the Second World War when the United States was shipping meat overseas to soldiers and allies, increasing the price of meat at home and decreasing domestic meat consumption. The U.S. government, concerned about the lack of protein in the American diet, funded Lewin's research. At one level, the purpose of the research was to change American women's negative perceptions of certain meats (e.g., kidneys, brains, hearts). Lewin formed two groups for the study: a lecture group and a discussion group. All the women were taught the same food facts and food preparation skills. However, in his comparison of the two groups, Lewin found that the women in the discussion group were more willing to serve the organ meats to their families. Lewin concluded that the discussion group condition stimulated discussion of experiences and attitudes, and that a discussion group can exert influence that is constructive and creative. In short, the discussion group condition promoted active learning in a way that the passive lecture group condition did not (Lewin, 1951). These results are in line with modern research on adult learning that finds that the active participation and reflection (in combination) condition is more effective in influencing behaviour than the inactive, passive learning typical of the lecture condition (Kolb, 2015). Leaders of group therapy with psycho-educational goals should keep this in mind.

Lewin thought that the group process should be seen as a pattern of forces within a field. These forces influence each other so that the group as a whole becomes more than the sum of its parts. Thus, a group is not just a collection of individuals but rather a network of relationships that constitute a dynamic force field.

With this research on the group concept as his starting point, Lewin developed *the force field analysis*, which is a strategic tool for mapping restraining forces and driving forces. These two sets of forces are in opposition: the restraining forces try to maintain the status quo; the driving forces try to bring about change. The analysis is often used today; for example, in connection with organizational development. Lewin's analysis assumes a number of these restraining and driving factors always exist between the present position and the desired position. For an individual or group to achieve a goal, the driving forces must be stronger than the restraining forces. Lewin argued that an increase in the driving factors rarely prevents the increase in the restraining forces. Many actual experiences suggest his analysis was correct. If one focuses on removing or reducing one of the restraining forces instead, generally sufficient energy is provided by the driving forces to make the desired change.

Adjustment and over-adjustment

People have developed a strong capacity to adapt to the environments of the family, the classroom, the work team, and so on. They have also adapted to society's norms, cultures, and religious tenets. While our mental adaptability and our psychic flexibility facilitate our ability to cooperate, this plasticity can nevertheless lead to destructive group processes. Our driving force to belong, to feel safe, and to achieve status may assert itself in a group such that we become aggressive, fixated on self-preservation, conformist, and sectarian. We may bully and exclude others as our ruthlessness and cruelty increase. We tend to reject any information that challenges our prejudices. In extreme cases, the consequences of destructive group phenomena can be catastrophic. One extreme example is the tragedy of the Jonestown cult in north-western Guyana that was led by Jim Jones, a charismatic preacher and faith healer. In 1978, under Jones's coercion, a total of 918 people died (at least a third of whom were children) in what was described as "mass suicide" (also "mass murder-suicide") from drinking a poisoned soft drink beverage.

One remarkable element of group dynamics is that the group may gain strength from its opposition to a (perceived) external enemy. A fragile group, especially a group with internal conflicts, increases its cohesion by uniting against an outside threat. As fragile groups prepare their defensive posture, initially they experience a strong sense of community, power, and even euphoria. They favourably contrast their members' similarities with outsiders' dissimilarities. Common examples of group similarities are religious beliefs, ethnic affiliations, or even support of the same football club. Not infrequently, extreme group solidarity leads to fanaticism and violence.

Examples are plentiful of political world leaders who have conducted wars and engaged in genocide based on this group dynamic. Fortunately, there are also examples of leaders who have demonstrated the very antithesis of this dynamic. For many people, Nelson Mandela (1918–2013) of South Africa is the world's best example of such a political leader. While serving 27 years in prison for political violence, he became a pacifist. Following his prison release in 1990, he laid the foundation of a unique leadership approach that emphasized empathy and forgiveness among the blacks, the coloured, and the whites of South Africa. As President of South Africa, he helped end the long years of apartheid.

Mandela, the son of a traditional leader of the Xhosa people (a Bantu-speaking ethnic group), was influenced by the African tribal values of Ubuntu and Inimba. The Ubuntu philosophy teaches that you cannot be human on your own because humanity is interpersonal: "I am what I am because of who we all are." Inimba is the body spirit that responds to another with empathy and forgiveness. For example, a mother's instinct is to comfort her crying child. Others who experience this spirit act altruistically. The Bantu-speaking tribes of Southern Africa owe their community spirit to these values. Dutch colonization from the seventeenth century onward and British colonization from the nineteenth century onward opposed and exploited these traditional tribal values. The greatness of Mandela and other leaders like Archbishop Desmond Tutu can be attributed to their ability to return people to their traditional cultural values in ways that helped reconcile South Africa's deep societal divisions (Battle, 2009; Mandela, 1994; Smith, 2011; Tutu, 1999).

From the 1930s to the 1960s, influential findings from many important social psychological experiments spread among scholars and even among outside academic circles. The well-known conformity experiment conducted by Solomon Asch (1907–1996) is an example (Asch, 1956). In this classic experiment, a group of participants examined a line drawn on a paper and then discussed which of three other lines was the same length as the first line. The participants then gave their answers aloud in the group. With one exception, the participants were actors who had been instructed to give a wrong answer. The point of the exercise was to see if the actors' behaviour influenced the non-actor participant. In the various trials of the experiment, 76 percent of the non-actor participants responded incorrectly (in agreement with the actor participants) although the correct answer was obvious. Asch concluded that individuals are reluctant to oppose group consensus. The experiment is often interpreted as evidence that people will deny an obvious truth in order to conform to the group.

Because groups, as well as individuals, require ongoing exchanges with the outside world to test their beliefs, a closed group is at risk of developing a rigid and uncompromising world view. In the 1970s, Irving Janis (1918–1990) created the concept of "groupthink" to describe the phenomenon of conformity pressure on closed groups. Groupthink causes an overvaluation of the group's ideas and opinions; only information that confirms these ideas and opinions has credence. One of the most famous examples of this phenomenon was the catastrophic invasion by Cuban exiles (supported by the U.S. Government) at the Bay of Pigs in Cuba in 1961. President John F. Kennedy's inner circle of advisers, notably from the U.S. Central Intelligence Agency, made a number of miscalculations influenced by a lack of critical thinking and an inability to process information that did not confirm their image of reality. The botched invasion resulted in large losses, both human and political. The Bay of Pigs is a dramatic example of the disastrous consequences of groupthink. However, it is by no means an isolated example. In fact, groupthink has frequently been observed in different degrees of severity in many organizations (Arnold, 2010).

When groupthink prevails, there is a tendency to exclude information that does not support the group's ideas and opinions. Nevertheless, a group needs boundaries that separate it to some extent from the outside world. Therefore, a group must develop its own culture if it is to create a community. Developing a group culture means norms must be agreed on, either explicitly or implicitly. "Who we are? How do we think? How do we act? How can we express our disagreement?" These norms, which define the group, communicate behavioural expectations to the group members. Without agreed-upon norms, conflicts arise in groups that can only be resolved through constant negotiation since legal guidelines are inapplicable. If a group's boundaries are not totally closed, others may challenge its norms by testing them against other ideas and opinions.

The necessity of group boundaries has relevance for therapeutic groups where information on group members must be held in strictest confidence. The members often share sensitive and private information in the group. Without group boundaries, the confidence and openness needed for the group to function are at risk.

Obedience and destructivity

In 1961, Stanley Milgram (1933–1984) conducted a famous social-psychology experiment that focused on obedience (Milgram, 1975). The experiment was designed to test if people would compromise their own values under pressure from an authority figure. In the experiment, which was conducted at Yale University, participants were divided into two groups: the teachers and the learners. The learners were, in fact, hired actors. When the learners gave wrong answers to the teachers' questions, the teachers administered electric shocks to the learners in increasingly higher voltages. In actuality, no shocks were administered. The experiment showed that 65 percent of the "teachers" were prepared to deliver, in principle, even fatal-strength shocks if strongly encouraged by an authority. It is worth noting, however, that more than one-third of the teachers opposed the authoritarian coercion. Philip Zimbardo's Stanford Prison Experiment, conducted in 1971, is another classic social psychological experiment that demonstrated people's inclination to respond to social pressure (Zimbardo, 2007).

Typically, these kinds of experiments are used to call attention to the dangers of peer, group, and authoritarian pressure. If such pressure is great enough, people are capable of very destructive actions. Yet there is a contrary argument. People are also capable of altruistic and constructive actions when supported and honoured by their peers and their groups. Everyday life offers many empirical examples of heroism, selflessness, and courage. For example, people risk their lives to save strangers, volunteer as aid workers in war zones, and adopt abused children. Some of these actions are reported; most are not.

One conclusion from the study of groups is the importance of group leadership in dealing with potentially destructive group processes. This is a conclusion that has significant relevance in the context of group therapy. As contributors to this book, our hope is that these chapters show how a group leader can strengthen a therapy group's constructive potential and weaken its destructive potential. It is also important that there is support for group leaders in the immediate organizational surroundings and that this support is exhibited transparently. A therapy group leader without encouragement risks being drawn into destructive group processes. In the worst case, such a leader may assume an authoritarian leadership style that is harmful to the group. At that point, the very purpose of the therapeutic treatment is defeated.

The group as a whole

Communications and interactions in a group are sometimes familiar and understandable to group members and sometimes strange and incomprehensible. The personalities, needs, and emotions of the members are complex, varied, and interconnected. Thus, a group climate (an emotional atmosphere) often develops in therapy groups. Sometimes it is helpful to express the experienced climate in words in order to increase the understanding of what is going on in the group.

The group can be viewed either as a collection of individuals or as a whole. One may compare the group to an orchestra – a group of musicians who play different instruments but together perform the same musical compositions harmoniously (or discordantly). Foulkes often used the orchestra metaphor when he described the "the group as a whole".

The group leader who views the therapy group in terms of "the group as a whole" attends to the group's themes and moods in its particular setting. This perspective is evidenced by the individual mental and social processes evident in the group's communications and interactions. Foulkes referred to this concept as the group's *matrix* (see above and Chapter 5). The matrix is the repository of all the group's experiences (conscious and unconscious) that direct the group communications and interactions (Foulkes, 1984). Every group has its own dynamic matrix – the psychological basis of its unique character, mood, limitations, and resources.

The group therapist (i.e., the group leader) should see the group as a whole. The therapist is advised to lead the group through group processes rather than to respond only to the individual members' needs and issues. The following example is illustrative.

> Members in a group for the elderly at a primary healthcare centre are talking about the lack of confidentiality in healthcare. The discussion is lively. As the discussion continues, however, the group leader realizes that the essential point of the discussion – patient confidentiality – has been ignored. The group leader wonders how to make the subject relevant to the group as a whole so that the members will see that it concerns them personally. The group leader says: "You complain that the healthcare staff discloses information about their patients. Does our group follow the duty of confidentiality?" Now the discussion becomes somewhat more heated, especially with the revelation that trust in the group leader and trust in the group are in question. However, in the following discussion of the duty of confidentiality as it relates to the group, the tension in the room decreases. A member says: "It is good to understand that what is said here will not be talked about elsewhere. Now, I want to talk about something else that I find very difficult in my life". At this point, the trust that was threatened is restored.

Seeing the group as a whole means taking a holistic perspective on group processes with individuals as part of these processes. The group leader who takes this perspective can overcome communication obstacles and elicit individual responses. In the health centre example, the group members felt safer when the problem of distrust was addressed.

Regardless of the therapeutic goal and method, viewing the group as a whole is a worthwhile exercise. This perspective, which increases the group leader's understanding of the group's processes and dynamics, is essential for safer interventions. The starting points in group therapy are the members' past experiences and acquired knowledge; the members' mutual group goal is to gain new experiences and new knowledge.

Summary

In this chapter we describe the group. We show that a collection of people in the same setting is not necessarily a group. A group forms when people interact with each other in pursuit of a common goal. The group then becomes more than the sum of its members. Social psychological research reveals that group pressure strongly influences group members, even to the extent that some members are willing to adapt their behaviour to conform to group norms. Groups are capable, therefore, of exerting both a constructive and destructive influence.

Chapter 4

The group as a learning and healing environment

A therapeutic group is a learning and healing environment. The group creates a space in which group members can have invigorating conversations. In these conversations, they learn to know themselves and to strengthen their ability to manage relationships and their own lives. Members in a therapeutic group have the opportunity to explore their feelings, impulses, and desires. It is here that they can be themselves as they strive to achieve their fullest potential (Barwick & Weegmann, 2017; Foulkes, 1983; Lorentzen, 2013; Schlapobersky, 2016; Yalom & Leszcz, 2020).

The history of group therapy

Dr Joseph H. Pratt (1872–1956) was a pioneer in group therapy with his treatment of tuberculosis patients in the early twentieth century at the Massachusetts General Hospital. He observed that waiting room patients talked to each other about their experiences of their illness, and that they seemed to take comfort from these conversations. Inspired by these observations, he started to meet groups of patients, and inform and talk with them. Pratt's conclusion was that such groups enhanced the patients to cope with their illness in a more constructive manner. After the sessions, the patients become more healthy and less fixated on their illnesses. Pratt's patient therapy groups may have been the first psycho-educational groups (see Chapter 8).

Alfred Adler (1870–1937), an Austrian physician and psychologist, was another pioneer in the development of collective group therapy, especially group therapy for children and adolescents. In the early twentieth century, in collaboration with Sigmund Freud (1856–1939), Adler founded the Vienna Psychoanalytic Society. Like Carl Jung (1875–1961), Adler broke early with Freud. Perhaps the foremost reason that Adler broke with Freud was his conviction that the social context has as great, if not greater, an influence on the formation of the individual personality as the inner psychological dynamic.

At about the same time as Adler developed an interest in groups, Trigant Burrow (1875–1950), an American psychoanalyst and psychiatrist, also did pioneering work in group therapy. He is regarded as the founder of group analysis in the United States. Burrow is remembered, among other things, for allowing a patient to "analyse" him (Sándor Ferenczi, a Hungarian psychoanalyst, also tried this experiment). This experience led Burrow to challenge the authoritarian approach that then prevailed in psychiatric treatment. He questioned whether the physicians' perspective, interpretations, and suggestions always were the most true and meaningful, and he started to value the patients' contribution in a different way. These doubts provoked Burrow's interest in interpersonal and social relationships and their relationship to intrapsychic dynamics. This approach was an early example of the intersubjective, reciprocal perspective. As with John Bowlby (see Chapter 2), the psychoanalytic community ostracized Burrow for these radical views.

Jacob Moreno (1889–1974) was a Romanian-American psychiatrist and psychosociologist, and the founder of *psychodrama*. He studied in Vienna, where he was influenced by Freud. He was a pioneer in the development of psychodrama, a therapy that is based on improvisational theatre. In the 1930s, he continued his work with group therapy after he immigrated to the United States. Moreno theorized that because man is a social creature, the social system must be involved in therapy if it is to make lasting changes. Similar to Gestalt therapy developed by Fritz Perls (1893–1970), a German-born psychiatrist and psychotherapist, psychodrama is based on action techniques. For example, in psychodrama therapy, the patient's inner world is illuminated in staged conflicts in group settings where memories and fantasies are evoked. When a group member (or members) takes the role of the protagonist's inner representations, then communication patterns, beliefs, and the propensity for action can be examined, processed, and changed. Action techniques such as psychodrama and Gestalt therapy are sometimes integrated into verbally based group therapy.

Psychodrama and Gestalt group psychotherapy are strongly represented internationally in the field of mental health and organizational consultation.

Few researchers show interest in such action methods despite the undoubtedly ambitious aim among practitioners of advancing research on their application. However, some empirical research gives support to these methods, in the case of psychodrama, mainly as an approach to treatment (Arn et al., 1989; Kipper & Ritchie, 2003; Orkibi & Feniger-Schaal, 2019). For the same reason that we do not describe systems-centred therapy (SCT) (i.e., because of the complexity of the method and the theory behind it) we do not include action techniques in this book. We find the study of verbally based group therapy challenging enough in itself. However, we believe that our book can be useful in the introductory phases in the training of psychodrama as well as in SCT and Gestalt therapy.

The flourishing years of group therapy

Psychiatric group therapy was increasingly used in clinical treatment in England and the United States after the Second World War. Returning soldiers with "war neurosis" (a catch-all term for complex mental issues caused by wartime trauma) were placed in therapy groups, often with inexperienced psychiatrists as group leaders. Despite the crudity of this mental health treatment, many soldiers nevertheless recovered unusually quickly. The result was explained, at least in part, by the soldiers' dialogue and exchange of experiences and feelings.

Many Londoners who had survived the German bombing campaign (the Blitz) were injured, had lost loved ones, and were traumatized. They were in need of both physical and mental care. Many children, some in overcrowded orphanages, were among these survivors. London soon became the locus of various treatment homes, therapies, and developmental psychological theories. Donald Winnicott, Bowlby (see Chapter 2), and others were influential in this development. Thomas Main (1911–1990) and Maxwell Jones (1907–1990) were among the influential figures who developed the "therapeutic community". This experiment was first tested at the Northfield Military Hospital near Birmingham, England. Returning soldiers suffering from shell shock were treated at the hospital. The experiment, which today is considered the first example of this kind of treatment, took a group-based approach that was later developed as treatment for mainly severe psychiatric conditions (e.g., personality disorders and drug addiction). Initially, the experiment was mainly for residents – thus, the hospital became the therapeutic community for residential treatment. At present, outpatient treatment programmes are more commonly used.

Two physicians, Wilfred Bion (1897–1979) and Foulkes, were crucial in the work at the Northfield Military Hospital. Bion's book (1961) about his experience with group therapy had great significance for the theoretical development of group dynamics. Foulkes, who was perhaps more pragmatic and more sensitive to the needs of patients than Bion, was more successful as a group psychotherapy practitioner. His work with group analytic psychotherapy has been particularly influential in Europe. We describe his theoretical concepts and practical recommendations in this chapter and Chapter 5.

In the United States, Samuel Richard Slavson (1890–1981) was a pioneer in group therapy and contributed to its recognition as a scientific discipline. He was a founder of the American Group Psychotherapy Association, which, among other things developed guidelines for qualified training in group therapy. Slavson's idea of group therapy has been described as focused on the relation between the group leader and each individual member, while giving less attention to the interaction and communication between members.

There was also an independent, Latin American school of group analysis, which originated in Argentina as a result of the work of the psychoanalyst Enrique Pichon-Riviere (1907–1977). He introduced the theory of *operative groups*, which is a whole way of thinking and acting. In spite of the fact that they developed their ideas independently in different parts of the world, the writings of Pichon-Riviere and Foulkes are interrelated in many ways (Tubert-Oklander & De Tubert, 2003)

In the 1970s groups of various kinds that focused on personal development in treatment, educational, and organizational settings gained popularity, at least in the Western world. As is often the case with new theories and methods, the belief and even idealization was considerable. The groups often had an experiential and experimental spirit that promoted full expression of feelings, often with a naïve approach. However, some participants suffered trauma or distress because of the group leaders' lack of preparation and competence, and because the leaders' responses to group members' interests and issues were inadequate. Many people today fear the effects of treatment in groups. If group leaders are not sufficiently knowledgeable and competent, that fear may well be justified. Our conviction is that the guidelines this book presents will help group leaders create a safe environment for group therapy and will counteract the destructive potential that is always present in groups.

Many types of group therapy training programmes are offered in different parts of the world. However, a decrease in educational opportunities to learn this kind of therapy has been observed in approximately the last 20 years. One can only speculate on the reasons for this development. Perhaps the explanation may relate to society's more individualistic culture and to people's increased use of the Internet to meet their social needs. Yet we are convinced that this scenario will change in due time. As we described in Chapter 2, man, as a social being, must exist In Real Life for communicating with and understanding others. People need to be in eye contact, something not even modern online techniques can offer, even if one can observe facial expressions and body movements in Skype, Zoom, and Teams meetings. Human interaction is severely handicapped without cues from facial expressions, body language, and sometimes subtle signals from other sensory organs. Even cognitive functions are impaired by the lack of emotional signals (Gantt & Agazarian, 2010).

Does group therapy work?

In the last 30 to 40 years, various trends have emerged in the research on group therapy. Even earlier, in the 1960s and 1970s, when group psychotherapy was first attracting attention as a modality for treatment, it was natural for researchers to ask whether group therapy has the intended effect.

Mary Lee Smith and colleagues (1980) made one of the earliest investigations of group therapy in their book *The Benefits of Psychotherapy*. The book presented a meta-analysis of 475 controlled case studies on psychotherapy of which almost half (233) analysed group therapy that lasted around three months. They introduced an index for use in comparing different therapies, the so-called *effect size*, which is still used in psychotherapy research to report the effects of treatment. The effect size is a simple way of quantifying the difference between groups; for example, the results on symptom scales before and after group therapy. The index illustrates the average degree of change in the whole sample in relation to the standard deviation. If the effect size is 0.2, for example, it is small and trivial even if it is statistically significant. A size of 0.5 is considered medium; a size of 0.8 and above is considered large. When Smith and colleagues compared the outcome of the studies of individual psychotherapy with the studies of group therapy, they found no difference. Mean effect sizes were 0.83 for group therapy and 0.87 for individual therapy. The conclusion was that group therapy "worked" as well as other forms of psychotherapy.

In the 1980s and 1990s, many researchers studied issues related to the so-called "form equivalence"; i.e., the similarities and dissimilarities in the results from group therapy and individual therapy. Several meta-analyses have reviewed research projects that compare the results from individual therapy and group therapy. Some analyses reached the same conclusion that Smith et al. (1980) did – essentially there is no difference between the two therapy forms in terms of results (Piper & Joyce, 1996; Tillitski, 1990). Yet, in some cases, the reverse effect was observed as reported by McRoberts et al. (1998). These researchers found the effect size was 0.76 for individual therapy and 0.90 for group therapy.

On the whole, however, the general conclusion from the research is that the results are the same regardless of whether the treatment takes place in group therapy or in individual therapy. A German meta-analysis that included new research showed similar results for the two therapy forms (Tschuschke, 1996). No differences were found in 11 of the studies; individual therapy produced better results than group therapy in five studies; group therapy produced better results than individual therapy in six studies. Burlingame et al. (2004) confirmed that the research strongly supports the conclusion that essentially no differences exist between the two therapy formats' results. Nevertheless, further research is needed to explore if patients with certain diagnoses or other characteristics are better suited for either group therapy or individual treatment.

Effectiveness of different patient groups

In recent years, several studies have shown good treatment results from group therapy for conditions such as depression, stress-related illness, social phobia, panic disorder, obsessive-compulsive disorder, eating disorders, addiction problems, intimate partner violence, trauma/post-traumatic stress disorder, physical illness (e.g., breast cancer), personality disorder, and schizophrenia (Berg Nesset et al., 2019; Burlingame et al., 2003, 2004; Delafield-Butt & Trevarthen, 2013; Fuhriman & Burlingame, 1994; Knauss, 2005; Lo Coco et al., 2019; Mahoney et al., 2019; McLaughlin et al., 2019). Good results from group therapy have also been reported for family members of seriously ill people, for HIV-positive and AIDS patients, for psychosomatic patients, and for people of all ages with other psychiatric problems (Bieling et al., 2006; Burlingame et al., 2013; MacKenzie, 1997). In a Swedish study of group therapy for patients on long-term sick leave due to exhaustion syndrome (Sandahl et al., 2011), good improvements were observed. However, no differences in the results were found when focused group therapy (see Chapter 12) and cognitive behavioural therapy (CBT) in groups were compared with individual therapy.

Long-term group therapy

Most group therapy studies involve relatively short therapies (usually fewer than 20 meetings). However, there are exceptions. For example, research in a Norwegian setting showed good symptom and social function improvements among a psychiatric patient group. The sample of 69 patients in 10 groups was studied after an average of 100 meetings in group analytical psychotherapy (Lorentzen et al., 2002). An earlier study, set in Canada, found that long-term group therapy yielded better results than short-term therapy (Piper et al., 1984). Volker Tschuschke and colleagues (Tschuschke & Anbeh, 2000; Tschuschke et al., 2007) followed more than 450 patients in 28 groups in a natural therapy course. They found good symptom improvements in the patients in long-term, group analytical therapy. Satisfactory results were also reported for extended therapies with patients with eating disorders as well as with sexually abused women, addicts with personality disorder, and young adults with mental health issues (Knauss, 2005).

Lorentzen et al. (2013) conducted an ambitious and unique study in Norway in which the results from short- and long-term manual-based (i.e., using specific guidelines) group analytical psychotherapies were compared. The short-term group met for 20 weekly sessions; the long-term for 80 weekly sessions. The average effect size for both groups was 0.80. However, a difference emerged in the follow-up study on the patients with personality disorders who were in the original study. For that group, the long-term therapy produced better results (Lorentzen, Ruud et al., 2015b). An analysis of data from a seven-year follow-up study on these patients revealed an interesting difference between the two therapies. The patients in short-term therapy maintained their improvements in symptoms, in management of interpersonal problems, and in psycho-social functions. The patients in long-term therapy continued to improve in these areas (Lorentzen, Fjeldstad et al., 2015a).

Historically, group therapy has usually been targeted at patients with a moderate degree of psychopathology such as depression, anxiety, or relatively mild relationship problems. Patients who have difficulty with impulse control or who experience serious relationship problems are generally not considered suitable for group therapy (Rutan et al., 2007).

However, some positive research results exist on homogeneous patient groups with personality disorders (especially borderline personality disorders) (McLaughlin et al., 2019). Some major studies that combine individual therapy and group therapy have also shown good results for mentalization-based therapy (Bateman & Fonagy, 2009) and dialectical behavioural therapy (McMain et al., 2009). Marziali and Munroe-Blum (1994) compared interpersonal group therapy and individual therapy in extensive research. They found that both therapies had positive and similar outcomes although group therapy was superior from a cost perspective. However, they found that the therapists preferred group therapy for other reasons – it was easier and less tiring to relate empathically to patients when they met them in groups. This research concludes that group therapy as used in psychiatric treatment contributes to a more positive work environment for therapists.

What is the significance of the group dynamic?

Many topics fall under the heading "Group therapy research". Probably the most common topic is the kind of group therapy this book describes. This is group therapy in which the focus is on the group members' interactions and communications, which are regarded as the central psychotherapeutic factors. However, it should be emphasized that the overwhelming majority of published group therapy research deals with CBT.

Only a few controlled studies address therapies in which group process is the central starting point. Even fewer studies compare CBT with process-focused therapy. One exception is the research on the treatment of alcoholism. Two studies (Kadden et al., 1989; Sandahl et al., 1998) conclude that CBT in groups is best suited for patients with severe alcohol dependency. People with mild or moderate alcohol problems benefit more from process-focused therapy, interactive treatment, or psychodynamic treatment. Some empirical research also supports the conclusion that patients with a lower degree of alcohol dependency and a lower degree of psychopathology benefit most from group therapy that focuses on the interpersonal and dynamic interaction in the group. Patients with more severe alcohol problems benefit more from the behavioural and cognitive elements in therapy (Sandahl et al., 2004).

As mentioned above, most scientific studies on group therapy focus on the use of CBT. However, Burlingame et al.'s (2013) review of group therapy research highlights an interesting paradox. They found that many researchers who study CBT in groups point to a problematic inconsistency in their studies. The theory behind the treatment of a certain patient population does not explain their research results. Burlingame and colleagues think the researchers overlook important information when they pay insufficient attention to well-known and measurable group characteristics and processes such as cohesion, group climate, group development, and the experience of the group as a whole. They conclude that CBT researchers simply do not see themselves as specialists in group therapy or group dynamics. Instead, CBT researchers see themselves as specialists in a particular diagnosis category (e.g., depression) or as advocates of a particular theoretical perspective. Therefore, according to Burlingame and colleagues, these researchers are not particularly interested in studying group processes using the available research tools.

Another explanation for CBT researchers' lack of interest in group processes has to do with how CBT has been used in psychotherapy. Traditionally, CBT has been described and practiced as a treatment for individuals. Thus, no group theory has been proposed or developed for CBT. This may seem strange given that CBT has been practiced in groups since the 1970s. Initially, the argument for the use of CBT in group therapy was that more patients could be treated in groups than could be treated as individuals in the same period of time (Hollon & Shaw, 1979). Therefore, as the demand for cost savings in health and medical care increased, it became necessary to adapt CBT to group therapy. CBT therapists have succumbed to this pressure, particularly because of the recent success of CBT in groups.

Convincing empirical data are now available on the positive treatment effects of group therapy. This research has tended to focus on well-defined issues that affect patients and therapists and on the structural aspects of group therapy. The issues of interest include the frequency, intensity, and length of group therapy as well as group size, occurrence of follow-up meetings, and the care context. *Context* refers to outpatient or inpatient care or to psychiatry or primary care.

For example, a group therapy study of patients in Canada with complicated grief responses revealed that the patients with more stable object relationships benefited most from psychodynamic group therapy (Piper et al., 2001). This finding is consistent with findings from studies on alcohol-dependent patients (Kadden et al., 1989; Sandahl et al., 1998). Similarly, Piper et al. (ibid.) found that patients who find it difficult to think and reason about internal psychological motives and conflicts – i.e., those with a lower degree of "psychological mindedness" (cf. *mentalization ability*) – received greater benefit from the structured group therapy. In the same study, a positive correlation was identified between treatment results and both psychological mindedness and group cohesion.

In addition, consideration should be given to the special nature of group therapy; namely, group dynamics and group processes. The issues include group cohesion, group members' communications and openness, and the development of therapeutic group alliances. How do we view the group as a whole – i.e., the group as a unit? What do we know about the group tendency to develop in stages, of which the most crucial stage deals with premature independence and conflicts concerning roles and status?

However, an important point should be made about group CBT. In several controlled studies that compared CBT with other therapies, the results from the control groups (that unintentionally applied group process factors) were positive.

Similar results from studies of several different patient populations support our assumption – group process factors are highly important in group therapy (Burlingame et al., 2004). According to Fuhriman and Burlingame (1994), if a technique used in individual therapy is to be equally effective in group therapy, it is necessary to utilize these unique group process factors. If these factors are not considered, individual therapy will most likely prove to be superior to group therapy.

The challenge for group therapy researchers today is how to address issues related to group cohesion and therapeutic alliances as well as the group experience as a whole. Other topics to explore further are how group leaders exercise their leadership, how group members interact, and how group members and group leaders develop their relationships (Burlingame et al., 2013). In summary, although the extensive research on group therapy is convincing as to its effectiveness, it is not as comprehensive as the research on individual therapy.

Can group therapy cause harm?

There is no doubt that groups may exert a destructive influence on group members. Most people have painful memories of school groups and agonizing recollections from their adolescent years. Even as adults, many people have experienced bullying, hostility, scapegoating, and ostracism from groups. We all have been part of groups that are stupefying, groups where it is impossible to take personal responsibility and use one's competence. At best these groups lead to inaction and paralysis, at worst to destructive acting-out. Morris Nitsun (1996), the English group analyst, refers to these phenomena as "anti-group". He argues that anti-group phenomena can also appear in therapy groups. However, more positively, Nitsun claims that courage in confronting these destructive phenomena can turn them into creative forces.

Researchers who have investigated *anti-therapeutic factors* have mostly concentrated on leadership characteristics. For example, charismatic group leaders, some of whom express a desire to "save" group members, can have a negative influence on members, especially when the leaders use control and/or rejection measures. Yalom and Leszcz (2020), in their review, argue that group leaders who exhibit impatience, authoritarianism, or uncooperative behaviour usually encounter problems with their groups. Passive and withdrawn group leaders can also contribute to destructive group processes by making group members feel insecure and abandoned because of their lack of group engagement. It is well established, in the field of leadership research, that passive and disengaged managers, with a so-called *laissez-faire* attitude, have a negative effect on work environments and employee health (Romanowska et al., 2018).

Most research on the negative or harmful effects of group therapy has been conducted in inpatient group therapy and in therapeutic community settings (Korda & Pancrazio, 1989). Erickson (1987), in a review of many of these studies, found no evidence for the conclusion that group therapy is more harmful in these settings than, for example, in settings when medications or individual therapy are used. Lambert and Bergin (1994) found that negative effects appeared on average in 10 percent of all patients in all forms of psychotherapeutic treatment. Yet these findings do not mean that the possibility of negative outcomes from group therapy should be dismissed. Probably the least-worst outcome of a harmful group therapy experience is that patients will leave the group. Other harmful outcomes are far more serious.

Korda and Pancrazio (1989) listed the various causes of the negative effects of group therapy (paraphrased) as follows: (1) unrealistic expectations, (2) fear of intimacy and self-reflection, (3) feelings of rejection and attack, (4) values that differ from the group values, (5) simultaneous life crises, (6) the emergence of stereotype sub-groups, (7) aggressive leadership attitudes, and (8) leadership disengagement (mental or physical).

Korda and Pancrazio (ibid.) offered the following recommendations to minimize these harmful effects (paraphrased):

1   Evaluate the competence of the group therapist.
2   Evaluate the competences of co-therapists.
3   Make appropriate patient assessments and preparations.
4   Decide on the security measures, including clear rules.
5   Address conflict management, transparency issues, and the emergence of stereotype sub-groups.
6   Avoid group leader absenteeism.
7   Manage the patient drop-out issue constructively.

If an inadequate process is used to select patients for a group, the potential for destructive group responses increases. For example, if the group members are very dissimilar or if one member is very different from the others, members are likely to have difficulty relating to others' life situations (see Chapter 6).

Active therapeutic factors in group therapy

Group cohesion, with its strong connection to positive treatment results, is the most studied active therapeutic factor in group therapy (Lorentzen, 2013). Group cohesion exists when group members achieve a state of mutual loyalty and solidarity, and when group members identify with the group's goals and cooperate to achieve them. Group cohesion counteracts the tendency towards fragmentation or dissolution of the group. In the initial group phases, it is important that the group leader contributes to a group climate that promotes group cohesion. Group cohesion is a prerequisite for other therapeutic factors.

Another important active therapeutic factor is the collective spirit of equality among group members that strengthens when they exchange *information* on symptoms and problems and offer each other *advice*. When people in group therapy *identify* with other members after making comparisons of similarities and dissimilarities, psychological differentiation increases at the same time as empathy and therapeutic understanding are exhibited. Through identification, transference, and projection, members can, for example, *re-live*, *process*, and *resolve* family and other conflicts in new ways.

The discovery by group members that their contributions can support others has significance for their own self-esteem. The group therapy literature refers to this active therapeutic factor as *altruism* because it concerns helping others by sharing experiences without expectation of reward. It is important not to underestimate the significance of this experience for group members. Sandahl's not-yet-published observations from interviews with members in the so-called Backstage Groups for Managers and members in CBT groups for social outsiders revealed an unexpected similarity between these two socially disparate samples. In interviews conducted after the group intervention, a majority of the interviewees said they were very surprised by how much useful knowledge they could offer other participants. They said this result (one of the most important results from the group experience) had had a therapeutic effect – it increased the self-esteem of both groups. A similar pattern was found regarding the active therapeutic factor of *universality* – the state of being when people recognize that others share their problems. This research also found that group leaders are initially responsible for the *hope* active therapeutic factor that strengthens as members see that other group members benefit from the therapy.

Yalom and Leszcz (2005, 2020) list 12 therapeutic factors that have been studied and that, in varying degrees, have significance for patients in group therapy. These factors are as follows (paraphrased):

1 Altruism – support for each other.
2 Cohesiveness – trust, belonging, and togetherness among group members.
3 Universality – the discovery that people share similar feelings, thoughts, and problems.
4 Interpersonal learning – input and feedback from other members.
5 Interpersonal learning – giving personal feedback which contributes to adaptive interaction.
6 Socialization – the group provides an environment that fosters skills of communication and interaction.
7 Resolving primary family dynamics – the opportunity to re-enact early patterns of being, but in a corrective manner.
8 Imparting information – Advice or education provided by group members or group leader.
9 Catharsis – release of strong feelings related to past or current experiences.
10 Imitative behaviour – observation of other group members, self-exploration, and working through.
11 Instillation of hope – recognizing other members' improvement and developing optimism for own improvement.
12 Existential factors – members accept responsibility for life decisions.

While all these therapeutic factors are important in group therapy, different groups focus on different factors. To these factors, we may add the following, widely supported therapeutic factor: the *therapeutic alliance* (discussed below).

Three therapeutically effective common factors in group therapy

Sandahl and Lindgren (2006), in their analysis of various forms of therapy, identify three main therapeutically effective factors commonly found in group therapy, regardless of the theoretical focus (the so-called common factors): (1) support, (2) learning, and (3) action. Sandahl and Lindgren also describe how a positive group experience can have a positive influence on members (see Chapter 12), leading to the transfer of group learning to life outside the group. They also comment on the powerful reinforcement implied when members act in new and constructive ways in and outside the group. As a result, new learning helps people solve difficult situations that previously seemed unsolvable.

We describe these three common factors next.

Support

Group cohesion fails if there is too little support in a group. Without the therapeutic factor of support, members may attend meetings sporadically or even leave the group. Group cohesion is especially important when a group is first formed. It is at this point that group members decide if they will risk joining the group, will dare to talk openly about their problems, and will be receptive to learning from the group therapy. Studies of groups with a high degree of group cohesion are characterized by the members' *interest, contact, trust, support, care, willingness to listen, focus, collaboration, openness, feedback*, and *process orientation*. A fundamental requirement of the therapeutic process in group therapy is that the members agree to express personal emotions and thoughts frankly, regardless of whether these emotions and thoughts are associated with conflict, support, or care.

There is intrinsic value in engaging with other group members who have experienced similar difficult-to-handle situations and relationships. These shared experiences create an immediate affinity among members and reduce the potential embarrassment that openness about personal problems may evoke. Compared to individual therapy, group therapy requires a slightly longer introductory period before the actual psychotherapeutic treatment begins. Typically, it is a challenge to get the group to function as a therapeutic instrument and to create a sufficiently secure group climate. The process takes less time in individual therapy where only two people (therapist and patient) need to establish a relationship. The process is much more complex in group therapy. However, this sometimes-lengthy introductory process is useful because it allows the group members to learn how groups will function and develop. This is learning that can be used in other settings as well.

We describe the therapeutic alliance, which is part of "support", in a later section of this chapter. The topic merits its own section owing to its central importance in treatment outcomes.

Learning

Learning is a therapeutic factor that is present throughout the duration of the group. People are unwilling to join groups or attend group meetings if they are not convinced there is something to learn from the experience. The learning may take various forms: learning about yourself, learning how others function, and learning new information relative to your particular life situation. Group members can acquire more effective life competences from emotionally meaningful communications in groups.

A positive spiral begins in the group when people begin to show their vulnerability by telling personal stories. It is then easier for others to tell stories that reveal their own vulnerability. The stories are important, especially when they are authentic and emotionally charged. When group members tell stories, other members experience shared continuity, wholeness, and identification.

Action

Action, as a therapeutic factor, is about trying new ways of being, mastering difficult situations, and developing the ability to communicate. If learning in group therapy is to have any relevance for group members, action must follow. Action can begin in the group or in any other setting where group members are willing to risk failure. There is no better reinforcement, to the use of learning-theoretical reasoning, than to master something that you were unable to master previously. Group therapy, with its focus on interaction and communication, provides a unique opportunity to try new ways of being in a relatively secure environment.

The therapeutic alliance

A prerequisite for the success of the therapeutic process in group therapy is that the group offers sufficient security that members are comfortable expressing their thoughts and emotions as freely as possible. The group leader has a particularly important role in developing therapeutic alliances with group members. A therapeutic alliance is an agreement between the group leader and the group members in *a relationship of sufficient mutual trust about the group's purpose, goals, methods, and areas of responsibility.*

The concept of the therapeutic alliance is well known in psychotherapy research, especially in individual therapy. However, the concept is more difficult to define and describe in group therapy than in individual therapy. Group therapy researchers have primarily been more interested in the factors related to common group experiences, especially *cohesion* and *climate*. Some researchers argue that *alliance* is a concept more closely associated with the therapist, while *cohesion* refers more to the group in the sense of belonging. Researchers have even struggled to agree on the definitions of these words (Piper et al., 2005).

In fact, the concept of the therapeutic alliance has only recently been recognized as a key issue in the research on group therapy. In part, the explanation may be that the group is thought of as a composite entity consisting of many complex factors. For example, group therapy includes several sub-systems: the group leader, the group members, the group as a whole, the sub-groups, and the organization behind the group. In addition, the interrelationships among these many sub-systems evolve over time.

A constructive therapeutic alliance in the group is created when there is a sense of group cohesion and when each group member agrees with others on why they have joined the group, how the work should progress, and what the group's goals are. If the group leader and the group members can create a positive therapeutic alliance, it is more likely that difficulties in the development of the group can be overcome. The research on therapeutic alliances in groups has shown a link between a high degree of alliance and positive treatment results. The research also points to the importance of the group members' alliance with the group as a whole in the interpersonal work stage (Lindgren et al., 2008; Piper et al., 2005). Obviously, a constructive therapeutic alliance in the group is only possible after group cohesion has been established.

In the process of building a group therapeutic alliance, the first step is to establish an alliance with the group leader. This alliance will be the basis for the members' alliance with the group. Thus, it is important that potential group members meet with group leaders in advance of the group meetings. In these meetings the group members require information about the group's goals, boundaries, and rules, as well as establishing a relation to the group leader. Without this information, it is difficult for members to understand how they can benefit from group therapy and how their participation can benefit other members. Thus, these one-on-one meetings give the potential group members the opportunity to ask questions about their problems, express their concerns about the group environment, and communicate their expectations about the therapy. The meetings are also an opportunity for group leaders to set realistic expectations. In this way, group leaders and group members work together as they determine the goals and focus of the group therapy (see Chapter 6).

The group members' alliance with the group leader should be specific and well-founded so that the alliance will be sustainable in all meetings of a time-limited group. All group members should have enough confidence in the alliance to sustain them through the inevitable periods of uncertainty and anxiety in the group. Although alliances develop gradually, their continued stability depends on how events occur, how the group interaction is perceived, and whether members feel secure. Security is essential for the members' reflection and learning. If members do not feel they are in a safe environment, they will take in less information. They will divert their energy to coping with perceived threats in an unfamiliar environment.

The potential group members' attitudes and personalities influence the success or failure of the initial meetings with the group leader. It is here that the group leader discovers, for example, the members' willingness to receive information and their capacity to trust. The group leader also has to manage various expectations, fears, emotions, and ideas before the group starts. Has the group leader engaged in this work voluntarily? Or has the sponsoring organization required the group leader to conduct this work? Is the therapy required by the particular care unit? How committed is the group leader to this work? Which emotions are evoked in the group leader by this work? If group leaders are new and inexperienced in this role, do they bring positive and negative emotions to the current group situation? In sum, the group leaders' professional experiences and competences as well as life experiences and personal growth are all factors that influence the creation and development of the therapeutic alliance.

The group leaders' organizations also influence the likelihood that constructive therapeutic alliances will be created between the group leaders and the group members. The likelihood that a stable alliance will develop increases if sponsoring organizations recognize that the group experience can contribute to their organizational goals and purpose. Organizations will then be more likely to support the group therapy and the group leaders.

The authors of this book have experience with the formation of therapeutic alliances and know which conditions are conducive to their formation. We next describe therapeutic alliances as they developed in two of our research projects.

We conducted two research projects with patients with exhaustion syndrome. The patients were randomly assigned to three treatment alternatives. We acted as group leaders for the short-term groups (according to the focused group therapy model; see Chapter 12). The conditions of the alternatives had some similarities as well as significant differences.

In the first research project, a physician and a psychologist made an initial assessment of the patients. The psychologist conducted psychological tests of the patients and created an individual focus for each patient. The psychologist also conducted the patient interviews and collected patient data. The group leader, who did not participate in the preparation work, did not meet the patients before the group meetings began.

In the second research project, the patients received written information about the therapy prior to the planning and composition of the groups. Unlike the first research project, the group leader conducted the patient interviews (usually three interviews). This interview process, which involved patient information acquisition and patient assessment, included the design of an individual focus for use in the group therapy.

The therapeutic alliances between the group leader and the patients were thus created earlier in the second research project than in the first research project; therefore, the second group's alliances with the group leader were stronger and deeper. When the group meetings began, the patients had already formed therapeutic alliances with the group leader. As a result, the group leader–patient interaction in the second research project took place in a more secure and more engaged environment than in the first research project.

Our conclusion from these two projects is that the therapeutic alliance, which was established in the individual meetings with the group leader, had a positive influence on the group's future work.

Group-specific factors

A fundamental principle of process- and interaction-oriented group therapy is that communication among group members have a healing effect. Foulkes argued that everything that advances personal communication between people leads to better social integration and thus to stronger mental health (Foulkes, 1984). In Foulkes's view, mental disorder is caused by the inability to communicate, resulting in isolation and alienation. In group therapy, if the atmosphere is one of tolerance and patience, group members can learn from the group, especially when they see how others react to their behaviour.

Foulkes also described some so-called group-specific factors (i.e., group properties not found in other therapeutic forms). We consider these factors next.

In the group analytic tradition, the therapeutic group's capacity for *socialization* is considered one of the most important group-specific factors. Group members learn how groups function and indirectly how families, society, and work-life function as well as their own role in these contexts. Group members constantly reveal their being to themselves and to other members. They also receive direct responses to their behaviour from others.

A therapy group has been described as a mirrored room. The group members, to a greater or lesser extent, reflect fragmented aspects of other group members. During an extended period of communication and exchange, these fragments of the self may join in new ways such that certain aspects strengthen and others weaken. In modern psychology, this *looking-glass phenomenon* has yet another connotation – the idea that one is seen and acknowledged by the mirroring effect. To experience meaning and connection in life, people require a kind of affective feedback in their interactions. This feedback, which helps allay doubts, confirms that experiences are real. It also seems that group members are more able than group leaders to provide this kind of spontaneous and explicit confirmation. Group leaders, who are constrained by the professional role in a way that group members are not, provide less direct and personal feedback

The *interpersonal learning* that occurs in the *exchange* of experiences and opinions is unique to group therapy. The positive therapeutic effect is assumed to increase if the feedback given is specific, closely associated with the cause of the feedback, emotionally charged, and focused on the person who provides the feedback (i.e., feedback not as judgment but as an expression of personal reactions). Ideally, such feedback should be non-judgmental and should illuminate the relationship between the feedback sender and the feedback receiver. The group leader's responsibility is to encourage and support the members involved so that the feedback results in a constructive and positive experience (Yalom & Leszcz, 2005, 2020).

Learning from emotional experiences in the group setting

Being able to read other people's affects is sometimes essential. In certain circumstances we need to recognize the existence of threats and react immediately to them without reflection. In everyday life, this ability is reflected in intuitive behaviour based on our gut feelings. For example, when you board a bus or an underground carriage, almost without conscious thought you pause for perhaps a fraction of a second to look for unruly gangs or deviant passengers. Instinctively, you avoid eye contact and sit at a distance. Or, as you cross the street, out of the corner of your eye you glimpse a speeding car coming towards you. Without thinking, you jump back. In both examples, you have no time to plan an action strategy or to take a defensive position. Afterward, when the danger has passed, it takes a while before your breathing and heart rate return to normal. Then, with some distance as you dwell on the "what-might-have-been", you process the learning from such frightening experiences.

All our experiences in life, especially the implicit, non-verbal experiences from early childhood, are embedded in our emotions. Our emotions and others' responses to these emotions create our innermost core, which in everyday speech we often refer to as the *self*. The basis of self-esteem is built from such early emotional experiences and from others' responses to them. We recognize the physical aspects of such emotions. We have all described them using metaphors: strong as steel, taut as a violin string, happy as a lark, heavy as lead, and so on.

In recent years, many psychoanalysts and psychologists (Fonagy et al., 2004; Schore, 2003; Schore & Schore, 2008) have focused on the theory of human affects, in particular the regulation of these affects that are driving forces in human development. These researchers conclude that an important task for parents and others engaged in children's development is teaching children about human emotions. Even in the first year of life, children learn which emotions their parents respond to and which are ignored or regulated. For example, if children see that their primary attachment person responds negatively to their temper tantrums (by rejection and distancing), gradually they moderate their behaviour and learn to control their anger. This result is similar to the group's complex format with its revitalizing, intersubjective mutual encounters in group sessions.

Group members, through human communication and interaction, can practice managing their own and others' emotions and behaviours. Peter Fonagy, the British-Hungarian psychologist, thinks all psychic difficulties and disorders in large measure can be understood as shortcomings in the mentalization ability.

Therefore, he argues that all psychotherapies, even more than they do today, should focus on the patient–group intersubjective mentalization in the present (Fonagy et al., 2002).

People are more inclined to remember and activate negative emotions than positive emotions. They therefore either deliberately or subconsciously avoid situations they think may provoke negative emotions (McClusky, 2005). For this reason, it is essential that group leaders create a group climate of trust that provides a safe haven for group members where they can connect with their emotions and needs, dare to be open with each other, and risk talking about the emotions evoked by the group setting and the group interaction.

The group format provides an opportunity, in the communications among group members and with group leaders, to co-create new experiences in which affects can be observed, received, and empathetically regulated. The group format can also help members understand how their own behaviour can arouse strong emotions in others – in and outside the group. The group becomes a practice arena where emotions are recognized and expressed. Foulkes's (1984) thesis on "ego training in action" describes how our emotions form part of a mutual and emotional exchange.

The group provides an opportunity to test new ways of being with others

The group leader's inner and outer work with emotions in the group is of great importance. The group leader's emotions that are evoked by the members and the interactions in the group are sources of important information. The group leader's personal feelings provide cues as to what else occurs in the group – for example, members' expressed emotions in the moment or members' repressed and unexpressed emotions.

In the group example (below), the group members have met a few times and have created a group climate in which they feel secure and trust one another. The therapist, who observes that the conversation is a little sluggish, notices that one member is quiet and seems tense and under stress. In the following example, "GL" is the therapist; "A", "B", and "C" are group members.

GL [to B]:   You haven't said much today. I wonder why.
B: I don't know if I want to talk or not. I probably should.
A: You don't seem well. Why? I'm curious. But don't talk just for my sake.
C: I have been sitting here and thinking that you don't seem yourself today. You usually say something important.
GL: As you can see, several of us are wondering how you are. With all due respect, you are the one to decide. I think you know how important I think it is to express your feelings in the group. *[It is important to encourage B to talk because B's body language expresses clearly that something is bothering him. If group members leave the group in highly emotional states, there is a risk they will not return.]*

B: You know that I was counting on an inheritance from my father. But I received nothing. It feels like I don't even exist. He left everything to his new wife.

A: That doesn't seem fair. You have half-siblings. What do they say?

B: [*downcast, with head bowed*]: They avoid me. It's just as I always knew it would be. My father didn't care at all about me.

C: I really recognize this feeling of being left out. It was the same for me. I got nothing from my grandfather and grandmother, who took care of me when I was a teenager. Still, I got nothing. I wasn't even contacted when my grandfather died. I read about his death in the newspaper. It was simply too damn unfair.

GL: Now I understand why you seemed so upset. I wonder how you feel now that you have told us the reason.

B: I don't know exactly. Both good and bad. It feels good, C, that you understand how I feel. But it feels embarrassing also.

C: I get so damned angry. Actually, I think anger is a protection. I had pushed away these thoughts about being ignored, but I have them again when you describe your feelings.

B: I have such a hard time being angry. I'm just ashamed to be me. No one wants to know me. It would be nice to react, but I can't. I just feel empty and anxious.

The group continues to work with the various emotions expressed. The goal is to encourage the group members to understand that their reactions are reasonable, and that they can identify and communicate their emotions to others. In this way, the group becomes an arena where they can rethink old ways of being and receive the attention their families do not provide.

In many groups, two group leaders work together. Our experience is that different group members affect group leaders emotionally in different ways. Paying attention to these various emotions and reflecting on them are helpful ways to achieve a more complex understanding of the whole situation.

The following example is from a group-based, integrated, and relationship therapy group for infants and their mothers. "A" is a mother; "GL1" and "GL2" are therapists.

A: My mother telephoned today to wish me Happy Mother's Day. I became stiff and fended her off. I don't feel like a mother. I absolutely do not want to be congratulated on being a mother.

GL1: How did you think about yourself as a parent before you had your own children?

A: I felt almost nauseated when my husband said, 'Just think, in a couple of months you will be a mother.'

B: But that attitude is not evident. You take care of your child and seem to care about her.

A: Yes, I do, but it is difficult to explain. I take care of her, but I feel that something is missing – a happiness that others have – like you, for example. I do not feel like a mother at all. I like her and feel responsible for her. She is a nice baby, but it feels like she could be anyone's nice baby.

GL2: It is difficult to put feelings into words. This difficulty begins early in life – when you were the same age as your children are now. That was the time before you could speak and think in language. The important thing is to think and talk about it here in the group. I know it works and makes it possible to eventually change your feelings.

A: I think the word 'mother' immediately makes me think of my own mother and my feelings about our relationship. I'm afraid of those feelings. They might make me feel even worse.

Then the other women/group members in the example, taking different points of view, begin to discuss how they feel about their relationships with their parents.

The two therapists listen to A's story empathically as the fundamental theme (harbouring negative emotions) appears. They establish an atmosphere of serenity and hope. They offer sympathetic remarks such as "We have heard this before" or "Others have had the same experience." They exhibit a theoretical understanding of the woman's emotions (psycho-education and cognitive understanding). They link the theme to other group members (broaden, deepen, and develop it) in an approach that leads to conscious reflection by the entire group. In this way, the group's emotional and experiential landscape increases. The therapists work interactively with the group, using both psychodynamic and cognitive and relational interventions at the "here and now" level that links to the "there and then" level.

Sharing experiences and feelings

Group leaders often encourage group members to describe group interaction openly and honestly. The following comments by a group leader exemplify such encouragement.

> Peter, you say that you have observed a pattern in how Minna finds space in the group and makes herself heard. Try to tell her about this pattern from your perspective so that she understands how you think and feel.

> One of the group leader's most important functions is to give the group members the opportunity to share experiences and feelings. Typically, a group leader will call attention to the fact that the concept of communication originates from the Latin word *communicare* – to make something common.

When communication works well in a group, the members experience an affinity with each other. When they feel connected, they can express thoughts and emotions that are mirrored by others. When people share their inner world with others, their thoughts become clearer to themselves and their emotions are easier to understand.

When communication works poorly, we usually feel frustrated. We may turn this frustration either outward or inward. When our frustration is turned outward, we think the poor communication is "someone else's fault". We then attribute that individual's lack of understanding to specific personality traits that explain an inability to comprehend or use language. When our frustration is turned inward, we blame ourselves. We feel isolated. We have negative thoughts about ourselves. People who are in long-term relationships where the communication has broken down, or is negative and defensive, are at risk of losing their self-confidence and self-esteem. Many people join therapy groups when they find themselves in such situations. Therefore, an important task for group leaders is to encourage open communication and to work actively to prevent potentially destructive communication.

Constructive and destructive forms of communication

How do we know if communication is constructive or destructive? Drawing from the work of North American psychologist Anita Simon and the founder of the *Theory of human living systems and its systems-centered practice*, Yvonne Agazarian (1967, 2000), Ben Benjamin, Amy Yeager, and Anita Simon, in their book *Conversation Transformation* (2012), describe how to identify communication patterns that either increase or decrease the probability of successful problem-solving in human interaction. Their work elaborates the coding patterns identified in the SAVI (System for Analyzing Verbal Interactions). SAVI was developed by Anita Simon and Yvonne Agazarian (2010) as a way of identifying which verbal behaviours are likely to transfer information and which are unlikely to do so. Agazarian et al. (2020) then applied this understanding in her work in SCT in recognizing the importance of identifying sufficient similarities in views, thoughts, and experiences among the people we are trying to communicate with. If our points of view or our information are too dissimilar, we do not recognize ourselves in what others say. Therefore, good communication requires conversational patterns where one can recognize and relate to what is said and to build on others' experiences and thoughts. In this way, we are able to share experiences and emotions. Simon and Agazarian (1967, 2000) introduced the idea of a traffic light metaphor to describe communication. "Red light" communication increases distance and conflict. "Yellow light" communication is neutral. "Green light" communication creates closeness and new learning opportunities.

In "red light" group communication, you attack yourself, others, or the entire world. You may complain and use sarcasm. Or you may act evasively by gossiping or claiming you are "just joking" when you make snide remarks. Or you may act competitively by interrupting, asking provocative questions, raising objections, or rudely dismissing others' ideas.

In "yellow light" group communication, you reveal impersonal information about yourself or objective information about the world. You communicate facts that are useful in orienting yourself and in making decisions. You ask encouraging questions, express uncontroversial opinions, and offer suggestions. Neutral reinforcement (by nodding, humming ["Mmm"], or remarking "I understand") lets others know that you understand them.

In "green light" group communication, you (and others) are inspired by the group's open and safe climate. You express your understanding of others, you share their emotions, and you mirror their experiences. You answer their questions honestly, restate their ideas supportively, and present your own ideas clearly. You agree with (and value) others' contributions and use them to develop your own contributions.

To establish a constructive conversation climate early in the life of the group, group leaders should encourage all members to build on each other's opinions and experiences. For example, a group leader might look at the members and ask: "Do any of you recognize yourself in what X is describing?" The group leader should react to members arguing or making deliberately provocative statements. In the fragile climate in the early stages of the group this kind of communication can evoke fear and fight/flight behaviour.

If a group member is met with silence and lack of response, especially if it happens several times, the group member tends to withdraw to silence and maybe abandons the group. It is the responsibility of group leaders to react and ensure some kind of response, either by responding oneself or by inviting the other group members to respond. In the following example, we suggest what a group leader might say:

> There was no response in the group to Giorgio's fear that he could not return to work. Before we go any further, I wonder if anyone recognizes what Giorgio is telling us?

"Noise" in the communication

In Claude Elwood Shannon and Warren Weaver's classic communication model (1949), communication is described as a process in which information is transmitted between transmitter and receiver, and in which "noise" makes information transfer difficult. Their model describes two categories of noise in communication: (1) vagueness, and (2) redundancy. When SAVI (see above) was developed as an operational definition of Shannon and Weaver's communication model by Simon and Agazarian, they introduced contradiction as a third source of noise in conversation (Simon & Agazarian, 2000). Let us look at those sources in more depth:

1   *Vagueness* describes communication that is unclear, evasive, and open to alternative interpretations. People who communicate vaguely often have an imprecise idea of the message they wish to deliver. Or, because of self-doubt, they fear challenges and personal attacks. They often feel misunderstood

because of the several alternative interpretations that are possible due to the vagueness of their communications.

2   *Redundancy* describes communication in which a message is repeated without new information. In a therapy group, as well as in other contexts, a certain level of redundancy improves the conversational flow and clarifies the intent of the speaker. A message often needs to be repeated by the sender (or re-stated by others), and perhaps formulated in a slightly different way so the receiver understands it. However, when communications are overly redundant, receivers tend to "tune out". When no one listens, no messages are received.

Communication redundancy also occurs in "information overload" situations – when too much information is sent. Messages with too many details, facts, and examples are difficult to understand and to respond to. Where should the receivers begin? Group leaders should be attentive to redundancy and steer the conversation in more meaningful and focused directions.

3   *Contradictions* describe communication in which two (or more) conflicting messages are sent simultaneously. As an example, someone may say: "I really care about you and what you have to say. But honestly, I am not that interested in you." A verbal message may also conflict with the body language message. As an example, someone who appears nonchalant or cheerful may say, "I really feel sad and blue."

People who use contradictions often speak ironically or sarcastically. Their intent is to convey a meaning that is the opposite of what they have said. Irony may have a humorous, non-specific aspect while sarcasm often has an aggressive, direct aspect. Group leaders should call attention to ironic or sarcastic statements in the group and ask the speakers to clarify their meaning so that misunderstandings are avoided.

The following introductory phrase is another common example of contradictory communication: "Yes, but ..." Sentences that begin with this phrase immediately indicate the speaker both agrees and disagrees with a previously expressed idea or opinion. While the speaker's intent may be to soften an objection and reduce the risk of conflict, often the effect is quite the opposite. "Yes, but ..." tends to evoke another "Yes, but ..." as a response, which often results in a argumentative conversation that easily escalates to conflict.

Dialogue and flow

Shannon and Weaver's model describes communication between a transmitter and a receiver. Another way to describe communication is to identify it as the dialogue among group members in a learning and healing environment. The group environment creates a common space where dialogue can flow as members share thoughts, emotions, and experiences. Foulkes describes this flow as *transpersonal*, by which he means that group participants become part of the group's communication process (Foulkes, 1984).

Communication, of course, is not limited to speech. We communicate with our gestures, our body language, and our actions. It is impossible for group members not to communicate. Even silences communicate something, although they are a difficult-to-interpret type of communication. Silences are often misinterpreted, for example, as fantasies, objections, even confirmations. Therefore, group leaders are advised to invite silent group members to participate in the conversation. However, caution and respect on the part of the group leader are recommended. People who are inclined to silence should be handled sensitively; it may take considerable courage for them to speak in the group.

It is not uncommon that some members in a group participate by listening and reflecting rather than by speaking. Sometimes patients who are silent and seem withdrawn can benefit greatly from the group experience. In such cases the patient may flourish and open up in other contexts, and make use of the communication skills they acquired in the group.

Group leaders, like group members, are part of the communication flow but with one important difference. Given their special role, group leaders have more opportunity to partially distance themselves from the group by adopting the so-called meta-perspective. This is the perspective in which group leaders view themselves from outside the group and use their analytical ability to understand the group communication. Taking this perspective, group leaders can direct the communication towards achievement of the group's goals.

Summary

In this chapter we describe the history of groups with a focus on patient groups, dynamics, and therapies. In particular, we look at emotions, experiences, and communications in the group context. A secondary focus is the role of group leaders in facilitating communication and dialogue in groups. A main theme of this chapter is that through reflection we can better understand ourselves and others as we examine our inner emotions, thoughts, and driving forces. In this way, we analyse our inner selves and our behaviour patterns. In groups, we review and update our experiences and relationships as we examine them. Thus, groups help us heal, improve our ability to communicate, and better manage our lives.

Chapter 5

Group therapy

Despite our observation that group therapy is used much less than individual therapy and counselling, our impression is that many countries offer various kinds of group support in the care sector. There are, for example, self-help groups, psycho-educational groups, mindfulness groups, and a variety of other groups. We find them in primary care, psychiatric care, and addiction care, in correctional services, churches, non-profit organizations, treatment homes, and various other contexts.

Groups offer support and personal development to people in numerous and varied ways. For example, groups provide safe havens for the vulnerable, offer the comfort of shared experiences, make daily life more manageable, treat addictions and psychiatric conditions, create social networks, support the self-esteem of insecure parents, and offer access to knowledge and self-help tools. It is very likely we have omitted some support groups and some support treatments. New kinds of groups seem to appear continuously.

Group structure varies depending on the group type. In some groups, the group members are responsible for the group's continuation after the group leader initiates the group. Other groups have no leaders. In many groups, members are encouraged to socialize with each other outside the group setting as a way to counteract loneliness and isolation. The main purpose of such groups is to offer something to the participants that they lack in everyday life. Arranging such groups is certainly a very valuable and meaningful activity; however, explaining how that can be done is not the subject of this book.

In this book, we focus on describing how to develop and conduct time-limited group therapy using the group process as a tool. It is our conviction that the group process is underused in many group interventions. Our goal in this book is to describe the core of the group therapy process – what it means, what its prerequisites are, and what the requirements are for its emergence and sustainability.

Time-limited group therapy

A time-limited therapy group meets regularly during a fixed time period, usually weekly or twice-weekly, in the same room, on the same day(s) of the week, at a fixed time, and with the same group members and the same group leader(s). If group leaders are not working in private practice, organizations and associations appoint the group leaders. These may be private healthcare, public healthcare, social care, or non-profit organizations/associations. Group members, who are carefully selected, are prepared in advance for group meetings (see Chapter 6).

The decision on the most suitable treatment for group members is based on their needs, conditions, and goals. The group leadership (i.e., the group leader's personal leadership style and education), the organizational context, and overall purpose of the group influence many decisions on the group goals, boundaries, activities, and dynamics.

The group leader, who plays a crucial role in the development of the group, also decides on the group's structure and content. Some groups have a written manual that the group leader follows closely. Other groups, which take a less formal approach, are governed by treatment orientation, goals, and client agreements.

Later in this chapter we use examples to show how group leaders decide which groups suit which members. Our intention is to describe the boundaries and conditions that influence group leaders' decisions.

Therapy focus

The common feature of all time-limited group therapy is the need for a treatment focus for the group as a whole and a therapy focus for every group member. The time limitation means strategies are needed that can efficiently manage the entire time-limited process (Lorentzen, 2020). These foci set a clear direction for the therapy.

The group focus derives from the group members' *common issues* (needs, conditions, and goals). This focus guides the work of the group. The following examples are illustrative.

Example 1:

A group for people with work-related stress. The group provides group members with the opportunity to meet others who suffer from work stress.

The members share experiences, reflect on their condition, and explore possible solutions.

Example 2:

A group for people with a gambling disorder. The group provides group members with the opportunity to meet others with the same condition. The members share experiences, examine the origins and consequences of their addiction, and discuss future plans and coping strategies.

Another group focus derives from the group members' *diagnosis categories*. The following example describes the "depression group" category.

Example:

A group for people who suffer from recurrent depression. The group provides group members with the opportunity to share experiences, to learn what living with depression means, and to explore possible ways to feel better.

Although potential group members are aware of the relevant group focus, they still need more information about how to work in the group. In process-oriented group therapy, the group leader needs to spend time with the client to formulate an individual focus to work with in the group. This is done in the preparatory interviews. The group leader examines the potential group members' specific problems and their hoped-for results – as evidenced by emotions, thoughts, behaviour patterns, and relationships. In the following example, a potential group member addresses a specific individual therapy focus (social withdrawal/detachment) with the group leader.

Example:

When I feel bad and just want to sit silently in the group, I will try to explain how I feel, even if I am embarrassed.

The example illustrates how the potential group member creates an early therapeutic alliance with the group leader in their joint effort to develop an individual therapy focus. This joint work enhances the client's motivation, participation, and understanding of the problems and to some degree what to expect from group therapy. (See also chapters 6 and 12.)

Therapeutic group processes

Perhaps the primary characteristic feature of group therapy – when the group potential is taken advantage of – is the *therapeutic group process*. This process consists of the *communications and interactions among the group members as well as their subsequent experiences*. Mood and atmosphere are continuously changing. The therapeutic group process can be a destructive or a constructive force, depending on how group leaders manage the process. Group leaders' task is to facilitate constructive processes as they work directly and indirectly in the various interventions at the individual, sub-group, and group-as-a-whole levels. We return to the role and responsibility of group leaders in later chapters. (See, in particular, chapters 6 and 7.)

Foulkes, the founder of group analytic psychotherapy (see chapters 2 and 3), considered the communication in the group the most important factor in the therapeutic group process. As group members (and group leaders) we "train ourselves to be ourselves". As he wrote, this process is "ego training in action" (1984).

Group process is an elusive phenomenon. The process continually evolves as it profoundly affects the group members who experience it. In interactions with others, group members can relive experiences and relationships from, for example, their family of origin and their early social networks. When this happens, past experiences and relationships with significant individuals are re-enacted in the group. This happens unconsciously, but when it occurs there will be an opportunity to understand and learn. The phenomenon illustrates one very important aspect of the therapeutic group's potential: the opportunity to relive and process previous experiences and relationships, make them conscious, and work them through.

Reconsideration of such relationships and experiences may lead to changes in certain repetitive and automatic behaviours and emotional responses (some of which may have been harmful). This kind of work is a preoccupation of long-term psychodynamic group psychotherapy. However, sometimes time-limited group psychotherapy can also be effective in bringing about beneficial changes of this kind. Regardless of its length, a prerequisite of group therapy is that group members feel sufficiently safe that they dare to reveal their vulnerability to other group members.

The group as an organism

It can be helpful to differentiate a group's basic structure from its process. We begin with commentary on group structure followed by commentary on group process.

Burlingame et al. (2013) compared the group's structure to the anatomy of the human body. Easily recognizable elements form the human body (e.g., the spine, muscles, heart, lungs, brain). The group is also formed by certain obvious elements. These elements include the group members and group leader, the organizational context, the group goals, the group setting (meeting time and place), and the group membership criteria (open or closed to new members).

During the life of the group, certain structures and characteristics develop such as rules, norms, and connections among the group members. Various, often vaguely defined, sub-groups may form, as evidenced, for example, by conversations in which some members are included but others are not. Or some members direct their comments exclusively to the group leader rather than to other members.

The emerging group structure is a function of many different factors. The group leader's professional education and experience certainly play a role. However, the group members' personal characteristics (e.g., age, gender, personality, and cultural background) are also relevant. For instance, Punter (2009) illustrated this diversity in therapy structures in an article that compared group therapy in Egypt and England. Punter argued that in Egypt, where the national culture emphasizes greater respect for authority than in England, group therapists have a much more interventionist style than English therapists, who have a more dialogue-oriented leadership style.

At best, the group structure is stable and predictable in a way that creates a sufficiently safe group climate in which interpersonal exchange (i.e., the group process) functions as intended. Absent stability, predictability, and safety, the lack of group structure contributes to group members' mistrust and to group chaos.

As mentioned earlier, the group process is about the interaction and communication between group members and with the group leader, and how the group dynamic evolves over time. Burlingame et al. (2013), in their human body and group elements comparison described above, link physiology to group process (see Figure 5.1). In all groups of the kind mentioned above, where people meet to cooperate in solving a common task, it is possible to identify well-known, psychosocial phenomena such as conformity, power, conflict, leadership style, decision making, roles, and social identity.

In addition, the therapeutic group process develops from therapeutic factors such as interpersonal interaction, group member openness and feedback, group cohesion and climate, therapeutic alliances, and more. (See Chapter 4.) Moreover, the theory of change used in the treatment model influences group process – that is, the theoretical concepts used in, for example, psychodynamic, existential, interpersonal, or cognitive behavioural therapies.

As shown in Figure 5.1, the therapy group is an organism that, in one perspective, can be described in a number of dimensions that are shared with all kinds of groups. In another perspective, the therapy group has a unique "individuality" derived from its combination of structure/characteristics and processes. The therapy group as a whole is thus obviously more – and something other – than the sum of the group members' contributions. It is challenging to view and experience the therapy group as a whole. This is especially true for new group leaders who tend to be more concerned with individual group members and with issues related to their cooperation, opposition, and task orientation.

The interplay among the group members as a whole

Group leaders should take both the individual perspective and the group-as-a-whole perspective, in a similar way to conductors of orchestras or to leaders of jazz groups. Group leaders must also listen to each member's contribution to the overall "sound" of the group.

Group as a vehicle of change

Group Structure – "Anatomy"

Emergent
Structure
(e.g. norms)

Imposed Structure
(e.g. group
composition)

Formal Change
Theory
(e.g. FGT or CBT)

**Group Properties and
Processes**

Patient and
Therapist Factors
(e.g. age or
culture)

Interpersonal exchange as
mechanism of change
Group Processes – "Physiology"

Foundational
Social Processes
(e.g. Social roles
and leader style)

Emergent
Processes
(e.g. Openness and
cohesion)

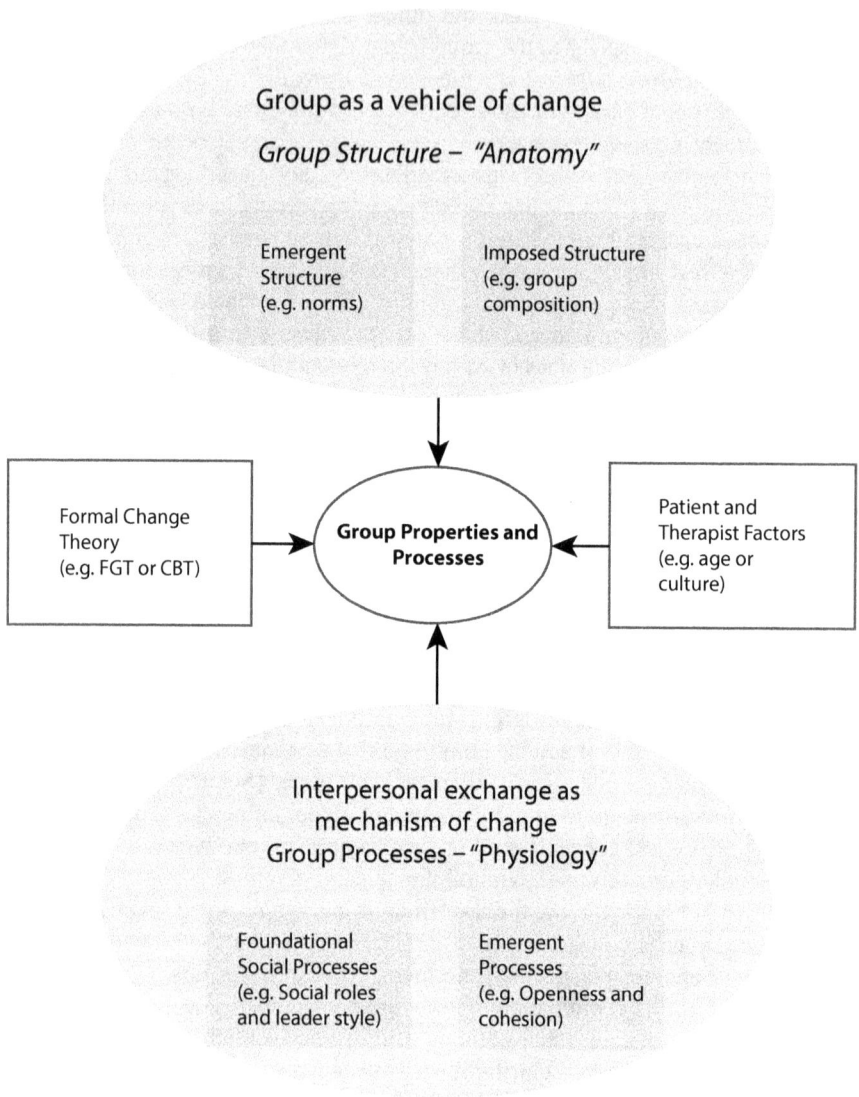

Figure 5.1 Structure and process in group therapy.

(adapted from Burlingame et al., 2013)

Sometimes group leaders must shift back and forth between several perspectives. Consider the following example.

> People in a therapy group are discussing their shared condition: exhaustion
> syndrome. One member complains that the condition creates work pressure

and family problems. The group leader observes the group's behaviour as a whole and the group members' individual responses. Some members listen attentively and nod affirmatively. Others slump in their chairs and look down at the floor. The group leader watches for changes in the group. Is the group energized or stifled by the complaint and the discussion? Do subgroups form around certain opinions, emotions, and relationships? Does one sub-group exhibit a hopeful and solution-oriented attitude while another sub-group exhibits resignation and hopelessness?Group leaders who ask themselves these questions and consider possible outcomes are engaged in both group structure and group process.

Even the most sensitive and empathetic group leaders find it impossible to observe everything that happens in a group. Therefore, group leaders must be realistic about their observation powers as they try to focus on those aspects that are needed to create a safe and open group climate. Their own experiences and emotions, which inevitably have some influence on the group, are important sources of information because they often mirror similar experiences and emotions in the group. Group leaders should also examine their own emotions after the group meetings. Are they pleased, reasonably satisfied, or frustrated? How did the group evoke these emotions?

The group matrix

Foulkes formulated the group matrix as one aspect of the group process (Foulkes, 1948/1984; Foulkes & Anthony, 1957/2014; see also Ahlin, 1984/1996; Lorentzen, 2013; and Chapter 3, where we describe Foulkes's concept of the matrix).

The Swedish group psychotherapy pioneer Göran Ahlin (a group analyst, a psychiatrist, and Associate Professor in Psychotherapy at the Karolinska Institutet, Stockholm) construed an observation method (originally in Swedish) for studying group psychotherapy processes: the Matrix Representation Grid – the MRG (Ahlin, 1996; Ahlin et al., 1996).

He proposed eight *group determinants*, graded from 1 to 5, of the group process that appear in the interaction between the group members and the group leader:

1   *Communication flow* (from silent to hectic).
2   *Imagery* (from factual to mythical/incomprehensible).
3   *Emotional climate* (from indifferent to pressing).
4   *Self-disclosure* (from prevented to dominating).
5   *Acceptance* (from scanty to engulfing).
6   *Relating pattern* (from social to ritualistic).
7   *Authority pattern* (from "laissez-faire" to totalitarian).
8   *Boundary character* (from denying to secluded).

The MRG was originally construed as a research tool for studying group interactions and group themes as well as the interrelationships between emerging group themes in group therapy sessions and between group sessions and the dynamic matrix. Readers who wish to know more about the MRG are advised to read Ahlin's doctoral thesis (Ahlin, 1996).

Structure provides safety for the group

Group leaders are responsible for creating conditions in which group members can explore their emotions and responses in their interactions with others, reflect on the group climate and discussion, and thereby discover opportunities for change. Group members are tasked to contribute by speaking as honestly as possible, share reflections and associations, respond to what is happening, and explore all this in close cooperation with the rest of the group. These are not the typical actions and practices of everyday life outside therapy groups. The kind of direct communication encouraged in therapy groups is usually unwelcome in social and family life. Such direct communications may be regarded as impolite and insensitive. Therefore, group leaders should devote time and attention to guiding members as they learn how the group can be useful to them.

Groups have a strong tendency to waver between working with their task and avoiding their task. In the latter situation, groups find other ways to use their time. This is a topic that Wilfred Bion, an English psychoanalyst and physician, addressed. (See Chapter 4.) Textbooks that discuss group psychology often reference Bion's ideas about group processes, which have had significant influence on group psychology, perhaps most in the organizational context. His theories are not easily adaptable as practical clinical guidelines.

Bion (1961) described how groups often move back and forth between a focus on its main agreed task, the working group, and the group's emotional defensive response, the *basic assumptions*. According to Bion, the three basic assumptions that influence human behaviour in groups are *dependency, fight–flight*, and *pairing*. If the group responds according to its basic assumptions, it fails to address its main task. Among group members, subconscious factors contribute to such behaviours. The dependency basic assumption describes the group's desire to feel safe via the protection of a strong and all-powerful leader. The fight–flight basic assumption describes how the group assumes it must secure its safety from hostile threats, within or outside the group boundaries, by either fighting or running away. The pairing basic assumption describes how the group has fantasies about its survival revealed in the creative "intercourse" between a pair of members or a sub-group that guarantees reproduction, giving relief and hope to other group members.

For the group process to develop in a way that is helpful to its members, group leaders need to establish and maintain a clearly defined and reliable holding structure. Only when a safe and therapeutic space is created, with clear boundaries and constraints and that offers steady leadership, can group members interact with each other more openly than they do in settings outside the group. This group structure creates and supports the conditions needed for the work of the group as a whole and the work of the group members as individuals when the group process detracts from the group's task. Group leaders should be sensitive to the group's expressed and unexpressed emotions. Even when conditions require that group leaders adapt their leadership styles, they should keep the group's goals and focus in sight. The following example is illustrative.

Example:

A group of rather isolated patients in psychiatric day-care meet for a few hours each week to talk. The conversation turns to the meals they are served. Everyone wants better food. On the whole, their focus is more on the quality of their meals than on their lack of personal relationships.

After the group had met for half their sessions, they began to express personal emotions and experiences. Their interest in their meals seemed to diminish. A male patient described a nightmare that he was unable to shake off. The group leader then raised the topic of fantasies and dreams with the group. Two female patients were very upset with this turn in the discussion. They said they wanted to leave the group. Other patients were unwilling to share deeper emotional experiences. The group leader quickly realized she had crossed a dangerous line. She had eagerly and mistakenly allowed the group to wander from its goals and focus.

In the next session, the group leader reviewed what had happened in the previous session. She admitted that she had directed the group to a discussion on fantasies and dreams. She acknowledged that this discussion had caused considerable discomfort among some group members. She apologized for allowing the session to take this direction.

Thereafter, in all subsequent sessions the group leader held the discussion to the group's goals and focus. She turned aside descriptions and discussions of fantasies and dreams. The anxiety in the group immediately diminished. The productive relationship work among the patients resumed. No one left the group prematurely. This example illustrates a common occurrence in group therapy. When a group member changes the topic of conversation, other members react negatively. In our example, the member's description of his nightmare did not fit the group's agreement regarding content and goals, in this case limited to food preparation and meals, not fantasies and dreams. The group leader soon realized the importance of sticking to the original discussion topic. She understood it was necessary to call the group "to order".

The nightmare account might have worked in a different group – perhaps a group focused on changing relationship patterns. Sharing dreams with others in such a group might have deepened the members' relationships and advanced their work. However, this was not the result in the example. The lesson from the example is that group leaders, who have a highly sensitive role, should be attuned to the responses of group members. *A leader must pay close attention to the group climate and, when necessary, return the group to the group's goals and focus when members try to redirect the conversation.*

The group leader's main tasks involve listening to group members, relating to their concerns, and facilitating the group process. Group leaders facilitate this process both directly and indirectly. Making comments to individual members, sub-groups, or the group as a whole is an example of direct intervention. (See Chapter 7.) Creating a group protective structure that sets and regulates boundaries is an example of indirect intervention.

Authority, power, and control

Issues related to authority, power, and control are highlighted in group therapy – more or less openly. Group members soon form impressions of their leaders. Leaders may be thought of as positive, supportive, and knowledgeable or as judgmental, domineering, and arrogant, or as somewhere in between. A group member's view of a leader is related both to the group leader's ways of being in the group and the group member's own experiences and relationships with authority in other contexts.

Patients in individual therapy also form impressions of their therapists. However, these impressions are, to some extent, less visible than the group leader impressions formed in group therapy. Patients in individual therapy are highly dependent on their therapists for obvious reasons. A clear division of roles exists between the helpers and those seeking help. Therapists who treat patients individually must carefully consider their own responses. If they are too open, they may do more harm than good.

Of course, this caution also applies to group therapy leaders. However, their responses are somewhat different. Group leaders maintain their neutrality and are restrained as far as giving personal information about themselves. They must always keep the group members' needs in focus. They see themselves as servants to the group. However, personal revelations related to the group process may be appropriate when they provide some benefit to the group; for example, it might be expressed in facial reactions, tone of voice, gestures, or brief comments.

Group leaders are formal leaders who have the power to determine the group's boundaries, structure, and goals. Yet certain group members may compete for power in the group or even try to take leadership control. While the reasons for such "power grabs" vary, one common reason is that members perceive weakness in the group leader; they may think the group leader has acted too cautiously or too passively. If group leaders are too hesitant, their hesitancy can easily lead to insecurity in the group, allowing a group member to seize the leadership role. In the worst case, such an informal (member) leader will undermine the group cohesion. The probable results are group fragmentation and member drop-outs and absenteeism. However, even in groups with stable leadership, would-be leaders may appear among the group members and challenge the leader. If this happens early in the life of the group it can be an expression of a need for safety, which the group leader must respond to, maybe by being clearer and more active.

When group leaders provide a protective group structure that contributes to trust, they demonstrate their authority and responsibility. Group members then feel they can be open-hearted and spontaneous in their relationships with other members in a way that is seldom possible elsewhere. Yet there are always (healthy) limits to leadership authority and power in group therapy. One way in which such limits are set is the presence of other group members who reduce member dependence on group leaders. To test leadership authority, power, and control is usually a process that members can learn from and it is also a necessary part of the differentiation stage of group development. (See Chapter 8.)

For whom are different group models suitable?

Different group models suit different people. Matching clients with groups is an important part of initial group planning. For example, if group models already exist in a workplace, it is important to consider these models from the clients' perspective. Which clients are suitable for a particular model of group therapy? Should other models be explored for the clients? These decisions involve evaluations of whether potential group members, given their internal and external difficulties, can benefit from participating in a particular group.

Many other questions arise in group planning. How much space and time are needed for teaching, or for the exploration of self-knowledge and of relationships? What role does conversation have in the group? How should the meeting time be allocated between the group leader and the group members? Which goals are appropriate for the group members? Which group leadership style is best for a particular group? What is the group leader's mandate? Is the group leader given the freedom to plan and lead group activities?

It is common in psychiatry, primary care, physical care, and other treatment activities to plan a therapy group based on a particular diagnosis. Examples of groups based on a specific diagnosis are "depression groups", "anxiety groups", "eating disorders groups", and "relapse prevention groups". A shared diagnosis is not enough for group cohesion and meaningful conversation to take place. The group's potential will be taken advantage of. The group leader will have to spend a lot of time lecturing and guiding activities for the group to keep together. For some members this can be rewarding, but other members find it unsatisfying.

To get a group to become beneficial for its members, one needs, as we mentioned earlier, to use other perspectives than the purely medical one. This is also necessary for group therapy within the setting of medical care.

Resources and dominant concerns

We cite the late professor Dorothy Stock Whitaker (1925–2018), the English-American social psychologist and group therapy researcher, several times in this book. She proposed some interesting and inspiring ideas on group formation. She used two notions (discussed next) as starting points for forming a group and for setting its goals (2001).

Whitaker's first notion was that of *frontier*. This refers to the fact that every person has the capacity and resources to make choices which move them towards what they desire in life. There are also skills and resources that for some reason are not within reach, that are beyond a person's current capacity. The border between what a person already has and can do and what is just beyond him/her can be thought of as that person's *frontier*. Most people have the capacity to move beyond their current frontier. When people are very dissatisfied with their life situation, they might need to try and move their frontiers.

Whitaker's second concept is *the preoccupying concern*. That means any issue, worry, or situation which at a given time occupies most of a person's horizon and thoughts. The person is unable to make a change, to move forward in life, and feels incapable of managing the situation.

Different kinds of groups for different persons

Whitaker also discussed different categories of people who often seek help in psychiatric care, primary care, social welfare, or other therapeutic settings. She proposed categories as a way to think about how potential group members should be understood, evaluated, and grouped according to her group model (2001). (Readers who are familiar with Whitaker's work will observe we have omitted some categories that are not relevant to the current discussion.)

1   *People who have previously functioned adequately*. They are described as "normally functioning" using standard measures, but now face some form of life or identity threat.

   The people in this category have experienced a difficult situation that has decisively influenced their lives, identity, or self-image. For example, they may have suffered a physical trauma or have been extremely ill. They may have experienced the loss of a close family member, have gone through a traumatic divorce, or have been dismissed by an employer. Many events qualify as life-changing experiences. People who have had these experiences may require help in dealing with their effects. One-to-one contact with a therapist is often required to manage reactions to the crisis or trauma.

   When the first shock of a crisis or trauma has passed, people may also find that joining a time-limited, open therapy group (e.g., a group with eight to ten meetings and five to eight members) can help with their recovery (e.g., grief groups and divorce support groups). Another possibility is a psychoeducational group that includes educational elements (e.g., role play and lectures) such as we find in chronic illness groups (e.g., groups for cardiac rehabilitation or diabetes patient groups). Yet another possibility is a time-limited group that meets four to five times and features an outside speaker who offers practical advice on managing the new life situation (e.g., groups for dismissed employees).

All these group models require that the group leaders have relevant competences for both the planning and the treatment stages. Group leaders should also acquire a good understanding of the members' situations, in particular where they are in the experience and recovery processes.

2   *Relatives and co-dependents who have endured severe psychological stress for some time as a result of problematic conditions in their close relationships.*

The people in this category include parents of children with disabilities, relatives of criminals, children (including adult children) of alcohol- or drug-dependent parents, relatives of severely ill people, and others.

One possibility is a therapeutic group that meets 12–18 times. Such groups provide the group members with the opportunity to talk about their situation, to share their experiences with others, and to receive comfort, social support, and advice. These support groups focus on the relatives of the family member whose behaviour has caused their psychological stress (e.g., relatives of a mentally ill family member, relatives of victims of domestic abuse, and families of alcohol and drug addicts). A second possibility is a permanent self-help group in which the group leader helps group members structure the group so that it can continue on its own (e.g., groups for people with eating disorders or co-dependency support groups). A third possibility is a non-profit action group – an association of interests – in which the goal is to spread knowledge about certain illnesses and to provide support for certain disorders. There are many such organizations in many countries.

3   *People who are in the midst of, or face, a profound life change.*

The people in this category include expectant parents, parents with new-born infants, recently divorced people, retired and about-to-retire people, and newly arrived immigrants.

Theory, supported by research, proposes that voluntary and involuntary changes are often stressful. However, change provides an opportunity for personal development. People need to talk about their emotions regarding the change and about their misgivings about their new situation. They also need to think about the positive possibilities offered by the new opportunity. A group that meets four to eight times and that focuses on the positives and negatives of the change may be helpful. The group members focus on what has been lost and what has been gained.

4   *People who function more or less adequately in their current environment but are anxious or depressed. They do not function to their full capacity or they engage in self-destructive behaviours.*

The people in this category often seek psychotherapeutic help because of a specific difficulty (e.g., problems with close relationships, an inability to complete work projects, recurrent nightmares, and symptoms of anxiety or depression). They give vague descriptions of their difficulty, complain about their lack of goals, describe their loneliness, and are generally dissatisfied with life. They are unable to cope in daily life and can imagine no solutions for their problems.

These people need to understand why they are unable to use their personal strengths and resources. They need to overcome obstacles in their path and transgress their current boundaries so that they can move forward. A therapeutic setting is recommended to help them explore their communication and relationship patterns in the attempt to discover what purpose their self-destructive behaviour serves. Is such behaviour a shield against even more intimidating threats? If they were less aggressive, would they draw closer to others or would they be more frightened? The group can provide such people with a corrective emotional experience, which is an active therapeutic mechanism of change.

Problems of this kind require a more challenging therapeutic process that includes focused group therapy (see Chapter 12) or long-term group analytical psychotherapy.

In some units in child and adolescent psychiatric care, groups are formed for new parents and their infants with severe attachment problems. Such groups combine individual home visits, video-based interventions, family conversations, and meetings with other caregivers (e.g., psychiatrists and paediatricians). Psychodynamic and psycho-educational methods are combined to develop parents' mentalization ability and to initiate development-promoting interaction between them and their infants.

5 *People who have lost, or have never had, basic social skills or are unable to manage everyday existence.*

The people in this category often have become "institutionalized" after extended institutional residency. They may have limited intellectual capacity or, for various reasons, have never had the opportunity to acquire basic life skills. Their frontiers need attention and how their behavioural and interpersonal skills can be expanded. They require careful and sustained attention in psycho-educational or semi-pedagogical groups where they can learn and practice life skills. These groups provide practical knowledge as well as social opportunities. Because individual support is also needed, a combination of modified group therapy and individual therapy may be helpful. This complex therapy structure is probably only available at large healthcare organizations.

In psychiatric care and addiction care today, integrated, coherent, and intensive treatment in groups is one of several therapy methods practised. An example is DBT (dialectical behaviour therapy, which is a specific form of cognitive behavioural therapy) that is used with patients with borderline personality disorder, self-harm behaviour, and other mental challenges. The groups offer training in managing and regulating affects. In individual therapy, the technique of chain analysis is used to understand how the coping with feelings is connected to behaviours. All care personnel involved in the patient's treatment work in teams.

MBT (mentalization-based therapy, which is a form of psychodynamic therapy) is also used for the patients in this category as well as for people with addictions or for people with a dual diagnosis. Group therapy is central in MBT. One purpose with the individual therapy, which also is part of the programme, is to help the patients understand what is happening in the group and to strengthen the capacity to participate in the group. Patients receiving MBT are also treated by psychiatrists and other care personnel who are part of the treatment team. Multi-modal treatment requires a team effort in which all team members jointly exchange experiences and reflections, and take necessary action.

6   *People who have severe psychiatric, social, and related problems.*
    The people in this category have several psychiatric diagnoses that have persisted throughout their entire lives. People in Category 5 whose treatment has been unsuccessful may also be in this category. Many of these people require support but hesitate to seek help. Others depend heavily on physicians and support staff.

It may be useful for caregivers to define these patients' *frontiers* (Whitaker) and address their possibilities for moving forward in life employing the same resources used with Category 5 patients. However, even when the next desirable step for a patient has been identified, there is no certainty that the patient will take that step. The likelihood of recovery may not have improved.

A support group can provide psychological nourishment for patients in this category. The patients may meet informally in hospital community rooms and in adult day-care facilities, or formally in structured groups. For some patients, co-habitation with others can have a life-enhancing effect even with no change in their condition. A period of co-habitation in an institutional setting may help a patient function after leaving the institution.

The most suitable group for patients in this category may be the open group that does not have a firm conclusion date and that meets one or more times a week. Group members are permitted to join and leave the meetings at will. They decide for themselves. Group leaders of open groups must take a participative, transparent, and flexible role. They must be open to improvisation in the group, changes in the group climate, and revisions of group goals. Examples are psychopharmaceutical depot therapy groups and food preparation groups. Such groups often have a surprising spin-off effect on both group members and staff members. For example, disturbing outpatient episodes may decrease in number and in intensity. Primary care and social service users may become less demanding. Group members, with staff support, may even start a small business like a café or a cooperative of some kind.

Summary

In this chapter we describe therapeutic group processes: how they are understood and used in therapy. Both competent leadership and group structure are identified as essential for group safety and predictability. The challenges that group leaders face are also described as they work to understand the individual group members and the group as a whole. With Whitaker's group categorization as a guide, the chapter reviews six group approaches that are suitable for people with specific issues or problems. The implicit conclusion is that because there is no "one-size-fits-all" group model, people should not be forced or persuaded to join a group that they do not want to join, or a group that is ill-suited to their particular circumstances.

Chapter 6

Starting a therapy group

This chapter describes the conditions associated with the success of group therapy – how groups are started, how group members are selected, and how group leaders prepare the group members for the group therapy. The chapter also describes the knowledge and experience group leaders require if they are to achieve the group's goals. The chapter emphasizes the importance of the collaboration within the organizational context for the success of therapy groups.

The organizational framework and system

Various physical, psychological, social, and economic factors in the organizational framework influence group activities. The success of group therapy is, in part, dependent on how well this framework takes these factors into account. Success also depends on how positive and supportive the organization's management and staff are of group leaders and the group members.

A group is a bounded system. Because group boundaries vary, group to group, it is necessary in group therapy to consider each group's environment. The context always influences the group therapy, although in varying degrees of intensity depending on the extent of the permeability of the group's boundaries. However, the group also impinges on the surrounding environment, which can cause positive or negative reactions. The group environment is complex because it consists of group members' relatives and friends as well as representatives from the care community such as physicians, psychologists, and social workers. In general, the group's environment always exerts some influence by establishing the conditions surrounding the group's work. A group will reflect these conditions in the thoughts, emotions, and attitudes of the group as a whole and of the group members as individuals.

The group's environment can support or sabotage the group therapy. If certain elements in the group's environment oppose the group's goals, the likelihood that group therapy will succeed is minimal. When opposition to the group's goals interferes with the group structure and process, the therapeutic work becomes much more difficult. Such opposition can take subtle and not-so-subtle forms. Group boundaries can be attacked or undermined. For example, the group meeting rooms may be unavailable, or the group members may be called to other meetings with other staff members. In these cases, group leaders have to defend the group requirements if the group is to function. Without the support of others (e.g., the organization's management and staff and group leaders' colleagues), their protests will likely fail. The following example makes this point.

Example:

A young psychologist in group therapy training (one of the book's authors) worked at an outpatient clinic for alcohol addiction. As a part of his training, he arranged a short-term therapy group. His colleagues thought group therapy was a poor alternative to individual therapy. Thus, he experienced difficulty in recruiting patients to his group. In fact, his colleagues referred patients to him who had "failed" in other treatments.

Because the clinic had no suitable rooms for group meetings, he and the patients met in an uncomfortable basement room that was some distance from the clinic entrance. In addition, there was a scheduling conflict. Some patients, who were also in individual therapy, were advised by their therapist (i.e. colleagues of the group therapist) not to attend the group. Such conflicts occurred when their attendance at the group meetings was especially critical.

The young psychologist, nevertheless, completed the group therapy. However, few patients completed the group therapy owing to the problems described. The lesson from the experience is clear: organizational and collegial support is essential when starting a therapy group.

When there is no organizational support for group leaders, no agreement on group goals, and no agreement on how the goals will be achieved, group leaders must use a lot of their energy managing the inevitable conflicts and problems.

Before starting a therapy group, group leaders are advised to spend time consulting with their organizations and/or colleagues. Group leaders should make the group goals and methods very clear so that there are no misconceptions about the planned work. They should also be prepared for opposition to their plans. Hostility to group therapy may sometimes be expected, especially when staff personnel or clients' relatives want to protect clients from something assumed harmful to them. Some critics believe, contrary to the research, that it can be destructive for patients to meet other patients with similar problems. In such meetings, patients may influence each other negatively, it is argued. The best way to cope with such negative preconceptions is for group leaders to be informative and to engage in open dialogue with special attention paid to the group's confidentiality agreements regarding what kind of information can be disclosed about the group's development.

Sometimes several treatment alternatives are offered by the same treatment programme. Individual therapy, group therapy, and even psycho-educational therapy can function well in parallel if collaboration and communication among therapists and units are arranged in advance. For example, MBT (mentalization-based therapy), DBT (dialectical behavioural therapy), and attachment therapy for infants and parents are compatible. Eating disorders therapy, for example, can be used in both individual and group therapies.

Organizational prerequisites

In the planning phase for a therapy group, it is essential to arrange and then manage the organizational conditions. Group leaders must coordinate these plans with the organizational manager who has responsibility for the group therapy. Agreement is needed on the following topics:

- *Target group* – the patients who are suitable for the planned group therapy.
- *Group therapy type* – a cognitive or psychodynamic orientation; a therapeutic or psycho-educational focus.
- *Purpose and goal* – formulated jointly and agreed to.
- *Framework* – number, duration, and frequency of meetings; number of group members.
- *Location* – the same meeting room with suitable furnishings; all sessions booked in advance.
- *Time* – group leader preparation before sessions; reflection after sessions with time allocated for documentation.
- *Group leaders' competence development* – support, as necessary, for supervision of group leaders including the possibility for consultation as problems arise. Training and experience exchange provided to group leaders.
- *Resources and other support* – administrative procedures that assist both group leaders and members; for example, the welcome reception for group member latecomers and notification of group member cancellations to group leaders.

- *Routines for communications and feedback* – formal, regular reporting and documentation. Feedback, coordination, and exchange of information with therapists, contact persons, and others (e.g., reference individuals). Agreement on assurance of member confidentiality.
- *Evaluations* – specific assessment procedures adapted to group therapy (as necessary).

After the organization's management and the group leaders agree on these points, group leaders receive a mandate to start a therapy group.

The planning for group therapy also includes thinking about how to recruit people willing to become group members. Possible recruitment tactics are information sheets, advertisements, and direct approaches to patient contacts and to patients. Colleagues and external partners may refer potential group members.

Group leaders should be aware that member recruitment can sometimes be a lengthy and frustrating process, especially at workplaces where group therapy is uncommon. The engagement of the organization's management is crucial. The enthusiasm and interest that were initially evoked when the idea of a therapeutic group was introduced can easily fade away. Reminder requests are often necessary. Group leaders should not be discouraged by recruitment setbacks, however, because this is the very nature of the preparation work. Starting a group may take six months or even longer – from planning to the first group meeting. Yet opportunities to find constructive ways to move forward exist.

A side benefit of the recruitment process is that often the information and conversation about the group therapy provoke interest in developing other group activities. As group therapy becomes known and established in an organization, the perception grows that group activities have value. Demand for more such activities may increase.

Sometimes it may be difficult to provide potential group members with information about waiting times for their groups or to provide accepted group members with firm start-up dates for their groups. If these waiting times are quite long or the start-up dates are much delayed, people may suspect that the group planning and preparation were not well thought out. The confusion about when the therapy will begin may be a sign that preparations are insufficient. The result may be insecurity and lack of motivation among the accepted group members. They may then consider (and choose) alternative treatments.

Rules and boundaries

For group therapy to succeed, it is essential that clear and firm organizational rules and boundaries are established. As observed above, the organization's representatives and the group leaders have to agree on the rules and boundaries for a therapy group. Furthermore, the management and staff personnel must commit to supporting the therapy group and its leader.

Typically, group leaders have some kind of consultant relationship or employee position in a department or unit of a healthcare organization. In this position, group leaders form a cooperative alliance with the organization when they start a therapy group. Group leaders can, for example, work with each group member's contact person and with other therapists who are treating that group member (as necessary). To manage treatment, to promote consensus, and to avoid group fragmentation, an informal alliance is created that organizes the planning, collaboration, and development of the therapy group. In this process, a crucial issue is the assurance of group members' privacy and confidentiality.

Group size

It is important to decide on the number of group members in a new therapy group. Practical arrangements for the group (e.g., room size and location) depend on the number of group members. Group leaders may ask themselves: If I plan for a certain group size (e.g., six to eight members), how shall I manage a final group size of ten members or of only four members? Probably the only answer is to recommend that group leaders remain calm and flexible; there can be advantages to larger and smaller group sizes than originally planned. With experience, these situations become easier to manage.

Time and space

Therapy groups must have a specific meeting time and a dedicated space. This means that groups should normally begin and end on schedule with exceptions only in special circumstances. These times should be established and confirmed before the first group meeting. "This group will meet on Tuesdays from 3.00 p.m. to 4:30 p.m." Obviously, group leaders should be on time. Group leader tardiness suggests the leaders have other priorities than the group members. Usually, 15–20 minutes before each session, the group leader will check that the meeting room is well-ventilated, the seating arrangements are in order, etc. The room should be somewhat isolated with sound insulation so that the group conversations cannot be overheard by outsiders.

Attendance and punctuality

Group members should be encouraged to attend all meetings and to be on time for all meetings. When members miss a meeting or join a meeting late, the flow of the meeting is disrupted. Notification of absences should preferably be made in advance at group meetings. If such advance notification is not possible, then group members should contact the group leader well before the session starts so that the leader can inform the group.

Duty of confidentiality

Group leaders have to explain that no member comments or group discussions should leave the room. Every group member has this obligation to every other group member. Without such confidentiality, there is no assurance of group trust or security. In a group with a psychodynamic or interactional approach, group members should be instructed not to meet each other outside the group.

Conversations on group format, boundaries, and rules

Group leaders should send clear messages to the group members that explain the group format, boundaries, and rules. Such messages present and protect the conditions necessary for successful therapeutic treatment. If group members ask questions about decisions on the group structure and process, group leaders should respond and follow-up on the decisions. If unexpected or undesirable changes occur (e.g., meeting time and room changes), the group members should have the right to express their frustration, disappointment, and possibly their anger. Although the organization's management typically makes these changes, group leaders should refrain in the group from harsh criticism of the administrative staff irrespective of the reasons for the change, and avoid laying blame or playing the victim. Group leaders who are critical of administrative staff decisions should discuss their concerns with the people who have made those decisions.

The following example illustrates possible complications when group boundaries and rules about contact outside the group are vaguely presented or not presented at all.

Example:

The discussion topics among a group of young adult women and men were exclusion and personal relationships. The expectation was that the discussion would result in an exchange of experiences and reflections that would help everyone better manage these difficulties in their lives.

Lisa and Mark began the discussion, and soon the others joined in. Everyone was eager to describe their experiences and to listen to others' experiences. Gradually, the discussion became somewhat tense. Lisa tried repeatedly to persuade Mark to reveal more about his experiences, but he hesitated. He seemed to be somewhat conflicted: he wanted to maintain some distance from Lisa, yet he also wanted to draw closer. The group leader understood that more members in the group were fantasizing about interacting with other members outside the group. This was both exciting and scary. There was no agreement in this group regarding prohibited interaction outside the group. Now, at least Mark and Lisa were ready to move their therapy beyond the boundaries of the group and the therapist's responsibility.

The group leader made a quick decision. She reminded the group members of an important group rule: the group members should not have contact with each other outside the group. While the rule disappointed some members, they realized that it simplified and facilitated the work of the group. As the discussion continued, Mark and the group members felt more comfortable in recounting their experiences when they were assured of the confidentiality of their comments and discussions.

This rule applies in other group contexts. Personal acquaintances and friends do not belong in the same group. These relationships easily lead to sub-groups that may adversely influence the group format and process. If such relationships in the group are discovered after the group has formed and met, the group leader should disclose these relationships to everyone in the group. Transparency is clearly the best approach in such sensitive situations.

The following example illustrates how member contacts outside the group can interfere with group goals.

Example:

A group member remarks at the second group meeting: "We discovered last time that Sara and I live in the same suburb. She has offered to give me a ride home today. Given the group rule about outside contact, is this okay?" The group leader encourages the group members to talk about this question. Eventually they conclude that it is not a good idea because of the constraint it would imply in combination with the temptation to chat about the other group members and their interaction with them.

Group leaders should be aware that group members will often ask tricky and problematic questions. Asking the group members to discuss these questions may sometimes be the right approach. It is not uncommon that members want to change boundaries. The following is an example of such a situation.

Example:

At the first group meeting, a young man who seemed strongly motivated to participate in the group stated:

I have just started a new job. I get off work at 14.30. It takes me about 45 minutes to get here. Today I asked my manager if I could leave work a little early so I could be here at 15:00 when the meeting begins. My manager seemed annoyed and told me not to make a habit of leaving early. My question is this: Is it okay if I come 15 minutes late? Or could we change the start time to 15:15?

Although group rules sometimes seem rigidly bureaucratic, group leaders need to explain their importance for the proper functioning of the group. Problems may arise if exceptions to rules are made for individual group members. In the example, the group leader may simply have to enforce the rule while at the same time trying to be helpful. Perhaps the young man can negotiate some solution with his manager.

Practical preparations and arrangements

Care and consistency are at the foundation of stable group therapy. Therefore, group leaders should take plenty of time to prepare and arrange the practical arrangements necessary for group therapy. It is important that the group members feel welcomed and cared for!

As described above, group leaders should reserve the same meeting room for all group meetings. The room should be in a quiet area of the building and should have good lighting, good ventilation, and as few distractions as possible (e.g., no windows that face football fields or busy sidewalks). It is optional whether to have a small, low table in the room. The chairs (comfortable but not too soft) should be placed in a circle, somewhat separated so that people do not feel cramped. At the first meeting, group leaders should observe whether any adjustments are needed to the room arrangements. The group leaders are responsible for holding the meetings to the time schedules and for making certain that the meeting rooms are available and set-up.

Group leaders should let the group members know the dates, times, and locations of all meetings well in advance of the first meeting. Administrative information on registration, payment, refunds, and late arrivals is generally communicated by the management of the organization. However, group leaders may wish to confirm with the members that they have received this information. This shows the members that their group leaders are concerned with their well-being and security. It is also important that group leaders distribute their personal contact information so members can email or call them when necessary. However, communication with the group leader outside the group should be an exception. Normally, group members ask their questions and provide relevant information during the meetings.

These preparations and arrangements are intended to strengthen the cohesion of the group, create a safe environment for the group, and establish a group climate in which group members can work to achieve the group goals without annoying and avoidable interruptions. Group leaders protect the group members within this therapeutic framework in the same way the sponsor organizations protect the group leaders.

Finally, group leaders require sufficient time to make these essential preparations and arrangements. They also need time to prepare for each meeting, to respond to group members' messages, to prepare reports, and to deal with a variety of administrative matters.

The group members

The people selected to join a group will interact with each other at the group meetings. Will they be able to cooperate with each other and share experiences with each other? Openness and cooperation are much more likely if the group members have some essential characteristic or condition in common (*the preoccupying concern* as described in Chapter 5). This commonality is important for creating an inclusive group climate. Group therapy works best if members' conditions are presented as *communication problems with others: spouses, partners, friends, relatives, colleagues, and authority figures.* When these problems are described as knowledge and relationship patterns that others also experience, group members can better grasp how the group as a whole can support them. In this way, the group members learn new ways to manage their conditions.

Although the focus of group therapy is often a particular diagnosis that the group members share, they can differentiate themselves by also focusing on and changing their unique communication problems in their individual relationships. The following examples illustrate the important role of group leaders as they interview candidates for group therapy and help clients see how group therapy can benefit them.

Example 1:

Prior to planning a "depression group", the group leader interviews Peter, who is receiving medical treatment for depression. Peter is feeling somewhat better but still worries about his passivity. He is rather sceptical of the benefits of the recommended group therapy. He shows more interest, however, after hearing descriptions of group therapy. He now understands generally how group therapy works. He is intrigued by the idea of meeting others who have his condition.

In the preparatory interview with the group leader, Peter reveals he is most tormented by a "weakness" that causes him to withdraw from others. He feels excluded and very lonely. Outwardly, in interactions with neighbours and acquaintances, he does not reveal this difficulty. He fears others will dislike him if he reveals his true self. He can only talk about this "weakness" with very close relatives. As a result, he is despondent and guilt-ridden because he thinks he may be a burden to others.

The outcome of the interview with the group leader is an individual goal for Peter in the planned depression group. Peter's goal is to overcome his isolation and depression. The recommended strategy for Peter is to talk to the others about his emotions – his sadness and loneliness – even if he thinks this makes him look rather pitiful. He needs to talk about himself and hear the others' responses.

Example 2:

A primary health care centre is planning an "anxiety group". Sabrina's physician refers her to the group. She seems a good candidate for group therapy as she likes to talk about her anxiety and likes to be with people.

She imagines the group as a new bunch of friends with whom she can share experiences.

In the preparatory interview with the group leader, Sabrina realizes that the recommended therapy group will not be like her other social groups. The "friends" in the therapy group will have their own problems that they will want to share with her. Now Sabrina is a little concerned. She says she is prone to performance anxiety. She doesn't like being observed. She wants to know exactly how the group will function and asks lots of questions. It is important to her that she "do the right thing" and that others support and like her.

Sabrina and the group leader decide she should accept the challenge of becoming a group member. This means she should try to talk in the group when she wants to say something, in spite of the anxiety she might feel. She should pause to examine her feelings and then describe them to the other group members. She should set aside her fear of how others will perceive her and instead listen carefully to their responses. In this way, she may overcome her performance anxiety. After this dialogue with the group leader, Sabrina was hopeful that the group might help her manage her anxiety.

Who is suitable for group therapy?

Group leaders select the group members according to two criteria: (1) the group's purpose, goals, and focus; and (2) the group's composition specifications. Normally, group leaders decide well in advance of group member selection if the group, for example, will consist of only female members, only male members, or both female and male members. If the group will consist of women and men, then group leaders should strive to achieve a gender balance.

Groups with a diversity of group member personalities are typically preferable to groups in which the members are quite similar in how they talk and react. The group interaction may be more useful if members demonstrate *different expression modes*. Some members may be spontaneous and lively, while others may be reflective and reticent. When they select members, group leaders may ask themselves the following question: "Will this individual *benefit* from the group, *contribute* to the group, and *help achieve the group's goal*?" It is also important to learn how *motivated* group interviewees are. Can they *listen to others* and are they *interested in others*? Active listening is an important part of the therapeutic work in therapy groups.

Ideally, a member of a time-limited therapy group should be interested in and responsive to others, should understand the implications of the group commitment, should formulate problems (on their own or with the therapist's help), and should find solutions to these problems. Clearly, it helps if clients can patiently listen and talk to others while sincerely demonstrating a personal motivation to be an active group member. (Chapter 5 explores these characteristics in more detail.) However, it is not essential that every member of particular group has all these characteristics. If the group has a number of members who match these characteristics, an exception can be made for the individual who has perhaps only one or two of the characteristics. A stable group that has developed trust and cohesion can cope with increased disparity among its members.

Who is not suitable for group therapy?

People will not benefit from or contribute to group therapy if they *cannot verbally express* their problems, fears, and expectations. People who are *uninterested* in other people will find it difficult to engage with others' problems in group therapy. This lack of interest will have a negative influence on group development. People who are uncomfortable in groups and cannot describe this discomfort will not benefit from group therapy. Nor will people who are ill at ease in difficult-to-control situations or who have *acute problems* associated with severe crises, abusive situations, or psychotic episodes. In fact, these people may even be harmed by group therapy. All their energy is consumed by dealing with the current situation; they have no time or space for group discussions.

The following conditions and attitudes are associated with problems in group therapy. Group leaders should be alert to these conditions and attitudes when interviewing potential group members.

- Interpersonal conflict characterized by aggression, defensiveness, agitation, or hostility.
- Extreme shyness and loneliness in combination with lack of support.
- Frequent self-destructive behaviour, drug/alcohol abuse, suicide attempts, or irresponsible sexual activity.
- Psycho-somatic symptoms without interest in making any psychological connection.
- Dismissive attitude towards personal problems.
- Discomfort in groups and scepticism of the benefits of group therapy.
- Extreme paranoia.
- Inability to focus on the group tasks owing to cognitive problems associated with an inability to concentrate and with a high degree of anxiety.
- Indications that the client will have problems in relation to a certain group member.
- Threats to group security; for example, because of a member's impulsive and aggressive behaviour.

Each interviewee's particular condition and attitude must be considered when selecting group members. An individual who is found unsuitable for a group because of age or condition may be suitable for another group at another time. For example, people may be in the midst of crises such that they have no mental space for others' problems. Or, despite meeting the group admission criteria, they may have scheduling problems. For example, they may be unable to arrange reliable childcare, or their employer may not approve work-release time to attend group meetings.

Preparatory interviews

Strictly speaking, the group begins the treatment process at the first group meeting. However, for group leaders, the process begins with the group planning. The group is born, so to speak, in the group leader's mind long before the first meeting. For the group members, the process begins with the preparatory interviews. A group leader may conduct more than one interview with each interviewee. Regardless of the number of interviews, every interview should be conducted in a spirit of mutual trust where information is exchanged and evaluated. Group leaders should explain how group therapy functions. Interviewees should be allowed time to assess their confidence in the group leader and to evaluate the possible benefit of the group therapy. Group leaders should decide whether group therapy for the interviewees is likely to benefit them as individuals and the group as a whole. A conversation on the goals of the treatment, which are discussed below, is an important element of this evaluation.

In the preparatory interviews, group leaders can review interviewees' history of group experiences. What is (or was) their family role? Have they been members in other groups? If so, do they recall any positive or negative group experiences? Previous therapy group experience is especially relevant.

Group leaders will also find it useful to examine interviewees' life experiences. Group leaders ask why interviewees think they need treatment and what their expectations of and concerns about group therapy are. These initial conversations about the interviewees' current and past life situations, relationships, and motives for seeking help and change create connections with group leaders. Thus, the therapeutic work actually begins in these preparatory interviews. What were the interviewees' successes and failures? How do the interviewees look back on these experiences? If they have had therapeutic treatment for managing these experiences, what is their opinion of that therapy? Are they suspicious of more therapy? Or do they have positive memories of therapy? The responses to these questions will help group leaders decide if therapy can be beneficial for the interviewees.

In groups that have no clear psychotherapeutic goal (e.g., psycho-educational groups), preparatory interviews are less important. It is usually sufficient that someone briefly offers interviewees the opportunity to join the group. If they accept the offer, they register and then meet the group leader(s) at the first group meeting. However, these invitations should be carefully framed so that the target group criteria are met. This is necessary so that group leaders can make constructive plans for the group. (See Chapter 11.)

In two-leader groups, the group leaders may jointly conduct the interviews. More commonly, each interviewee meets with only one group leader in the preparatory interview. The group leaders may share the interview work as each leader conducts half the interviews. In any case, all group members should meet both group leaders before the first meeting so that the members have some familiarity with them. In preparing the interview questions, the group leaders must think about which questions to ask and how to ask them. Shared leadership requires that leaders communicate and interact with each other so that, for example, there are no disagreements on how the interviews should be planned and conducted. (Chapter 7 describes more broadly how group leadership can be conducted.)

Group leaders should formulate a *purpose, goal* and *focus* for the group therapy that should then be communicated to the interviewees. It is always useful to have written information to hand over to the clients at the first interview. At the next meeting, interviewees could then be given the opportunity to ask any questions that the information sheet provokes. Below is an example of how such written information might be formulated:

Information on group therapy

Group therapy differs from individual therapy in that much of the work takes place in the interaction and exchanges between group members; i.e., not only between the therapist and the individual member. In the therapy group all members have their individual treatment goal. However, group members begin group therapy as strangers, and they need to get to know each other to a certain extent before the group can reach its full potential.

Do people benefit from group therapy?

Group therapy, which has a broad range of applications, has been used as a standard mental health option for more than 50 years. Research has shown that group therapy is an effective mental health treatment. Group therapy offers a unique opportunity for group members to learn and to change as they interact with other group members. The group structure presents a social microcosm of the kind of relationships that people who seek psychotherapeutic treatment find problematic in their private and public lives. In groups, the members can observe each other, provide feedback to each other, and practice change strategies. In short, group therapy has a powerful healing and supportive function.

Common misconceptions of group therapy

New group members are often apprehensive about the whole idea of the group experience. It may seem too much like *group confession* in which members are expected to reveal their most private (sometimes embarrassing) life experiences. This is a misconception of group therapy. As the members become acquainted, mutual trust develops in the group. Then members are willing to talk about their relationships and the importance of these relationships. Such revelations can be either specific or general. Members decide, without pressure of any kind, to reveal as much or as little as they choose.

Other group members worry about a *contagion effect* in the group. As members talk about their difficulties, other members who identify with those difficulties worry that their conditions will worsen. This, too, is a misconception of group therapy. In practice, people often feel better if they have the opportunity to talk to others who share the same condition. Many patients in group therapy are surprised and pleased they can help others.

Still other group members are afraid they will *lose control* of their lives while in group therapy. Because this outcome is so rare, it is fair to say this fear is also a misconception of group therapy. Group leaders are attentive to the possibility that group members think they are losing control, and immediately intervene to calm and reassure these members.

Last, some group members fear *rejection or exclusion* by the group. They worry that other members will criticize them, laugh at them, or ignore them. They think they must agree to do or say uncomfortable or distasteful things in order to be included. They worry they will *lose their individuality* in the anonymity of the group. These concerns are also misconceptions of group therapy. The best thing is to talk about these fears early in the group, so they can be understood and possible to leave behind.

Group conditions

Confidentiality and *privacy* are essential in group therapy. Group members may talk about the group with relatives and very close friends, but only about one's own feelings and thoughts. However, it is preferable that group conversations stay within the group. Members should never reveal information about other members to anyone outside the group.

Attendance and punctuality. It is important that group members attend all meetings, be on time, and not leave early. The success of a therapy group depends on member participation, and everybody is important. Members are recommended to inform their group leader of unavoidable absences or of late arrivals/early departures.

Prohibited interaction outside the group [an exception is sometimes made for psycho-educational groups]. Group members are recommended not to meet outside the group, as it will influence the therapy negatively. In case it happens, it is important talk about it in the next session, to explore how this member interaction outside the group affects the work in the group.

How do group members benefit most from the group?

The more involved and engaged group members are in the group, the more they will benefit from the group experience. Perhaps the most important benefit from group therapy derives from the group setting as an environment in which learning occurs in the relationships between group members and in the relationships between group leaders and group members. The learning gained from these relationships can be applied to relationships outside the group setting.

Group leaders explain the group's format, boundaries, and rules to the interviewees. They explain the importance of attending meetings, being on time, and notifying group leaders of absences or early departures from meetings. Group leaders should also emphasize that each group member's participation in the group influences the success or failure of that member's group therapy experience.

Group leaders should also try to relieve any doubts interviewees have about the group therapy experience. Although people seek therapy for different reasons, they almost all suffer from some kind of life crisis, trauma, psychological condition, or relationship issue. Group leaders can explain that this commonality can be a bridge that links group members as they think about their own and others' situations. Group leaders should reassure interviewees that group therapy is designed to make them feel more secure in groups and more confident about their possible behavioural changes. Group members often have ill-informed fantasies and imaginary fears about group therapy. Therefore, it is important that such fantasies and fears can be verbalized and discussed in the interview.

When unexpected situations arise, sometimes a group member must leave the group prematurely. The departure procedure is explained to interviewees in the preparatory interview. The general rule is that group members should explain the reasons for their departure to the group, taking into account that one to three sessions are needed for the termination work. It is important for both the departing and remaining members to conclude their therapeutic work respectfully and cordially as they say goodbye to the group leaders and the other group members. This rule ensures that members who wish to leave abruptly, without any farewell remarks, understand the benefits of staying in the group until they can explain their reasons for leaving. A sudden departure by a member without explanation can be troubling to the other members, leaving them feeling confused and even guilty in some way. They cannot ask that member for clarification or reassurance.

All therapy groups have rules about early departures by group members. In the following example from a preparatory interview, an interviewee explains why that rule means she cannot join a certain group.

Example:

A woman at her second preparatory interview:

> I thought group therapy sounded very helpful. I am eager to be a member of the next group. However, since my husband and I are going on a cruise, I cannot attend the first three group meetings. We have already paid for the cruise, and I cannot cancel it. Is it okay for me to join the group anyway?

Group leaders must be prepared to deal with such questions in the preparatory interviews. Rather than responding immediately, they should take time to think about the question and possibly consult with a colleague or supervisor. There are no rulebook answers. Each question deserves careful consideration and a thoughtful response.

Group leaders should also review the *confidentiality rules* in the preparatory interview. It is essential to explain why group members have an obligation of confidentiality that prohibits them from socializing with each other for the duration of the group.

To conclude this section on preparatory interviews, we summarize Whitaker's (2001) list of common fears people often have about group therapy. If interviewees express any of these fears, group leaders should allow time to discuss them in the light of what is known about how most people actually feel and think in group therapy. People may have fears about the following:

- Not being liked, being thought of as stupid, being ridiculed or rejected.
- Losing emotional control (e.g., crying, becoming angry, or exhibiting sexual urges).
- Close proximity to others.
- Disappointing others.
- Being seen as crazy, emotionally disturbed, strange, or confused.
- Discovering something hidden about oneself.
- Becoming involved with others' emotional problems or illnesses.
- Revealing personal secrets.
- Losing control in front of others.
- Being hurt by others' insensitivity.
- Becoming too dependent or needy.

Choosing to participate in group therapy

Potential group members should be encouraged to make an active, independent choice about group membership. To make this choice, they require sufficient information on the group's purpose, goals, and size; meeting dates and times; the length of meetings; rules; and fees (if any). In addition, information on the group members' commitment to share experiences, emotions, and thoughts should be provided.

Near the conclusion of the preparatory interviews, the group leaders give their opinions on the suitability of the interviewees for group therapy. Then the *potential group members decide if they want to join a group*. Some group leaders may be tempted to persuade hesitant interviewees to join groups because they seem like ideal group members. Other group leaders, who need only one more member for their group, may try to convince sceptical interviewees to join their group. Group leaders need to resist this temptation if the interviewees are unsuitable for group therapy or have negative opinions of group therapy.

During group therapy, group members who were strongly persuaded to join a group may feel they were cheated and pressured. Group leaders and the group members may then try to persuade these disappointed group members to remain by talking through the situation. If a group leader and member trust one another, the hesitant member will be comfortable with making a decision about remaining or staying. If the discussion takes place at a group meeting, a message is sent that other group members also have the autonomy and power to decide what is best for themselves. They will feel liberated from the group pressure.

Of course, group leaders should anticipate the possibility of premature departures by group members. Therefore, in the preparatory interviews, groups leaders can indirectly explore this possibility. They should calmly ask the potential group members questions such as the following: "Are you sure?" "Have you thought about everything?" "Do you have enough time for this?" "Is there anything we can do?"

The importance of preparatory interviews

Most people are aware of the importance of preparation before starting new activities. This is especially the case with an activity as complex as therapeutic group therapy. If group leaders have thoroughly prepared the potential group members, they will be able to manage the inevitable doubts and fears that become apparent in the initial treatment phases. When group leaders sense potential group members are inadequately prepared, we recommend that they schedule additional interviews with those members before admitting them to the group.

Inadequate preparation can result in negative consequences for group therapy. We next list and describe six possible consequences.

- *Group sessions are dominated by a negative climate* – the conversations are restrained and guarded. Group members have many questions about rules and boundaries and challenge some group conditions. One possible cause is that not enough time in the preparatory interviews was spent on explanations and clarifications.
- *Poor group member participation* – members may leave the group before its termination. Possibly member motivation was insufficiently examined in the preparatory interviews.
- *Poor group rapport* – group members are too diverse. The reason may that the group composition was insufficiently considered at member selection.
- *External disruptions* – street noise, corridor noise, etc. Such problems result from inadequate organizational support that is required to protect the group so it can function optimally.
- *Over-dependence on the group leaders* – group members talk more to the group leaders than to each other. In such situations, group leaders must try to determine the reasons for this. Is something lacking in their own communication facilitation skills? They should seek advice from colleagues and/or supervisors.
- *Group discussions are dominated by one or a few members* – in such situations, group leaders might need to develop their skills in guiding and influencing discussions. Possible remedies are competence development and supervision.

In sum, thorough preparation is critical to the success of group therapy.

Planning the evaluation

Formal evaluations of group therapy programmes are typically made after the group therapy concludes. However, it is a good idea to think carefully about the evaluations in the planning and initial treatment phases. Useful evaluations deal with the group's purpose and goals. Did the group therapy serve its purpose and achieve its goals? Before treatment begins, we recommend that group leaders decide if they will make

1   A *formative* evaluation during the process (which can be used as a feedback and a guide during treatment).
2   A *summative* evaluation after completion of the therapy.
3   Both of these evaluations.

Part of traditional clinical work of group leaders is to evaluate each meeting after its conclusion, which would be a simple formative evaluation. They want to know, for example, if the group has "stayed on message" by concentrating on the group's purpose and goals. They want to know how the process developed and, not least, if they, as group leaders, contributed (positively or negatively) to the meetings. Group leaders usually find that contemporaneous journal entries and memoranda are helpful for recalling details and impressions (caution: group leaders' impressions may not match group members' impressions). Feedback from the group members can therefore be very useful.

One type of formative process evaluation, which is useful in some types of structured group therapy, such as psycho-educational, systems-centred, and cognitive behavioural groups, is that group leaders use the last five to ten minutes of each meeting to ask the group questions. Some sample questions are the following: "What did you learn?" "Were you surprised by this learning?" "What parts are you satisfied with and what parts are dissatisfied with?" In answering these questions, group members reflect on and verbalize their impressions. This can be a useful exercise for both group leaders and group members.

The evaluation of psycho-educational groups should address whether the group's learning objectives were achieved. Groups leaders may pose knowledge and attitude questions to group members that determine what they have learned. (See Chapter 11.)

Questionnaires

Questionnaires are often used in group evaluations where anonymity of responses is desirable. Another advantage of questionnaires is that respondents are inclined to answer the questions more truthfully than if the questions are asked in one-to-one exchanges or in group settings. In psychotherapy research, studies reveal that different therapists with the same focus can have very different results; for example, on the extent of the change in symptoms that patients experience after the therapy meetings (Norcross & Lambert, 2019; Wampold & Imel, 2015).

An essential feature of the group leaders' work is the solicitation of feedback from group members in therapeutic treatment. It is important to analyse, among many other things, how the therapy affected members' conditions, how members experienced the group climate, and how the therapeutic alliance developed. Formative evaluations conducted in one-to-one conversations are unusual in everyday clinical work. Despite their usefulness as training exercises for therapists, such evaluations, however, are often too costly because they require long hours of data entry and analysis.

A cost-effective solution is to use self-assessment questionnaires – perhaps before, during, and/or after treatment. It is especially useful to ask group members to complete a questionnaire before the first meeting. The results of that questionnaire can then be compared with the results of a subsequent questionnaire. Questionnaires may also be used in connection with the clinical assessments after the groups have ended or at some specified follow-up point.

Of the numerous available questionnaires, some relate to the treatment choice while others focus on treatment processes and outcomes. For example, Strauss et al. (2008) describe the CORE-R battery questionnaire, which is a tool kit for evaluating group selection, process, and outcome.

Regardless of which evaluation method is selected or how it is conducted, some form of evaluation should be part of therapeutic treatment. Group leaders may lack sufficient resources, including time, to make an extensive evaluation. However, even small-scale evaluations are useful if they add to the organization's knowledge bank that influences how resources are used. Frequently, group therapy benefits from such evaluations.

Summary

In this chapter we describe how to start a therapy group. We discuss preparatory interviews with potential group members; the group member selection process, including the suitability and unsuitability of potential group members; and various forms and uses of group evaluations. Our emphasis is on the importance of thorough group therapy planning and group member preparation. We also describe the importance of clear boundaries and rules and address various problems that group leaders might encounter, such as uncooperative and suspicious group members and disruptive external factors.

Chapter 7

Conducting a therapy group

As a group leader in a therapy group you have to manage several tasks and challenges. This chapter describes the group leader's complex role. The focus is on leadership in time-limited group therapy based on interaction and communication.

The leadership role

The concept of "role" encompasses all the demands and expectations related to an individual in a particular situation. When you take on a role, you act based on your own personal prerequisites, your understanding of what you wish to achieve, and how you interpret each situation. Thus, although different leaders may perform the same leadership role in different ways, they can be equally effective. When you assume the leadership role, you have to be yourself in that role.

Taking the role of the group leader in a therapy group means you are at the centre of the group. In this position, you are highly visible. Given this prominent position, inexperienced group therapy leaders may find the leadership role quite challenging. They may feel insecure, vulnerable, and worried about not being able to live up to the needs and expectations of the group. They may also be concerned about the complexities of the leadership role, and about the communication on many levels in the group; conscious, subconscious, between individuals, sub-groups, to the leader, and more. All this is sometimes somewhat overwhelming. Group leaders need time to digest and reflect on all the information and impressions received from the group experience.

As a group leader, you are advised to safeguard your professional identity by maintaining a careful balance between your private and professional identities at the same time that you reveal your personality in the role. Certainly, this is a delicate balancing act! Another challenge for the group leader is that you become a part of the group dynamic. This affects how you interpret what happens in the group and how you evaluate your own actions. It is therefore often invaluable to seek outsiders' observations and opinions on how you interact with the group members.

While this outside assistance (e.g., supervisory and collegial support) is valuable for group leaders throughout their careers, it is especially crucial for the inexperienced group leader. The inexperienced group leader can benefit greatly from co-leading therapy groups with more experienced leaders. Dual leadership creates an opportunity for both parties to explore different aspects of the group leader role. If an inexperienced group leader lacks the opportunity to co-lead with a more experienced group leader, then training and supervision should be provided so that the inexperienced group leader can grow into the role. (See our Concluding Remarks at the end of the book, where we address learning how to conduct groups.)

In order to take the role of group leader there must be an agreement regarding the purpose, goals, and tasks with the organization of which the group is a part. Group leaders need to understand and deal with the dynamics of both the group and of the organization, and sometimes of other actors in the context of group members. Group leaders need to monitor the opportunities that the organization offers as well as the limitations it imposes. Another aspect of this responsibility is that group leaders need to coordinate certain management responsibilities with the organization with respect to group member selection and various practical arrangements. (See Chapter 6 for more information on how to start a therapy group.)

The leadership function

The leader role in group therapy differs from many other leader roles, such as the roles of football trainers or business executives. The primary tool in group therapy is the group process; i.e., the interaction between group members, including feelings and thoughts that are communicated, and the sum of common experiences in the group. Therefore, the group leader's most important task is to support an open dialogue in the group. The group leader strives to create a group climate of openness and trust among the group members. This is more a "show" than a "tell" function because group leaders create the group climate by the way they act and speak in the group. Group leaders create a sense of safety in the group by visibly encouraging and caring for group members and by demonstrating respect for their integrity.

In previous chapters, we compared the group therapy leader to an orchestra conductor. We described how the orchestra conductor interacts and communicates with the musicians. In the same way, group therapy leaders interact and communicate with the members in the therapy group. In both cases, the whole is greater than the sum of its parts. In fact, in the discussion and literature on group therapy, group leaders are often described as "conductors".

The way in which group therapy leaders exercise leadership functions depends on the nature of the group – its purpose, goals, and composition. Group leaders have to act flexibly when groups develop in their various stages because different leadership functions are required in different stages (See chapters 8 and 9 for more information on group development.) An analogy with parental care can clarify this point. Parents act differently during the various stages of their children's development. When children are very young, parents provide an enormous amount of care and support. As children gradually mature, parents give them more space to exercise their independence. In the same way, group therapy leaders gradually exercise less active leadership as the group develops and members learn the working of the group. Leaders also expect the group members to take more responsibility for the work of the group. Another similarity between a group leader and a parent is that neither of them totally withdraws from the leadership function; they are always available if needed.

Leadership functions in group therapy can be described in terms of four main tasks:

- *Concern* – the leader provides support for and care of members. The leader shows warmth, acceptance, and genuineness.
- *Clarification of meaning* – the leader clarifies what happens in the group and in the interactions and communications between the members.
- *Emotional stimulation* – the leader initiates activities that emphasize confrontation, emotional release, and risk-taking.
- *Executive function* – the leader manages the group and sets group boundaries. The leader initiates group rules, asks questions, sets the pace of meetings, intervenes, and handles disruptions.

The management and leadership literature describes rather similar leadership functions. However, as mentioned above, the main tasks of the leader in therapy groups are to drive the group's process forward, to nurture the group climate and the relations in the group, and to express and give meaning to phenomena that group members are unable or reluctant to express.

Last, group therapy leaders have a responsibility to safeguard the group's norms and rules so that a group climate is created that supports the group's goals. This responsibility includes responding to rule violations (with sanctions if necessary). In therapy groups, it is usually sufficient that rule violations are noted and discussed. However, if group members break rules in a way that threatens the group's work, such members may have to be excluded from the group (e.g., if group members are intoxicated or make threats against other group members). Such situations, which are unusual, are often caused by a failure in preparation. The group leader may not have had the opportunity to choose the group members or may not have correctly assessed a potential group member's suitability for the group. Alternatively, the problematic group member may not have been sufficiently prepared for the group experience. It should be noted, nevertheless, that destructive processes can appear in groups despite good preparation. However, if all parties are well prepared, disruptive situations are usually easier to manage safely and effectively.

Two-leader groups

Some therapy groups have two leaders. There are several benefits of shared leadership. One can support each other to facilitate the group process, and the members' learning and development. Shared leadership facilitates more observations, more confirmation of observations, more interaction and communication with group members, and more analysis and evaluation. For group leaders, it can be fun, educational, and inspiring to share observations and reflections with a colleague. This is especially the case if the two group leaders have different occupational and educational backgrounds (e.g., a social worker and a physiotherapist working together with rehabilitation after a serious accident). More knowledge and more skills are then brought to the group.

When a therapy group has two group leaders, it is necessary to clarify how to deal with the situation when one leader is absent. Some two-leader groups have a rule that requires both leaders to be present at all group meetings; if one leader cannot attend a meeting, then the meeting is cancelled. The reasoning behind this rule is that both leaders are needed for the continuity and stability in the group. However, other two-leader groups have a rule that even if one leader is absent, the group will still meet. As a practical matter, this rule means fewer group sessions are cancelled. Yet there are disadvantages to this rule. For example, the absence of one group leader can have a negative effect on the therapeutic alliance. Poor attendance by group members may be attributable to leaders' absences. A group member complained to a group leader who had not attended all group meetings: "It seems that you don't think that we are especially important. You prioritize others before us." It is often a good idea for group leaders to think about such situations in the context of how the group leadership affects the group.

Cooperation between two group leaders

It may seem a two-leader group is more easily managed than a one-leader group, but this is not always true. The two leaders need to cooperate closely in planning and leading a dual-leader group. They need to think carefully about their own interaction and communication. The work will go much more smoothly if the two leaders know each other fairly well and have chosen to work together. It will be much easier to manage difficulties in the group if the two leaders trust each other and have a consensus view of how to lead the group.

In two-leader groups, the planning phase has an extra dimension. This phase provides an opportunity for the two group leaders to get to know one another and to strengthen their cooperation. They should take time to think how they can best interact and communicate as a team with the group members and how they should manage their different leadership roles. They should also plan when they will reflect on their group observations and ongoing cooperation and on how they will record their impressions (e.g., in journals and notes). This is an often-overlooked administrative task in organizations with limited experience of therapy groups. In the following example, we see how two group leaders cooperate in group therapy.

Example:

A group with young women with anxiety symptoms are in a two-leader group with a psychologist and a physiotherapist as group leaders. The leaders have completed the planning work together and have discussed how they will divide the leadership tasks and responsibilities. According to their plan, each group session begins with gathering the members in the group, catching up with each member, and engaging in group dialogue. Next follows a body awareness exercise. To conclude, the group members describe what was important for them in the session.

The psychologist will be in charge at the beginning and end of each session. The physiotherapist will lead the physical exercises. They will cooperate in following the group process and in taking an active role in the group dialogues. The leaders will meet for 30 minutes before the sessions to discuss and reflect on their cooperation and the group process. To increase their competency in leading groups and to strengthen their cooperative efforts, together they will meet with a supervisor for a few hours each month.

Of course, problems may strain two-leader cooperation from time to time. These problems may be caused by certain demands or interference from the surrounding organization. Other problems may result from the leaders' different views on the group direction and purpose. When the group is in the differentiation stage of its development – when members are testing the group boundaries and encountering the group challenges – some group leaders find themselves competing for authority and space in the group. It is therefore important that group leaders allocate enough time for internal reflection and external supervision so that they can monitor and develop their cooperation in harmony with the group's process.

In the following example, a two-leader team works to resolve what has become almost a group therapy "turf war".

Example:

Two group leaders, after a period of joint group therapy work, realized they had become increasingly irritated with each other. The background to this uncomfortable realization was that a group member had commented on the leaders' different approach to the group. The leaders took the problem to a supervisor, where they explained the group's situation and their leadership difficulty with the group that was in a help-seeking phase. The leaders had responded differently to the group members' demands and sense of help-lessness. One group leader readily offered advice; the second group leader was more withdrawn. The group members seemed to like one leader more than the other. They also criticized one group leader more than the other.

When the two group leaders understood that their conflict was a reflec-tion of the process in the group, they worked to understand the interaction. They asked themselves: "Does the group benefit from our advice?" "How can we support the group's self-confidence and independence?" "How can we prevent our leadership roles from being stereotyped as active or pas-sive?" They decided they should pay more attention to the group's abilities than to its helplessness. They tried to achieve a more balanced approach in their interactions with the group. They also saw that they should take more time to reflect constructively on their observations and impressions, and should give each other feedback after every session.

As these examples reveal, in addition to the usual leadership concerns, two-leader teams have an extra concern. Group therapy leaders have to work together harmoniously even when their education and experience may have prepared them quite differently. They have to learn to reconcile these differences. To that end, two-leader teams should share their knowledge and skills, examine their leader-ship styles, and reflect on their teamwork. Each has to protect their own need for competence development and possible need for further training.

Group leaders in leadership teams often conclude the experience increases their professional stature. These leaders learn to be more flexible and conciliatory when working as teams. Yet there are risks if the cooperation fails. For that reason, proper supervision that supports two-leader teams is essential.

The group leader's tasks

Dorothy Stock Whitaker (2001), a former professor of Social Work at York University, described the work of the therapist (i.e., group leader) as follows (paraphrased):

1   The therapist gathers information and creates images of the individual group members. The therapist may be surprised when the group members increas-ingly reveal more of themselves in the group than they did in the preparatory interviews. The therapist adds the new information to the images.
2   The therapist follows the development of the group as a whole during every group session and over time. With experience, the therapist's ability to observe the group dynamics increases. The therapist pays close attention to the group climate and culture and to the themes under discussion.

3   The therapist constantly observes aspects such as the following: how do sessions begin? How is the conversation mediated? Who turns to whom? Does one group member dominate the communication? What is the tone of the meeting? Who speaks? Do they speak loudly or quietly? How do the members appear? How do they interrelate? Do they make or avoid eye contact? What pattern has emerged – is there, for example, silence in the beginning and lively exchanges in the end? Do the members seem eager to leave? Are they silently watching the minutes on the clock tick by, waiting for the session to end?

4   The therapist constantly engages in self-reflection. Am I comfortable in group sessions? How do I feel about attending the sessions? Am I nervous? Expectant? Energized? Have my emotions about the group changed during the course of the treatment? Am I engaged or disengaged with members' problems and conditions? The group leader needs to sort through all these thoughts and emotions before, during, and after the group sessions.

According to Whitaker, the therapist works with the four tasks simultaneously. The tasks are related and complementary.

Steinar Lorentzen (2013), the Norwegian group analyst, agrees that the therapist must manage many tasks. We can say that a good therapist is a "multi-tasker". Therapists advance the group development, maintain and safeguard the group structure, and respond to group members' individual needs. The therapist is always observing the group as a whole as well as the group members as individuals.

Therapeutic alliances

Establishing a therapeutic alliance with the group leader is each group member's first step in establishing a therapeutic alliance with the group. When potential group members meet with the group leaders in the preparatory interviews, they can ask questions, express their concerns, and state their expectations. It is important that group leaders describe group therapy in a way that creates realistic expectations. The potential group member requires the space to describe the problems and trauma that have led to the search for help. The potential group member then will need help from the group leader to "translate" these problems into interpersonal terms – how these problems manifest themselves in patterns of problematic relations with others. The group leader and the potential group member should then agree on the goals and focus of the group therapy.

The interactions in the preparatory interviews between group members and group leaders are necessary preparation for the actual work in the group. The alliance with the group leader can be crucial for helping group members with the insecurity and anxiety they experience in the initial group sessions as well as in the turbulent times that may appear later in the process. Each group member's alliance with the group as a whole develops if the group is perceived as sufficiently safe (mirrored in the cohesion), if the group members have similar views

on the goal of the work in the group, and if they understand the general principles for interacting in the group. The alliance with the group develops gradually,
depending on how the group process unfolds, as the group members feel more
comfortable in revealing themselves and explore thoughts and emotions that are
mirrored by others in the feedback exchanges.

In the initial stage of group therapy, group members usually turn to the group
leader for guidance and support. (See Chapter 8.) As group sessions continue, the
focus changes. The leader–member therapeutic alliance gradually develops into
the therapeutic alliance with the group as the members interact and talk to each
other. When the group cohesion increases, members develop a sense of belonging,
the group seems important and the group members prioritize the group (e.g., by
regular attendance and timely arrival to sessions) and they find the goals of the
group meaningful and important. The group members contribute to the group and
take active responsibility for its development and understand how they can use
the group to reach the individual and common goals. The alliance with the group
is then established. This alliance will develop (and endure) only if the members
are secure in the confidentiality of the group. They then will dare to make intimate
revelations, explore their emotions, and be open to feedback.

Both therapeutic alliances – leader–member and to the group – change during the course of the group's development. These are not neutral changes; they
either strengthen or weaken the alliances. For example, group members' trust in
the group leader or in other group members may increase or decrease. Perhaps
some members support the treatment methods and activities, while others doubt
their usefulness. When these alliances weaken, it is crucial that group leaders
pay attention to this development and safeguard the boundaries of the group. The
recommended way for group leaders to manage the processes when the alliance
weakens is usually to remind the group of its purpose and to invite everyone to
participate in open and exploratory dialogue regarding the doubts and difficulties
the members experience. (See Chapter 8 on changes in therapeutic alliances.)

The group leader's attitude

Group therapy leaders have a big responsibility. For inexperienced group leaders,
the responsibility may seem very daunting. A closer look at this responsibility
might be instructive. In the kind of group therapy that this book describes, group
leader responsibility refers more to the leader's responsibility for the development
of a therapeutic group process than to the leader's self-presentation as an omnis-
cient expert in mental health issues or as the leader at the centre of the group's
focus. In our opinion, group leaders are responsible for developing this process
such that the group itself becomes a therapeutic tool. In a sense, responsible group
leaders develop group members as co-therapists.

The language used by group leaders should be casual and simple – rather like
the language used in other social contexts. Group leaders should avoid theoretical
explanations and long-winded descriptions. On the contrary, they should strive to

make their comments concise, inclusive, open, and non-judgmental. Group leaders are also advised to avoid imitating the group members' language and modes of expression when significant differences in backgrounds and cultures exist between them and the group members. For example, when a middle-aged group leader with a middle-class background tries to imitate the language of young drug addicts, the group members will see through it and react negatively.

In group sessions, group leaders pay close attention to the group's mood. They listen carefully and watch attentively. Their attitude towards the group is that of interested observers who are trying to understand all that is said and all that is implied. Group leaders encourage this same attitude in group members.

Example:

The group leader looks around the group. She leans forward. Her facial expression is visible for all members in the group, as is her posture and other expressions of her personality. The members listen to what she says, but also hear how she speaks slowly in a moderately strong and somewhat tense tone of voice. All is noticeable and possible for the members to react to. She tunes in to the atmosphere, lets time pass, and finally abstains from making any further intervention and leans back in the chair.

The group leader's activities will change to adapt to the needs of the group and are dependent on the stage of group development. Generally speaking, group leaders are most active in the first group sessions, and less active during the period when the group members are working most intensively, and increase activity again during termination. (See chapters 8 and 9 on group development).

When a group leader takes an active role in the group, it implies that there is less time for members to speak. However, sometimes it is important for leaders to step in; for example, when the group is unable to use the time and lapses into long silences. The members may need help to explore what prevents them to move on.

Interventions and group leaders

An intervention is a conscious effort to influence the group process. When group leaders observe, listen, and try to understand and evaluate what is going on in the group, they are at the same time influenced by the dynamics of the group. Interventions by group leaders are, therefore, complicated and not always obviously necessary. Interventions may be verbal or non-verbal: in spoken comments, by facial expressions, or by body language. Because interventions are complex and sensitive actions, group leaders should intervene with care and then reflect on the effects of their interventions. The purpose of interventions is always to serve the group. Group leaders should not intervene to satisfy their own needs/desires; for example, to be wanted, important, competent, or something else which has its roots in insecurity. Such needs should be dealt with in supervision or in dialogue with colleagues.

Unavoidably, some interventions will not accomplish their intended purpose. Group leaders who worry a lot that they will make misguided interventions should examine their emotions and thoughts related to what is happening in the group, the stage of development, and the process of working through. Is their concern related to a "right–wrong", or a "good–bad", or an "either–or" theme in the group dialogue? It can be quite helpful if group leaders are curious enough to examine why interventions are not received as hoped for. It is less helpful if group leaders are looking only for their own mistakes and trying to blame themselves.

Certain actions are not interventions, although they can nevertheless influence the group. For example, if a group member begins to cry, a group leader may offer a tissue. This might be a comforting act, or it might be something caused by other kinds of emotions in the group leader. How facial and other physical expressions are combined with words will influence how the members interpret the meaning of the action. Probably the group's reaction is determinative. If the group leader is in tune with the group climate, the group members will see the action as natural and adequate.

Group leaders should usually avoid individual interpretations of subconscious intentions or transference reactions that seldom benefit the development of the group. This caution, however, does not apply to group members. It is quite common in groups (that have been working for a while) that the members will interpret others' actions and words in ways that may have powerful therapeutic effects.

The group leaders' interventions have different purposes in the four stages of the group's development. (See Chapter 8 for a discussion of the four stages).

1   In the *engagement stage*, the interventions focus on creating a climate of security and community. This climate creates a reassuring environment for all group sessions.
2   In the *differentiation stage*, the interventions help the group move away from creating a community to accommodating differences and variations.
3   In the *interpersonal stage*, the interventions develop and deepen the processing both for the group members individually and for the group as a whole.
4   In the *termination stage*, the interventions assist the group in the work of separation. The goal is to maintain group community as members examine their emotions when working with separating from the group.

To whom should group leaders direct their interventions?

Group leaders intervene in groups at various times and in various ways. A group leader's intervention may focus on one group member, two group members (a pair in some respect), the group as whole, or a sub-group. Regardless of the focus, the aim is to help group members communicate with each other. Group leaders may ask simple questions, such as: "What do you think of what Matthew just said?" Or group leaders may look at a quiet group member and ask: "Do you want to describe what is going on with you right now?" If a group member responds hesitantly or vaguely, a group leader may ask: "Will you repeat what you just said to Lena so that everyone can hear it?" All such group leader verbal interventions, which aim to open up the flow of communication, should be adapted to the group's purpose, maturity, and preparedness for the specific intervention.

If group leaders focus their attention on specific group members, the effect will vary depending on the group therapy stage. Group members, especially a targeted member, may feel threatened or exposed by leader interventions in the engagement stage. However, once group cohesion has been established, group members are more inclined to welcome group leaders' interventions, especially if an intervention is a response to a group member who seems in crisis. The intervention may offer relief to all group members, not just the targeted member. When a group is stable, safe, and cohesive, the group leader may help a member to make an important therapeutic experience related to what is happening in the here and now of the group. At this stage, the group can tolerate that one individual member is the subject of the group leader's attention.

Group leaders often focus on the group as a whole. This interventionist technique may be problematic if the group has not yet coalesced. To deal with this difficulty, group leaders may connect group members' accounts in a way that supports the group as a community of people with shared interests/conditions. In the next two examples, a group leader addresses the group:

Example 1:

"Andrew described his conflicts with his manager at work. Michael talked about his annoying and unhelpful landlord. Lisa related how her doctor responded unsympathetically to her description of her symptoms. The rest of you have probably had similar experiences with authority figures. Perhaps you see me in the same way – as the 'boss' who takes control of a situation, being unsure how I should cope with this responsibility."

Example 2:

"You heard Mary complain how an irritating cousin disrupted a family dinner and Jennifer complain how her uncooperative colleague slowed the progress of a project. These are not unique experiences. They are familiar to most of us. Does anyone want to share an experience that is like those I have just mentioned?"

If group members respond to this invitation, group cohesion increases. The group leader's intervention achieves its aim.

When should group leaders intervene?

We next describe several group situations (with examples) in which group leaders may need to intervene.

- When a *group member appears insecure* in the group. For the well-being of both the individual group member and the group as a whole, the group leader helps the member with the current issue so that it is possible for the member to remain in the group.
- When *group members are trapped* in a mutual behaviour (rooted in some fear or uncertainty) that obstructs group progress. The group leader relieves tension and refocuses the conversation.

   Example:

   In the beginning of a group therapy when members still feel insecure, some of them might direct comments to the group leader rather than to the group. In such a situation the leader can avoid maintaining eye contact with that member who is experiencing the difficulty, and instead look around in the group at the other members. The leader may comment: "I notice that you often speak to me. I think you probably have a lot to gain from speaking to the others. I know you have a lot in common. Speaking to each other will help you to get to know each other."

- When group leaders perceive that *group members' concerns and uncertainties hinder communication.* Instead of giving calming assurances – which will not help – the group leader can address the situation by inviting members to talk about what hinder them at this moment.
- When group leaders observe *destructive processes* in the group. An example is the situation when a group member is scapegoated. The group leaders can suggest that the scapegoated member may indeed express something that is relevant for the other group members.

   Example:

   The group leader addresses the group: "You all seem to agree that Anne is in the wrong and that there is no reason for fear in this group. It seems to me that Anne was dismissed without being given the chance to express her thoughts that something might be avoided. What are your thoughts on that?"

- When the *group climate becomes overheated.* In this situation, the group needs the group leaders' help to calm down, but also to try and find out what led to the heated exchanges and how the group members responded to this change in the group climate.

- When *group members show a great interest* in a specific topic. Group leaders should encourage all group members to express their views and share their experiences, thoughts, and emotions on the topic. Feedback might be encouraged to create the opportunity to explore others' views on the topic.
- When group leaders *realize a situation is of critical importance*. At this point, group leaders should seize the opportunity to intervene. The situation may involve a group member on the edge of an important emotional experience, which might influence that person's basic psychological patterns Or the situation may involve a sub-group engaged in an important dialogue.
- When the *group members cannot manage a situation*. For example, when a conflict occurs in the group that threatens group cohesion, group leaders should intervene to reduce the tension. This can be done by simply summarizing the situation.

Example:

"You began by talking enthusiastically about an important subject. But when you disagreed with each other, you became very angry. Now you are silent and refuse to talk to each other. Why is that? What do you think happened?"

If that is insufficient, one may continue suggesting, for example: "When one is angry and upset it can be hard to find any meaning in staying here. Is that the case for the two of you now?"

- When *a group member has (or risks) an adverse outcome*. Group leaders must act to protect the group member. The intervention should be handled very sensitively so that the group member does not seem to be favoured or infantilized. Group leaders may ask the group to halt a while and reflect in silence, and then initiate a discussion about what happened and how it was for everybody to be part of it.
- When the *group members reach a conversational impasse*. Although the group members are still engaged and motivated, they nevertheless seem to have exhausted their energy and ideas. The dialogue comes to a halt. Group leaders in this situation need to listen to their own feelings about what is happening in the group. This observation and exploration of the interactions in the group create material for forming a hypothesis that can be tested with the group.
- *To pave the way* for an important subject the group is unable to grasp. In such situations, the group leader can encourage the group with a comment such as:

Example:

"You are talking about abandonment. We are approaching the summer break. Soon we will not see each other for a while."

Jeff Roberts, an English group analyst, recommends that group leaders ask themselves the following questions before making interventions (Kennard et al., 1993, p. 6):

- What is the state I am observing?
- What processes are contributing to it?
- Do I judge it to be constructive, destructive, or neutral?
- Would it be advantageous to change this state?
- Is it possible to change it?
- What intervention(s) might influence the constituent processes and state?
- Is the necessary intervention within my repertoire?
- Is the time ripe for an intervention?

Examples of intervention

Group leaders might try the following examples of interventions. Some of the interventions may be used in combination. It is a good idea, as these examples show, to make the interventions brief. The intent of all interventions is to contribute to genuine dialogue in the group.

- The group leader may *deepen an emotional state*. Perhaps the group members need to explore and work with grief. The group leader can speak softly, in tune with the emotion of the group members.
- If the *mood is restrained*, the group leader may decide not to respond to the current group climate and instead provoke a different group climate using energetic body language or facial expressions.
- The group leader may *show interest* by leaning sympathetically towards a member or by nodding encouragingly. The group leader may offer the following brief remark: "Interesting. Is there more to say about this?"
- The group leader may *invite* other group members to participate – non-verbally by looking around the group, or verbally by asking: "Can you add anything? What do the rest of you think? Is this experience familiar?"
- The group leader may *summarize* a situation. The group leader might say: "You sat quietly until Jim began to talk about conflict in the Middle East. Then you had a long and engaged conversation on this topic."
- The group leader may intervene when *the group has no response* to a situation. The group leader might ask: "Everyone noticed that Alice was not here today. Yet why did no one remark on her absence?"
- The group leader may *comment on something that recently occurred* in the group by inviting the group members to reflect on the interaction in the group. The group leader might say: "What did you think and feel when Bob and Jane were talking just now?"
- The group leader may *invite group members to talk about a previous occurrence* by asking members to describe what happened and how they felt about

it. The group leader might ask: "When Kenneth was upset in our last meeting, what did you think and feel? How did you perceive what happened?"

- The group leader may *give direct instructions*. For example, if a member is on the verge of a violent outburst, the group leader might say: "Stop! Wait a minute! Let's sit down quietly and talk things over."
- The group leader may invite members to *talk about the consequences* of a certain behaviour. The group leader might say: "Your criticism was not directed at Hassan exactly. But you were very critical of his favourite football team. How do you interpret what happened after that?"
- The group leader may *help the group members talk openly* about a difficult topic that they are alluding to using metaphors and circumlocutions. The group leader might say: "You have talked about different situations where confidentiality has been violated in your contacts with healthcare. How do you think the things you say in this group are taken care of?"
- The group leader may *enlarge an individual problem to a group problem*. The group leader might say: "Everyone has tried to get Ann to change her behaviour at work, but we have not talked about why that is so important for you."
- The group leader may speak openly about something the *group members are reluctant to talk about*. The group leader might say: "Today we have avoided talking about something everyone sees. Rebecca has been angrily complaining that her mother has been nagging her about her weight loss. No one has commented. But we can all see [*turning to Rebecca*] that you have lost quite a bit of weight."

When should group leaders not intervene?

The needs of group leaders must always take second place to the needs of the group. If group leaders allow their emotions and prejudices to influence their interventions, their ability to listen, interpret, and respond is endangered. Group leaders should seek supervision or consultation if they think they are not sufficiently clear about how their own conflicts and struggles influence their interpretations of group situations and responses. At the same time, it is inevitable that the group processes will resonate with group leaders' emotions and unresolved conflicts as well as touch their own emotional scars.

For example, a group is strongly cohesive. Group members share intimate emotions, joke good-naturedly among themselves, and generally feel a strong sense of togetherness. This group cohesiveness can cause the group leader to feel excluded and alienated.

In situations where group leaders do not fully grasp the direction and content of what is happening in the group, the best response is to wait, watch, and let the group move forward. If group leaders are unable to resolve their confusion, they may admit to the group that they are somewhat perplexed and not in touch with what is happening in the group. The group leader might say: "I am not sure what is going on right now in the group. What is your view of what is happening?"

There may be circumstances in which the group members, consciously or subconsciously, exclude the group leader. If the exclusion challenges the group leader's authority, the group leader may be less able "to lead". The group leader should handle this situation with care so as to avoid creating a power struggle. It is usually helpful for group leaders to examine and process their own emotions and reactions when they sense they are under attack. The next step for group leaders is to try to understand the rebellion by individual group members and by the group as a whole. After this step, group leaders can move to interventions. They may simply and directly explain the situation to the group. A group leader might say:

> I have noticed that the group at the last session seems to have lost interest in what I have to say. When I try to contribute, I have been interrupted. I have not been asked for guidance. This response is a considerable shift from the response I received only a few weeks ago.

Yet another situation in which group leaders should refrain from intervening is when all group members are fully absorbed in a thoughtful and respectful dialogue. Even if group leaders spot an opportunity to focus on one group member's particular problem, they ought not to intervene. When a group is productively engaged in its work, there is no reason for the group leader to intervene.

It is easy for a group leader to be affected by performance anxiety. In this situation, it can be helpful to keep in mind that the most important aspects of the group are the group members' interactions with each other. Insightful interpretations, explanations, or interventions by the group leader are less important aspects. Group leaders can guide and facilitate the process, but the most powerful interventions are formed within the group itself. When the group leader tries to manage performance anxiety by hiding behind a façade or by trying to assume a false role, group members will typically spot the leader's lack of genuineness.

On a more positive note, we observe that with experience, training, and guidance, group leaders can improve their ability to make effective interventions. Group leadership is a craft that needs to be learnt and practised. As group leaders become more self-confident, they feel more secure and assume their roles more comfortably.

Summary

In this chapter we focused on the group leader's role in conducting group therapy. Like orchestra conductors, group leaders direct an assembly of diverse members, to allow all parts to be heard and contribute to the music The foremost responsibility of group leaders is to facilitate an open group climate and a group culture of exploration and acceptance. They use simple verbal and non-verbal interventions, carefully attuned to the group mood. They work to understand and support group members via their commitment, receptivity, mirroring, intersubjectivity, warmth, generosity, and dialogue. Group leaders are clear about the purpose, goals, and boundaries, and thereby provide members with a safe environment where confidentiality is assured.

Chapter 8

Engagement and differentiation

In the next two chapters we describe the typical development of time-limited group psychotherapy (normally 10–30 sessions), its stages, its alliances, and the role of its leader. The chapter is based in the general principles of group development and in the process-oriented interactive group model (MacKenzie, 1997).

Research and clinical experience support the claim that groups pass through various development stages. Groups that begin and end at the same time (i.e., time-limited groups) follow approximately the same development process. At the beginning, the group is relatively dependent and security-seeking. As time passes, the group becomes more contentious and counter-dependent. Then the group becomes more trusting and more structured. Last, the group enters the separation and termination stage. It is a development process that resembles the identity development process that people experience in life: childhood, adolescence, adult life, and old age (when preparing for death).

The stages of group development are easily identifiable in time-limited, process-oriented group therapy with permanent members and fixed beginning and ending dates. However, the stages described in the interactive group model do not apply to the development in slow-open groups that admit new members in later stages (as described at the end of this chapter) or in therapy groups that last several years.

Each stage in the group development process in a time-limited group has its special characteristics that differentiate it from the other stages. An understanding of these stages can be helpful for group leaders as they guide group members through the stages. As a meta-theory, the group development process provides a structure, a map, and a powerful tool for group leaders.

Many models describe the passage through these stages (i.e., the changes) in the development of groups. The commonality among these models is that all derive from the belief that the group development process is systematic and specific. The models describe characteristic patterns found in different types of groups. For example, the models describe group mood (or climate), member–member relationships, member–group relationships, and member–group leader relationships. They also describe how emotions are expressed and ideas and opinions are formed. This also applies to the kinds of themes that develop during the group sessions.

In this chapter, we describe the following four sequential development stages: (1) engagement, (2) differentiation, (3) interpersonal work, and (4) termination. In highly structured groups, the differentiation stage typically is not easily distinguishable or brief (see Chapter 12, which describes Focused Group Therapy [FGT]). We are inspired by the group model created by K. Roy MacKenzie, a Canadian psychiatry professor and psychotherapist and an authority in the field of group development. MacKenzie derived his model from his research on time-limited group psychotherapy (MacKenzie, 1997).

The four stages of group development

We describe each of the four stages of group development in three sub-sections: the group's purpose and goals, the group's therapeutic alliance, and the group leader's role.

In Figure 8.1, we present our adaptation of MacKenzie's (1990) model. The figure illustrates the change in the group's structure over time and the relatively fixed relationship patterns between the group members and the group leader.

The first circle in Figure 8.1 illustrates the engagement stage. Group members who have joined the group feel uncertain and nervous in this new situation. The small circles, ringed by dashes, represent the group members. The second circle illustrates the differentiation stage, in which group members (as solid-line small circles) have become more confident and have begun to establish relationships (dashed lines) with others. The third circle illustrates the interpersonal work stage, in which the group members have become more open, more cooperative, and more willing to accept mutual responsibility. Communication among group members has improved. All lines in the third circle are solid. The fourth circle illustrates the termination stage. The group leader's external position has changed. Group members accept responsibility for themselves, say goodbye to the other members, and express sadness that the group, which has been very important to them, is ending. The group members, who are no longer connected by lines, go their separate ways, carrying the group experience within themselves.

Engagement

The engagement stage of group therapy begins at the first session and lasts until the group members develop a "we-sense" – i.e., group cohesion. Typically, it

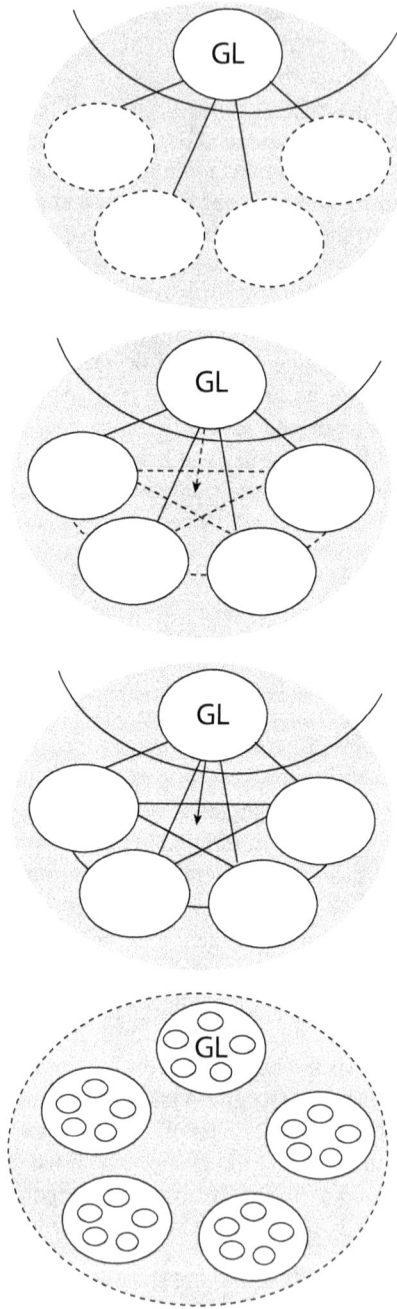

Figure 8.1 Group structure in the four stages of development.
(adapted after MacKenzie, 1990)

takes two to five sessions to establish this cohesion. The first session is especially crucial for the group development process. It is then that group leaders' attitudes towards the group and their leadership styles are revealed. Both group leader attitude and leadership style are highly influential in the group development process.

Group members bring different emotions, expectations, worries, longings, and other concerns to the group. They are often as curious as they are nervous. They may ask themselves questions, such as the following:

- How will I be able to cope with my need to become a member of the group?
- Will I get the help I require in the group?
- What will the others think of me?
- How can I find my own way together with all these people?
- Can I be myself?
- Will the others be receptive to my emotions and experiences?
- Will I fit into the group? Do I want to?
- Will I be an important part of the group?
- Will anyone care if I feel isolated in the group?
- Does anyone else think and feel the way I do? Is there anyone here like me?
- Will I really be helped by these meetings?
- Will the group leader direct the conversation?
- Will the group leader help me?

The way in which group leaders welcome group members, respond to their concerns and fears, and "hold" them creates a framework with protective boundaries. The aim is for group members to feel safe.

The group's purpose and goals in the engagement stage

The main task in the engagement stage is to create among the group members the sense that they belong to this specific group. The goal is that all members will adopt the frame of "We as a group" in a way that sets the group apart from "others outside the group". The bounded framework of the group separates the members psychologically from the outside world.

The group has achieved these goals when the group members, individually and collectively, agree to take an active role in the group by talking about themselves and by taking an interest in the other members. A spirited group climate is established when members contribute eagerly and welcome others' contributions. At this point, the group leader observes that the members' focus has shifted – from the group leader to the group itself.

This achievement will probably take a while. Perhaps the group must meet as many as five times before the members conclude "Now we are a group." The research literature on groups shows group cohesion (as just described) has a positive influence in group therapy outcome (Bakali et al., 2010; Lindgren et al., 2008). Figure 8.2 illustrates the group structure in the engagement stage.

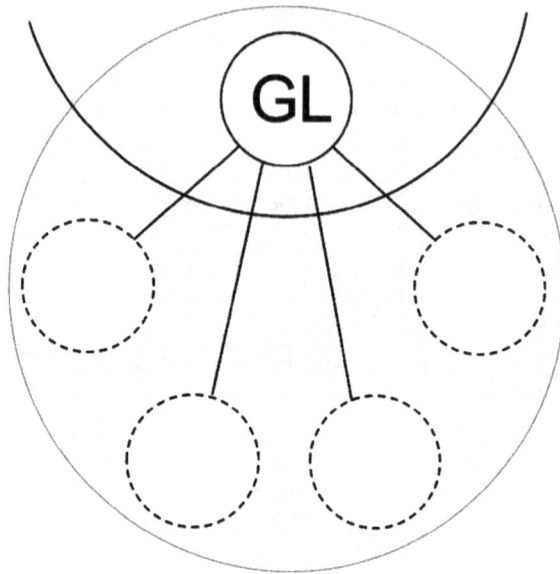

Figure 8.2 Group structure in the engagement stage.

The group's therapeutic alliance in the engagement stage

In the preparatory interviews (see Chapter 5), one wants to establish a therapeutic alliance between the group leader and the future group members. In the initial interviews, group leaders described the purpose and goals of the treatment to the members, answered their questions, emphasized the importance of confidentiality, and researched members' motivations and expectations. The hoped-for outcome is that mutual trust has developed between the group leader and the group members.

However, the group experience is new and strange to everyone. Members are somewhat wary of each other. They understand the nature of group therapy and how it functions – theoretically but not practically. No one is quite sure what will happen in the sessions. Will the group cooperate? Who will remain silent? Who will talk? What mood will dominate? Will positive relationships develop? These are only a few of the unknowns. It is impossible to predict with any certainty how the group will develop. Everyone, including the group leader of this particular group, is a neophyte.

In this stage, many group members look to the group leader for guidance in this new and unfamiliar situation. Group leaders help members address other members as they explain why they joined the group and how they now feel about the group. Members' accounts strengthen the therapeutic alliance to the group when other members respond to them.

At this point, as the emotional involvement of the members increases, the therapeutic alliance among the members is on its way to being established. However, the alliance is still under construction. The group climate might be somewhat constrained. For example, some members may think the conversations are somewhat superficial or too narrowly focused. Other members may begin to doubt the value of group therapy. It is critically important to encourage all members to express their worries and doubts, all of which, if unexpressed, can pose barriers to open communication in the group. The group leader's response to these complaints and concerns is of paramount importance.

The next example addresses this point. In the exchange, GL is the group leader; A, B, and C are group members.

Example:

GL: Some of you have talked about yourselves and why you are here. How do you feel now?

A: I am a bit worried. We don't know each other. I wonder how I will feel the next time we meet.

B: It was easier for me to talk after you spoke first and led the way.

GL: Some of you have not said anything. How do you feel?

C: I don't really know. All this is quite difficult for me.

GL: It is difficult to be here. You may feel unsafe and worried. You don't know how things will develop. Can you say something about this situation that makes it difficult and unsafe?

The conversations in the engagement stage reflect the group members' nervousness and insecurity. Perhaps they did not fully express their doubts about group therapy in the preparatory interviews. Perhaps they did not imagine the group experience would be so scary and confusing. Perhaps they see an inconsistency between what they agreed to in theory and what they have experienced in reality. The group leader in fact may have been ambiguous. Disruptions in agreed-upon routines (e.g., changes in meeting rooms and times) or in group composition can have that effect. A group member may say to the group leader: "I thought you would be more active in the group. I thought you would tell us what to do." When such comments are made, the group leader should offer reassurance and clarification directly. The group leader may say: "I understand that I should have been clearer with …" or "I have thought about what it means to you when I … What do you think?" The group leader should not rush members' responses. The members need time to reflect on how their first impressions may influence their sense of security and thereby influence the group's therapeutic alliance.

By the time the group has met several times (perhaps two to five times), the therapeutic alliance to the group is apparent. Everyone has been working towards the goal of making the group meaningful for everyone. The members are now sharing experiences and emotions, exchanging information, and taking an interest in others. They are comfortable with asking and answering questions and with reflecting on their own and others' revelations. The group leader, while still important for assuring the group safety, is less directly involved in facilitating the communication. The members have gained the self-confidence to initiate and carry on the conversations. Members are less hesitant to tell outsiders that they are in group therapy. Members now understand why they belong in the group and how the group may help them.

The group leader's role in the engagement stage

The first group meeting sets the tone for the group therapy and for the group leader's interactions with the group members. Group members will often replicate the communication style of the group leader in one way or another (Sandahl et al., 2000). Therefore, group leaders should prepare the first meeting very carefully. In their first group leader experience (following a long and demanding preparation process), group leaders may be quite excited. They will have both positive and negative expectations of the group experience. However, it is wise for group leaders to contain some of this spirit that might distract them from paying close attention to the members' concerns and hopes.

Prior to this first session, we suggest sending a written information sheet to the group members. Group members are informed of beginning/ending times, dates, and locations for all sessions. They are also told at the first meeting that the group leader will meet them in the waiting room and lead them to the therapy room. It is a good idea to have members assemble in the waiting room before the session begins. This procedure allows the members to avoid the discomfort of sitting together in a room, waiting for the group leader. When the entire group and the group leader have arrived, everyone enters the therapy room together. The room should be well prepared, with good ventilation, lighting, and the right number of chairs placed in a circle.

Group leaders should also be prepared for the unexpected at this first session. Some members may not attend; others may be late. It is important to create a notification system that members can use to pass messages to the group leader about delays, absences, etc.

Now the first session can begin. When the group leader closes the door, a boundary is created between the group and the world outside, between therapy and everyday life. From the first few minutes of this session, the leader's remarks and actions are important. It is then that the group community and the group cultural foundation are created. Although the group leader role is important for the members throughout the whole treatment process, the role is especially important in the initial meetings. Because the situation is unfamiliar, it is then that group members seek reassurance. They are acutely aware of the group leader's presence. Group leaders are the only people in the room who have met the group members and who have formed relationships with them. The members are strangers to each other. When they become acquainted, they will be less dependent on the group leader.

Group leaders are advised to take an active leadership role beginning with this first meeting. By "active", we do not imply group leaders should dominate the conversation, offer advice, or make opinionated judgments. However, the members need guidance in how to contribute to the group and how to interact with each other. The primary concern of group leaders is the group as a whole. While the group leader role may at first seem very demanding and complicated, group leaders can to some extent take comfort in the assurance that therapeutic factors will emerge spontaneously in the group conversations. Their responsibility is to facilitate the group members' work. Some group leaders, in the first meeting, will have to teach members how therapy groups work and how the members can contribute. To some extent, when they listen and observe, group leaders are role models for the members.

At the first session, typically the group members observe the group leaders and wait attentively for them to speak. This anticipation in the room is simply an expression of the group's first sense of community – the "We". Group leaders should not interpret this mood as either an indication of the members' appreciation or as a demand for some expected performance.

Group leaders begin the first session by welcoming the group members. Then they review the guidelines and rules that were previously presented in the preparatory interviews. Group leaders then ask the members to respond. The purpose of this exercise is two-fold – to draw all members into the conversation and to confirm that they understand the implications of the agreement on boundaries. Group leaders can correct any misunderstandings as well as present any new information (e.g., information from the sponsor organization). It is normal for a group leader to prepare a written memo on what to say so nothing of importance is overlooked. The group members also have the opportunity to provide new information (e.g., concerning a planned absence).

Members' questions should be regarded as important contributions even if the same questions have been answered previously or the answers are really quite obvious. Because group leaders have noted members' worries and concerns in the first meeting, they readily understand that some members may ask unnecessary questions. Sometimes a member just wants reassurance from the group leader. When such questions are asked, a group leader may turn to the group members and ask for their response: "Is there anyone who remembers how we covered that topic and can answer that question?" Or: "I know it is hard to remember everything I have told you. Probably some of you have the same concerns as Lisa. We can certainly review this material again. It is really important that there are no misunderstandings."

The group leader then invites group members to speak. A group leader might say: "We are all in this treatment experience together. I think I have said what I want to say at this moment. Now you are welcome to talk to each other." When the members' conversation slows, a group leader might say: "Some of you have explained why you are here and what you expect. We would like to hear from the rest of you."

Sometimes conversations begin with a "round" in which group members take turns speaking. Many people are familiar with this practice from other kinds of meetings. "Rounds" are useful for giving everyone a chance to speak and for limiting the length of time they speak. However, group leaders should be wary that this practice does not become a repeated pattern. Gradually, group members need to learn to be comfortable speaking spontaneously without prompting. It is also a group leader's responsibility to ensure that no member is completely silent, no member is ignored by the group, and no member dominates the conversation.

When a group member is late to the first session – when group members are already engaged in conversation – the best decision is to greet the late arrival quietly, and, for the moment, ignore the interruption and let the conversation continue. When a natural break in the conversation occurs, the group leader can introduce this individual to the group and summarize the conversation for that individual's benefit. A group leader might say: "Welcome, Mary. We have just heard why everyone is here. They can briefly introduce themselves to you. Then I would like you to tell the group about yourself." By asking the group members to speak first, the group leader safeguards the group and strengthens the group community. Everyone also learns that the time limit is an important group boundary.

At the first session, after everyone has spoken, the group leader can review the group members' similarities. Then the group leader should encourage further reflection. A group leader might say: "All of you joined this group because you have some problem or difficulty you wanted help with. What do you think when you listen to the others? Do you recognize anything in what you have heard?" Members are then invited to share experiences and to identify similarities.

Group leaders can help group members discover how they can talk to each other. A group leader might say:

> When Jane was talking, many of you asked questions. Some of you seemed very moved by her story. What were you thinking and feeling while she was talking? One way to get to know each other is to describe your thoughts and feelings as you listen.

Sometimes a group member who is anxious or tense may withdraw psychologically, ask the group leader critical questions, or generally launch a flow of words that dominates the conversation. Group leaders respond with respect and interest. This response indicates that everything that is said in the group is important.

Group leaders should thoughtfully address criticism from the members in recognition that members' comments are therapeutically valuable. At times, members simply need to give vent to their concerns and complaints together. A group leader might say: "It's good, Alex, that you brought this up. It is something we might need to look at together for a little while. How did the rest of you perceive it?" If no one responds, the group leader might continue: "It seems you have a lot to think about. Does anyone wish to tell us what these thoughts might be about?"

Inexperienced group leaders may be nervous at their first group meeting even if they look forward to an experience that should be exciting and interesting. The temptation when one is insecure is to fall back on something one is more familiar with – such as the individual therapy perspective. However, this response undermines the creation of the group as a therapeutic environment. Instead of asking members questions about their specific stories, group leaders should direct their attention to the group as a whole rather than to the members as individuals. To broaden the conversation from one group member to the entire group, a group leader might say: "Do you understand what John is describing? It seems somewhat unclear to me. Perhaps one of you can help. Or do you think we need to hear more from John?"

It is more likely that group therapy will produce positive results if group leaders take a holistic perspective. It is important to listen to the "the voice of the group"; it is this voice that speaks for all group members. Group leaders listen to what is said in the group with "two ears" – one ear for the individual voice and one ear for the group voice. At a tense moment in group therapy, a group leader might say: "George probably isn't the only one with these doubts." The group leader might add:

> It was not easy talking about this. What do you think? It is essential not to criticize others. You need to help the group overcome obstacles in your communication. Do you have any ideas on why it is difficult to talk in the group now?

As many of our examples show, it is quite common for group leaders to address group members by their first name. There are at least two good reasons for this practice. First, when members hear their names, they feel included and welcomed. Second, other group members are reminded of people's names. Although they heard everyone's name at the first round, the members tend to focus on the unknown situation, on what they feel, and on what they say. Therefore, it is not unusual that members do not remember which name went with which member.

In the first session, the members introduce themselves and identify their individual goals. The group leader makes sure that no one is left out of this process. If certain members seem too eager to tell their stories, it is wise to try to curb such discussions. The group leader might say: "Michael and Amira, you have described some important stuff that we should explore further. We will return to that subject in future sessions."

When the first session is nearing an end, group leaders are advised to ask the group members to give their impressions of the meeting. Usually, the members respond positively. They may say the meeting has actually put their fears to rest. They are relieved. Some members may even say they found the meeting a rewarding experience. If the meeting ends in a positive atmosphere, most members will leave the room with a hopeful attitude. They are looking forward to the next session. If the responses are less positive (e.g., critical questions were asked and doubts or strong feelings were expressed), group leaders should remark on this atmosphere. The members need to be reassured that it is acceptable to have doubts and strong feelings. Group leaders should state that these issues will be addressed in future sessions. In this way, group leaders express their confidence in the group therapy.

Next, we describe some more difficult situations that might emerge in the engagement stage.

When group members plan to leave the group

The beginning of therapy can be a disturbing experience for some members – especially when they reveal more of themselves than others do. In such situations, the risk is that these members have revealed emotions and experiences that surprise, even distress, them. They may be so frightened that they do not want to continue in the group. Group leaders, who must be attentive to such responses, should carefully help these members finish their stories at that moment. To reassure these members, a group leader might say (speaking to a member): "I can tell that you have many important things you want to share with the group." This same leader might then say (speaking to the group): "I am sure there are others here who recognize themselves in what you say."

When group members are silent and passive

The engagement stage can be a difficult time for group members. Many members are reluctant to engage in conversation and to respond to each other. They prefer to be silent and passive observers. It is likely they are experiencing insecurity and disorientation. They ask themselves: "What should I do?" In such situations, the group leader needs to actively engage all members by encouraging them to talk in the group. That is how the creation of a safe place begins.

The engagement stage – in short

Feelings emerge quickly in a group even when groups members do not openly share their feelings with other members. While members are often very curious about other members, they may initially fear some member (or members). They may distance themselves from that member even as they seek support from yet another member. Other members may worry that they will say something foolish or will be laughed at. However, as the group members gradually become acquainted, listen to each other, and start to communicate, they see that others have the same insecurities. At this point, when members share a common experience, the first building block of group cohesion is laid. Group leaders support development in the group by linking members' emotions and experiences. A group leader might say: "Anne, perhaps you can relate to what David has just described. Haven't you told the group about a similar experience?" Or a group leader might say: "Is there anyone who recognizes what Ellen has just described?"

Exchanges in group therapy, which can be verbal or non-verbal communications and conscious or subconscious revelations, foster cohesion, trust, and care among group members. Members sometimes increase their self-esteem when they contribute and realize they can support other members as they receive help themselves. A group member might say: "What you said last time, Yannis, meant a lot to me. I've been thinking about it all week." By the time the group has met a couple of times, all members have said something about themselves. They have experienced what it feels like to be listened to and to listen to other members' stories. A sense of fellowship and belonging has been established. A group member might say: "It is good that you understand. I used to feel so alone with this."

Summary of the engagement stage

Supportive group cohesion and a positive group climate are created in the engagement stage. Group leaders remind group members of the group boundaries: confidentiality, attentiveness, sincerity, and spontaneity in the conversations within the walls of the therapy room. These inner and outer boundaries set the necessary conditions for group therapy. Group leaders offer support and encouragement as they focus on the group as a whole by linking all the individual members' statements and stories. As similarities among the group members emerge, a group community grows. There is a feeling of "We" and "Now we are a group."

Differentiation

After the initial work and the established community in the engagement stage – thus founding group trust and security – the group members' need is to separate themselves from the "We" of the group. The group conversation becomes less harmonious, more confrontational, and there is a change in tone. The group theme "We Are Alike" is set aside as group members' as well as the group leaders' differences are explored and valued. Group leaders follow this process paying attention to the changes in the climate and supporting the differences and whatever issues that come up.

A greater emotional distance develops between group members. The driving force in this stage is the group members' need to establish their identities in the group and to examine how they relate to and interact with other members. When a member has experienced the feeling of being part of a group, enjoying the security of that group and the possibility to satisfy his/her needs, then it is also important to show who you are. The now existing secure atmosphere makes it possible to express one's differences and to be confident believing that one will be listened to. An apt analogy is child development, when a secure environment gives children the opportunity to differentiate themselves as they grow up, establishing their independent and stable identities. In this development work – for group members as well as for children – achieving independence often means conflict and tension with others, not least with the people closest to them. This is obvious in therapeutic groups and the dynamics can also be found in other contexts; for example, in work teams.

Research on group development concludes that the conflict and tension aspects of the differentiation stage are usually short-lived in clearly structured contexts

(Wheelan, 2005). Therefore, in groups with a high degree of structure, such as cognitive behavioural therapy and psycho-educational groups, the differentiation stage is relatively brief. Of course disagreements, rivalries, and leadership challenges appear in these groups, but they are usually rather uncomplicated and easy to manage.

The group's purpose and goals in the differentiation stage

The group's main task in the differentiation stage is to develop ways to manage the tension in the group that results from group members' differences and conflicts. This means that the members should stand, contain, and accept differences in the group without polarizing. The changing attitude appears slowly. It is perhaps first noticed when group members make complaints about an outside authority.

For example, some members may describe unsympathetic physicians while others talk about inexperienced therapists with questionable skills. Some members blame unsupportive parents or authoritarian work managers and experienced earlier unsuccessful therapies. These conversations may become quite emotional as members express and verbalize their feelings. Gradually, if the group leader manages, members may direct the criticism and protests at the group leader. Group leaders should calmly recognize the self-assertive aspects of these activities and be seriously interested in these complaints and emotions even when they are personally targeted.

The group leader may have difficulties with the challenging task of focusing more on the self-assertion and less on the content, the criticism. Otherwise the risk is that the opposition will stay in the group and drive the group members apart.

When the group has had the opportunity to test the authority and realize that the group leader can stand by and handle that confrontation, the group can then develop further as group members now dare to confront each other. Now the conversation reveals that the members want to differentiate themselves from the group even as they claim a position in the group. Now they want to talk about the difficulty that results when the group community makes them either conform to or revolt against the group ethos. They examine how they feel about their place and role in the group. They explore their relationships with their so-called siblings in the group. It is likely that as habitual roles and behaviour patterns appear in the group, an opportunity exists to rethink and change them.

In short, the group members in the differentiation stage have a need to liberate themselves from the feelings of control and the extent of the group leader's authority as it is symbolized in the group members' inner and outer world. They question the group norms, and new norms can be established. More and more, as group members assert their individuality, they define themselves in relation to each other and to the group leader: *I do not agree. I have a somewhat different opinion.*

If this process is successful, a deeper level of the presented difficulties and conflicts is exposed. More problematic aspects and feelings are described, like relational difficulties, embarrassing experiences, irritations, poor self-esteem, and fear of rejection and isolation. A skilled group leader can help group members link their experiences outside the group to the here-and-now group relationships to be worked on in the group. In this way, through the intensive and challenging meeting with others – and their mirroring feedback response – the people develop a clearer identity that becomes clearer in each other's eyes. The process also contributes to a greater understanding of the complexity of other human beings.

In this way, group members develop their inner strength and capacity to take responsibility for their own needs and a healthy self-assertiveness. This will create opportunities for important therapeutic experiences later on in the group.

A group that is unable to pass through the differentiation stage might remain in the experience of friendly fellowship and support. This outcome may be unproblematic, even desirable, if the group is a support group, a self-help group, or a psycho-educational group (i.e., groups not focused on relationships). The groups in focus in this book, however, have to pass through every stage in order to reach their full potential.

A group reaches its full potential and goal in this stage when group members agree to explore their relationships with each other and to examine the differences and conflicts in these relationships in spite of their disagreements. It is possible to explore this and to verbalize how one is affected and how that feels. Having done this leaves a feeling of conquest: *This is our group, not yours. You are needed, but this is our work.* At this point, the group leader is important but not central to the group's security. The group leader points out to the group that it has matured and is ready to move to the next stage. Figure 8.3 illustrates the group structure in the differentiation stage.v

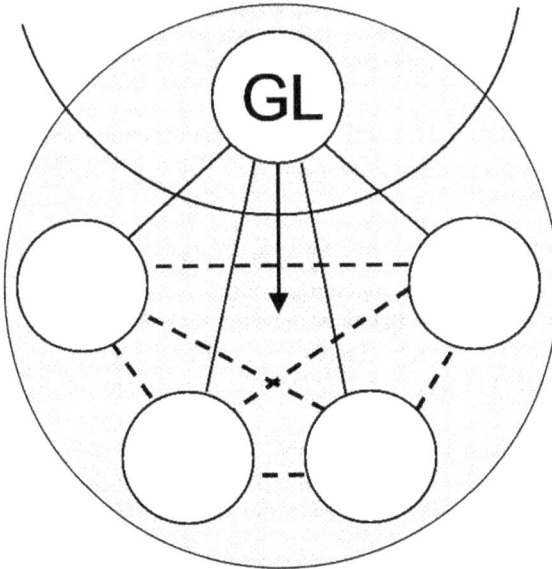

Figure 8.3 Group structure in the differentiation stage.

The group's therapeutic alliance in the differentiation stage

The differentiation stage can be experienced as the most difficult stage in group development and can be experienced as threatening for the group as well as group leaders. It can be unnerving to see the group's therapeutic alliance begin to shatter. Thus, members can be tempted to return to the good, secure atmosphere of the earlier stage, however fragile. This was based on an illusion of a forever-good community, which would be of no good to anyone and hardly anyone in the room believes in.

The initial alliance was built on common factors, on mutual recognizable experiences, shared conditions, and feelings of being alike. The authority of the group leader was uniting the group and provided the security. Members are now aware of their differences in the relation to the other group member as well as to the group leader.

The threats to the group's therapeutic alliance are evidenced by increased absenteeism and tardiness, objections to the therapeutic methods, and more complaints and criticism. As general dissatisfaction spreads among the group members, the group climate becomes tense. Group members avoid eye contact with each other. Sub-groups form. Some members are increasingly isolated. In the following example, the discussion is about how the group can understand one member's absenteeism and what feelings this awakes. GL is the group leader; A, B, and C are group members.

> **Example:**
>
> A [to B]: I probably feel a little different from you. I do not agree with you.
> B [to GL]: But what do you think? What is your opinion?
> GL: People think differently. Like the two of you. I would like to know what the others think. Perhaps there are other views.
> C: I do not recognize myself in either A or B.
> GL: It seems that the same situation can provoke different emotions. Because one person thinks and feels one way does not mean that everyone agrees.

People react differently to the difficulty of managing conflicts and tolerating disagreements. This lack of group unanimity may be very disturbing to some group members. Others are relieved that they can express themselves as individuals. The differences and conflicts become more obvious. The group risks polarization. The greatest risk is that the differences may split the group into sub-groups or shatter altogether.

The value of the group has now changed, the group members are less convinced of the group's benefits than before when it was obvious. Some members with difficulties in asserting themselves in a healthy way are threatened, withdraw, and distance themselves from the group. Group members who are less independent and less secure may find the challenges too difficult. *If I say what I think, the others will not like me. What if someone is angry at me?*

Others whose difficulties may be the closeness and intimacy, experiencing that atmosphere as too invading and threatening, can feel relieved and free. *I don't agree.* Yet members who are uncomfortable with the communal intimacy may miss the former shared cohesion and community from the earlier stage; they can experience this as a loss.

Also, in relation to the group leader the therapeutic alliance is changing. The differences in the distribution of the roles, with the group leader setting the boundaries and being responsible for guiding the group, come to mean security in the group. This can now be experienced differently and questioned and criticized by some group members wanting to influence the group setting. They may want to change the time frames and the meeting routines and exert an influence contrary to that of the group leader. Members may even become quite contentious.

The opposition can be so big that some group members feel guilty and shameful. They may be ashamed that they have exposed themselves in an unfavourable way, have fantasies about not being liked, or that they challenged the group leader. They may also be worried that they will be rejected, judged, ridiculed, or punished in some other way for these actions. It is painful knowing you have or will hurt someone you are close to. A member response may be to withdraw emotionally and physically: *Can I suddenly distance myself from that individual? I really don't like being so close.*

If group members cannot share these concerns, or explore them in an effort to understand and resolve them, the therapeutic alliance among the members is at risk. There is now a danger of negative, destructive group processes starting up. In a misguided effort to save the alliance and get rid of these strong emotions the group may scapegoat a member as the cause of the breakdown. Victims are typically members who have a unique position in the group, like upholding an unpopular attitude in the group, or who have forcefully asserted their individuality, thus being left alone in the group. No one wants to be connected or try to understand. The group avoids communicating with him or her and has for the moment reinstalled a calm and united group: *We do not want this person in our group.* The scapegoat member is excluded and in the worst case leaves the group with the unexplored problem. The group leader and the group are left to consider and understand the cause and the effect of the expulsion on the remaining group members.

The group's hard-won revival of the alliance is only temporary, though. It soon becomes clear that expelling a member does not restore peace and harmony to the group. The scapegoat issues, which are still unresolved, will return in some form until the group addresses them. The process has hurt the excluded member, who was ostracized or victimized. In some sense, the group members have lost more than they have gained because the expulsion damages deeply the group's self-image. Therefore, the group leader's responsibility is to intervene in the scapegoat process when there are hints of victimizing another member before it reaches the point of member expulsion. This can be done by paying attention to the ongoing process and by insisting that the members talk about the problem. It is essential to get everything "on the table" in order to explore what hinders the communication in the group and in order to stop blaming something outside the group or one special group member. The group leader might say:

> You are angry and frustrated right now. It sounds as if you want to get rid of your frustration by focusing on Kevin as the problem. He is the target now, but it could have been anyone of you. We need to talk about this situation now.

The therapeutic alliance needs to find a form in the differentiation stage unlike that in the earlier stage. As we know, people must feel secure in their relationships before they can acquire new knowledge from others. Security precedes curiosity and interest. In the engagement stage, group members took comfort in the security provided by the group cohesion and community formed from similar emotions and experiences. But in the long run comfort in security inhibits personal development and individual freedom. Now, in the differentiation stage, that group cohesion and community are less relevant when members' differences and conflicts are in focus.

In this situation, group leaders should take an active interest in these differences and conflicts. They can explain that group cohesion and community were necessary in the engagement stage, but now groups members are in a new stage. The former group unity is no longer appropriate for the long-term development of the group. Group leaders may invite the members to think about and how they experience how they differ from each other. The message is that differences and conflicts are normal. If they talk about their dissimilarities, they are less likely to feel insecure or threatened.

In this process with the new therapeutic alliance, in which differences and conflicts are accepted, group members discover how their opinions and thoughts, which once seemed obvious truths, can now be differently understood in light of their own life histories and earlier experiences. This way, the members' dissimilarities, in short, become therapeutically useful. The interesting diversity of the members' histories and their individual experiences can strengthen the alliance and make it more inclusive. Group leaders should support the respectful and curious communication around those differences and conflicts.

The group leader's role in the differentiation stage

The group leader's role in this stage is to observe, to listen calmly, and to support group members in their difficult work of managing their different powerfully expressed emotions and strongly-held opinions. The main task is not the members' actual expression of their negative emotions but the opportunity to explore the significance of the fact that these differences exists within the group. The intention for the group is to try to understand what underlies the negative feelings that arise.

It takes time for group members to learn to manage their differences and misunderstandings. Group leaders should assist by confirming group members' comments – not on the basis of "right or wrong" – but as legitimate expressions of points of view. In this work, group leaders should pay attention to the following levels of group developments:

- The group as a whole in a stage in which group cohesion, formerly based on similarities and agreements, now includes members' differences and conflicts.
- Group members clearly differentiating themselves from other members (Figure 8.3).
- Group members assuming some of the group leader's control over the group.
- The group leader's more advisory role: reminding the group of its purpose and goals, reviewing activities and methods, and giving members space to communicate and discover their own voices – their individuality in the group.

These group developments can be problematic and strenuous for everyone. The risk in this developmental stage is that the group may be so resistant to change that it returns to its former "good" situation in which member support, group cohesion, and the warmth of the community prevailed. The group may even split into sub-groups and some members will leave of their own free will or with the help of the group. People with poor experience of being together in groups are particularly at risk of this outcome. They are in danger of ostracism or they themselves rejecting others in the group. The group leader's task is to develop the capacity for "timing", to intervene at the right moment to divert this destructive possibility. (See Chapter 7 for a discussion of group leaders and interventions.) In the following example, we see how the group leader re-directs the conversation. GL is the group leader; A, B, C, and D are group members.

Example:

A [to B]: You want to talk about that again? I think we are done with that topic.
C: I agree. We can't talk about that every time.
D: I would like to talk about something that happened last week.
GL [to D]: We will return to that later. Now I think we need to talk about B's problem. He was upset. We need to know what really happened.

The group leader's most important task in holding the group together is to actively encourage the group members to talk about their dissimilarities – what it means and how they think and feel, how it is to disagree or experience oneself or someone else being different from others. When these contrasting positions can be communicated, the group tension decreases.

Sometimes group conversations are characterized by resistance when the group members are talking about some problem that is external to the group. This can be angry voices uniting around a topic outside the group's and the group leader's control. The task for the group leader is then to bring the anger into the group; for example, like this:

> I hear that you are upset about the traffic congestion today. This can really be trying. I wonder if you on another level are talking about our situation in the group. What trying obstacles to our communication do you find here in the group?

When the resistance is openly verbalized, the problem can be seen and heard by everyone. The protests, criticisms, and oppositions are contributions to be received and reflected upon. Sometimes it is a separate single person protesting; sometimes it is "the voice of the group" that verbalizes the protest. It is beneficial to discuss such protests openly in the group. The frustration can be caused by something in the relation between the group and the leader or in relation to the outside world. In either case, the group leader should ask members to voice their feelings and thoughts and encourage them to be receptive to critical responses.

When group members continue the passive resistance by a sulky silence, the group leader's task is more complicated, encouraging the passive protesters to talk about their negative feelings. A group leader might say: "You are all silent. No eye contact with me or with anyone else. What is happening?" It can be helpful if group leaders direct the negativity towards themselves, thus supporting group members to address the others in the group. A group leader might say: "Now you are definitely disappointed with me! Do you want me to intervene in some way? How?"

The fear of expressing anger, opinion, or criticism towards others may silence some group members. However, it is necessary to convince the group of the importance of giving one's opinions, of disagreeing with others, and maybe being angry when you disagree. Group leaders sometimes focus on how something is said rather than on what is said. A leader might say: "John, it is great that now you are talking freely. That was so difficult for you before." The group leader may invite others to confirm this observation. If the entire group is involved in a meaningful exchange, the group leader can listen, and then perhaps contribute supportively: "I am hearing many different opinions now."

A fear that many group members share is that these challenges will be destructive and threatening to others. For this reason, these members are not inclined to talk freely in the group because they think their opinions and emotions are unacceptable to the group. Group leaders should always listen closely to the members' reactions to what is said and done. When such topics and behaviours – like scapegoating, for example – threaten to creep into the group conversation, a group leader should interrupt, and invite the members to reflect on what is happening. This often means that the destructive process stops, and a repairing reflection starts. A group leader might say: "Now I want to stop for a while. What do you think of what is going on now?"

Group leaders may face challenges to their authority from the group. Some challenges are rather minor. For example, a group member may propose a change in the meeting time schedule. Another group member may propose the introduction of time-limited "rounds" in the conversations so that everyone has an equal chance to speak. On the surface, such proposals seem perfectly reasonable. The group leader's task is to stay in role when such proposals are made. They should not allow themselves to feel provoked or threatened. Nor should they give into members' demands and requests before the group has resolved these matters. As always, group leaders should lead the conversations so that all aspects are thoroughly addressed. A group conversation about the proposals will likely reveal members' underlying feelings and motivations. What does it stand for, what needs are involved? Does the suggestion about an equal amount of time have to do with envy or with a feeling of being offended, wrongly treated, and so on?

Sometimes such work in the group can lead to the implementation of minor changes that the group wishes to make. These changes are usually procedural. For example, the group members may ask that all session times/dates be posted in the meeting room. To a certain extent, the members have assumed the leadership role and have set themselves up as equals to the authority of the group leader.

It is helpful for group leaders to remember that group members need to explore their strength and to assert their independence. It also helps to understand that members' self-assertions are intended to test the group leaders' role and authority. These self-assertions should not be interpreted as personal attacks on the group leader. By asking questions, offering suggestions, and making criticisms, members show they are not wholly dependent on their group leaders. One can compare group members in group therapy to teenagers who need to develop identities that are independent from their parents. The advice for group leaders is the following: when the group asserts its independence, accept it as evidence of the group development process in the differentiation stage. The process, which is normal and expected, will be productive.

Next, we describe some more difficult situations in the differentiation stage.

When a group member deviates from other members

This situation often means that not enough consideration was given to the group composition. Problems in the group may arise if a group member does not have the same characteristics as the other group members. For example, the group member has no children (all other members are parents), is much older than the other group members, or is the only immigrant in the group. From the start, this group member is different in some way. There is a risk that this member will be exposed or by himself or herself takes the role of being special. The group member might say: "You can't understand. No one in the group has ever ..." The group leader must make a special effort to include such members to show that group members have differing views.

When a member makes an angry outburst in the group

People with problematic aggression can frighten the group. Typically, such people are considered unsuitable for time-limited group therapy with an interpersonal focus. Maybe this person should benefit better from alternative therapies. How-ever, if such a person is in the group, group leaders must manage the situation firmly by calling an immediate stop to the outburst. A group leader might say to the other group members: "Leave Anne alone with her anger for now. I know you are upset, too." The group leader may help the members see Anne's outburst as an expression of their and the group's own anger. The group leader might say: "It is unlikely that Anne is the only angry person here. Who else is upset? What stops you from talking about that?" At its best the angry member's voice is included in the choir of the whole group helping the other to express their anger.

When an angry or upset member rushes from the group room

This is a challenging situation. In a one-leader group, the group leader must remember (unless there is a physical risk to the member or to others) that the group takes priority over the individual members, so the group leader stays in the group and helps the group to talk about what happened. Perhaps a group member will try to persuade the member to return to the group. When a group member rushes from the room, that individual may need a few moments to be alone. In a two-leader group one of the leaders leaves for the member and, ideally, persuades him or her to come back. Furthermore, the group leaders are responsible in such situations for dealing with the member – should the situation just described arise – and the group leader should go on leading the group conversation. A group leader might say: "What did you think when Anne became so angry? How did you feel when she slammed out the door?" To have the possibility to reflect and calmly talk about how everyone experienced the same situation, what feelings and memories were aroused, deepens the therapeutic work in the group. If Anne returns, the group leader must handle her departure/return with great sensitivity. There is a possibility for her to describe her reaction, how she sees it now, and how it felt to rush out and be asked and brought back.

When an unhappy member leaves the group

Occasionally a member who is driven from the group in this stage contacts the group leader and informs him or her "I am getting nothing worthwhile from this group experience", or does not contact them at all. The group leader, who is aware that all group difficulties are part of group therapy, tries to get hold of the mem-ber, and says in the group what has happened and what actions are planned. It is important to let the members participate in this work, and to ask about their feel-ings and thoughts. This is another possibility to work with the different experi-ences and conflicting opinions in the group.

  If the person decides to definitely leave the group, the group leader should con-tact the drop-out member to explore the reasons for leaving and to try to persuade the member to return for a last session in the group to share the separation with the group. It is often difficult, maybe impossible, but it is important for the group to be informed of that attempt. And seeing the drop-out member in a final two-person session gives the group leader a possibility to help the member to sum up what work has been done and to get a good-enough separation from the group.

When a member becomes a scapegoat

The scapegoat group phenomenon was previously explained in this section. Scapegoating is a common tendency among human beings. The group offers the possibility to everyone to see the universal aspects of human interaction and the demanding difficulty to be a human being among others and be part of a democratic society. The group members can have deep experiences of how easy it is to exclude someone and what emotions causes these impulses. And they can reflect together on what consequences these mechanisms might have. While we often try to avoid differences, much can be learned from them.

If the scapegoat situation arises in the group, group leaders should, early on, take the opportunity for a group conversation on what feelings and thought are involved and what it means to blame a single individual for the group's difficulties as a way of avoiding these difficulties.

When a member is isolated by the group

Destructivity in the group can be very subtle and may take various forms: for example, simple neglect, casual avoidance, or, in extreme cases, outright rejection. The group's isolating behaviour can develop into exclusion. It is usually not difficult for group leaders to spot such behaviour. When they do, group leaders should make a special effort to include the isolated member in the conversations. A group leader might say: "I wonder how we reached this point. It seems that the group does not understand what John is saying. It is important that we talk about what he has said. What do you think? How do you feel, John?"

Summary of the differentiation stage

Differences and conflicts with respect to group members' behaviour, emotions, responses, and opinions appear in the differentiation stage. In the process of group development, the members are confronted with their differences and conflicts, but they are also rewarded with a greater sense of independence and individuality. Group leaders help members express and value their dissimilarities in ways that are productive to the group as a whole and to the members as individuals. Group leaders may also help members see the value of what they have constructed together; they have built a foundation that is essential for the difficult and important work the group is engaged in. Group leaders also deal with challenges to the group therapy model and to their leadership role. They manage sensitive situations when members feel isolated, angry, or scapegoated. The differentiation stage, in short, is a very complex stage in the group's development. For the group leader it is important to remember the group's developmental task for this stage: group members should express, cope with, and incorporate the differences in the group.

Chapter 9

Interpersonal work and termination

The work in the differentiation stage, with its differences and conflict resolution experiences, has increased the group members' commitment to, and trust in, group therapy. They are ready to work with their relationship difficulties, to explore their personal relationship patterns, and to learn from others. They are also ready to welcome feedback and to experiment with new approaches in the here-and-now group setting.

In the interpersonal work stage, group leaders encourage the group members to be spontaneous and open in their conversations. They also protect the group members from locking themselves into limiting forms of communication (e.g., not taking turns, talking only to the group leader, avoiding the group leader, or talking too much or too little). Group leaders can facilitate the conversations in this stage by describing the current communication pattern so that group members recognize the obstacles to open and free group communication.

Group members take more responsibility for the conversational content and development in this stage as they move towards more self-governance. They describe past events in their lives and talk about their lives outside the group. The group members' reactions to what is said are prioritized. The content of their stories is explored, if possible, in relation to the here-and-now.

Group leaders can sometimes make pedagogic interventions that help group members understand how the group works. They help the members discover what is relevant in the flow of information. They help members explore reactions and emotions when the conversation becomes impersonal or evasive. If group members have difficulties communicating, group leaders can ask the group members to discuss what is happening, the feelings involved, and their responses. A group leader might say: "You seem almost paralyzed today. What do you think about that?" It is helpful to the group when group leaders are open in expressing their reactions to members' accounts and communicate their reactions with facial expressions or brief verbal comments.

Interpersonal

The group's purpose and goals in the interpersonal work stage

In the kind of process-oriented, interactive treatment that is the focus of this book, one main goal in this stage is to understand the individual and group relationship patterns as they appear in the group. The psychological boundaries relate firstly to the individual's own intrapsychic sphere and secondly to the group as a whole (including the members' interpersonal exchanges and interactions).

One way to think of the group development process is to visualize it as a spiral movement of ever-deepening interpersonal themes. The topics from the engagement stage return in the interpersonal work stage when emotions and experiences are again recounted, now in a more intimate and self-revelatory way. The differences and conflicts from the differentiation stage return when autonomy issues are in focus. With this background, the interpersonal work stage focuses on key factors in identity development – for example, intimacy–distance, dependence–independence, and dominance–submission.

Members receive and give feedback. In this stage, it is a challenge for members to reveal more about themselves and to consider the meaning of what others say. As conversations become more personal, group members may feel more vulnerable. They may fear loss of self-esteem, or rejection. At the same time, the group offers an opportunity for individuals to deepen their understanding of themselves. As group members become more self-aware, they recognize the universality of their interpersonal relationships. The work on these issues increases the group's closeness and intimacy, its independence, and its self-definition in relation to others. Each group member's task in this stage is to achieve the following level of introspection: *I dare to be vulnerable. Others can understand me and accept me as I am.*

The group members' goal is to achieve self-acceptance and acceptance of others in equal, open relationships. The hoped-for result of this acceptance is that members will be able to function flexibly at the various group levels: the group-as-a-whole level and the individual member level – in relation to the group leader and to the self. Figure 9.1 illustrates the group structure in the interpersonal work stage.

The group's therapeutic alliance in the interpersonal work stage

When the group enters the interpersonal work stage, the group members and the group leader have met for nearly half the scheduled sessions. They have learned

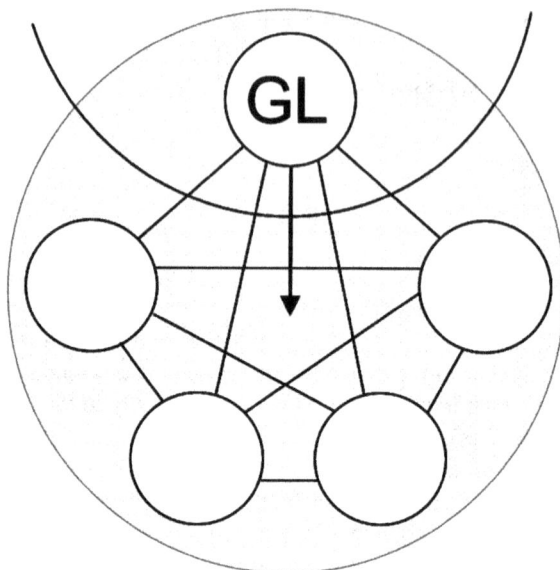

Figure 9.1 Group structure in the interpersonal work stage.

to work together. The therapeutic alliances are usually well established. The group cohesion is strong. Group leaders can relax somewhat as the group becomes more independent. From their previous meetings, group members know how the group functions productively. They can apply this learning in their conversations in the interpersonal work stage.

Security in the group is also well established in this stage. Thus, the group members are more comfortable talking about their experiences and emotions. They trust each other and the group leader. The members' stories are often emotionally powerful for both speaker and listeners. A window of opportunity is now open in which experiences and emotions can be explored more deeply than in the two previous stages. In the following example, we see how a group member opens up far more than before. A, B, C, and D are group members.

Example:

A [in tears]: It is so difficult when you [B and C] talk so intimately with each other. I can scarcely stand it. I have always felt like an outsider. Even in school, I was not allowed to join the others.

B: Goodness! That does sound really difficult. There is nothing worse than feeling excluded.

C: What happened at school? Did no one offer to help you?

A: No. No one knew what it was like for me. I told no one. I was too ashamed. I felt there was something wrong with me.

D: But now you are telling us. I think that takes a lot of courage.

Yet even when group security is well established, some group members are still apprehensive. They may be reluctant to reveal some very profound and sensitive emotions. For other members, because the group climate is reassuring and welcoming, they are tempted to tell more than they really intended. Afterward, although they may feel exposed and unprotected, they rarely leave the group in this stage. Sometimes just longing to be open can help members get in touch with strong feelings that can cause anxiety. In such situations, it might be wise for group leaders to provide extra support between group sessions.

The group leader's role in the interpersonal work stage

The group leader's role in the interpersonal work stage is to continue providing guidance and support as the group members develop their relationships. As mentioned above, this role is less visible than in previous stages. The group members, who are now actively engaged in the group therapy, have taken on greater responsibility. The group members are highly influential in the treatment. Now that they have learned to use the group process, they see how powerful a tool it is. Yet group leaders still have a role. They help the members understand, integrate, and apply these experiences. This is an essential leadership task.

The group therapy in the interpersonal work stage builds on the experiences and emotions revealed in earlier group sessions. The group members' relationship difficulties that arose in the group were already evident in their formative years. Now they have internalized these difficulties as self-perceptions. They have also formed expectations of how others will respond to them. The group work takes these issues to a deeper level when past experiences are addressed and repaired through new experiences within and outside the group. Making this work visible is part of the group leader's responsibility.

Feedback is an important group tool in the interpersonal work stage. According to the results of clinical studies (Yalom & Leszcz, 2020), individually directed and spontaneous responses are valuable, especially for those who give immediate feedback that is emotionally charged and involves some personal risk. Group leaders, however, should avoid using the word "feedback" because it has a negative connotation for some people, sometimes implying vague criticism. At this point, the group members know how to express their reactions in the group. The work now deepens. The "feedback" can be provided directly with comments, or indirectly with nods, facial expressions, or body language. In the following example, we see how several group members and a group leader respond to others. Some of the responses are positive; some are negative. GL is the group leader; the others are group members.

Example:

A [speaking to B]: When you talked, I was really happy. You have really changed. When we first met, you could barely describe your feelings. Now it seems so easy for you. I can understand you perfectly.

C [speaking to D]: Last week you said I should take a different job because I complain so much about my work. I am really angry at you. You can't understand how hard it is for me. You only want to give me advice all the time. You must always have a solution. You always seem to know best.

E [speaking to F]: I get the creeps when you talk. You don't seem to come to the point. You are so long-winded and boring. I really think you are very angry. Is that so?

GL [speaking to G]: When you spoke, you seemed to portray yourself as a victim, but I wonder if you were just letting it happen. I think you are much more competent than you describe yourself. I have thought this on several occasions. When we last spoke, you had some really good ideas. You are certainly not helpless!

Group leaders are now primarily listeners who carefully follow all that happens while refraining from intervening too quickly. Interventions by group leaders may be directed towards individual group members, sub-groups, or the whole group. In the following example, we see how the group leader interjects comments in order to keep the conversation alive. GL is the group leader; A, B, C, and D are group members.

Example:

GL [to A]: We understand that your life has been greatly influenced by what you have just described. What was the experience really like at the time? It would be good if you could tell us more. [And later] Do you recognize this in the group? Did something happen before that caused you to drop out of the conversation?

GL [to B, C, and D]: You three seem to have formed your own sub-group. You have shared a very special experience that means a great deal to each of you. Can you tell us about that?

GL [later, to the group]: What do you think after listening to B, C, and D?

GL [to the group]: This seems to have been a tough meeting for all of you. Everyone seems to have shut down, with nothing more to say.

Group leaders pay close attention to the meeting time so they know when sessions will end. It is unfortunate when a session ends while a group member is in the middle of an emotionally powerful account. Therefore, group leaders try to lower the emotional level in the room when they see that the session is nearing termination. A group leader may state how many minutes remain. The group leader may invite everyone to say something about the day's meeting and how it feels to leave the room.

Next, we describe some more difficult situations in the interpersonal work stage.

When a group member needs additional support

Some group members may be so strongly affected by their memories and feelings that they become acutely anxious. Remembering and describing a traumatic event may trigger an anxiety attack so severe that the group member is unable to recover before the session ends. The group leader might offer to remain with the individual until the afflicted group member has regained his or her composure. This action reassures other group members who are disturbed by the situation and might find it difficult to leave the person who is in pain. When the group meets again, the group leader reviews the event and asks the members, including the affected member, to describe how they felt about the situation.

When a group member contacts the group leader

Sometimes a group member under stress will contact the group leader outside of normal meeting times. Typically, the group member telephones the group leader. Their telephone conversation may provide the necessary reassurance. Yet sometimes a meeting with the group leader is necessary. However, the group leader should remind the member that all issues can be talked about in the group, including this particular issue. At the next session, members may have an opportunity to discuss the issue.

When a group member is at risk of suicide

Group leaders have to take immediate action if a group member appears at risk of suicide. It is essential to seek individual support for the member. Group members may be reassured if they learn that the member is under the care of a physician. If the situation becomes even more serious and, for example, the member requires hospital care, the group is strongly affected. If possible, group leaders can ask the in-patient unit to support the patient at the subsequent group meetings. Of course, it is very stressful if the group member is unable to return to the group. As always, the group leader should ensure that time is spent on what has happened and how each member has experienced the event.

When a group member exhibits avoidance behaviours

All group members, irrespective of their life experiences, have some worries and fears that forcefully affect their behaviour in the group. It is a very natural response to try to suppress these worries and fears by adopting avoidance behaviours as a form of self-protection. Such behaviours will influence the group as a whole. Whitaker and Lieberman (1964) concluded that the way in which the group members manage their fears determines the group climate or character. Group members' responses to their own worries and fears are critical. If the group does not deal with avoidance behaviours and instead uses what Whitaker and Lieberman describe as "restrictive solutions", it is difficult for the group to develop. So long as the group uses restrictive solutions, the scope of the therapeutic treatment is limited. Ultimately, the group leader's task is to guide the group to "enabling solutions" that lead to a group climate that is conducive to the emotional learning that psychotherapy provides.

It is essential that group leaders are not confrontational about such defences. Confrontation may increase the anxiety in the group, causing some group members to draw away. In dealing with such situations, the healthiest group leader approach is to call on the group's resources. For example, group leaders can describe the situation and encourage the members to explore what prevents them from addressing the disturbing issues.

If group members are unable to talk about their worries and fears, the group leader should explain that these feelings are universally held. Other members probably have similar worries and fears, although perhaps in a somewhat different form. Group leaders can encourage other members to talk about these feelings. It is important that group leaders take an explorative approach so that members understand how these feelings influence behaviour in interpersonal relationships – in and outside the group.

However, avoidance is a necessary aspect of the psychotherapeutic process. Such behaviours may reflect how the group has developed in response to the members' expectations of, or demands from, other group members and group leaders (i.e., the group's norms). The type and extent of the avoidance behaviours that people adopt may reveal useful information about their interpersonal dynamics and their emotional state as well as their fears.

We list some commonly used avoidance behaviours in group therapy:

- Staying silent.
- Talking only about impersonal or unimportant topics.
- Avoiding member interaction.
- Intense questioning of other members; assuming a leadership role.
- Intellectualizing issues and problems at abstract, unemotional levels.
- Harshly criticizing other group members and group therapy.

Avoidance behaviours in the group setting allow group members to control their anxiety to some extent. However, group leaders should respond respectfully when they try to help members reduce their anxiety by adopting more productive interpersonal behaviours. We recommend that group leaders explore these obstacles to improvement in an atmosphere of trust and safety.

Summary of the interpersonal work stage

As group members in the interpersonal work stage talk about various topics and feelings, the pace and tone of their conversations vary. Some conversations are more emotional than others. This conversational flexibility allows the members to explore many interesting avenues and to focus on many meaningful areas – all of which advance the therapeutic work. Attention oscillates between the group as a whole and the members as individuals. Group members feel more confident, more secure, and more relaxed. They are more comfortable with expressing their personal reactions, sometimes with a deep sense of gravity and at other times with distance and humour (e.g., joking about common memories or funny situations in the group). The mood can shift quickly from one of good humour to one of anger, sadness, or distress. The members' relationship with the group leader is more on an equal footing in this stage. By this point, the group leader has partially directed the group focus to helping the group members concentrate on their individual problems. The group has achieved a certain level of stability that is evidenced by the members' greater knowledge of how the group functions and their decreased need for leader interventions.

Termination

The termination stage in time-limited group therapy takes place in the last three to five group meetings. In this stage, the group's termination activities reinforce the core themes of members' identity and maturity development through life. When group members work through various termination aspects, the goal is for them to take full responsibility for their lives.

The group's purpose and goals in the termination stage

The group's main goal in the termination stage is to end the therapy positively and to manage the group separation constructively. The members need to accept the termination of the group as they return to their separate lives. The work in the group now revolves around the emotions that the therapy termination causes. This work facilitates the release of the group and its dependence on the group leader/ authority. The goal is for members to accept that all members are responsible for their own life, while recognizing the importance of the therapy group.

Unavoidably, some group members feel lonely and abandoned when the group therapy ends. When the group members share these emotions and thoughts with each another, stressful feelings about the group's termination are mitigated by their understanding of the existential, general aspect of all separations. It is part of the human condition that we all share. It is possible to think: *I can exist even if I am lonely.* In this work, each individual discovers a future direction with the realization that the group experience is preserved and internalized. *Somewhere within we are always together.* The curious paradox is that the members in some sense draw closer to each other during the termination stage as the group breaks up.

With the guidance of the group leader, the group members in the termination stage voice their emotions and recall important experiences from the group's common history. This shared memory increases the group cohesion, which strengthens the internalization – the inner, highly emotional memory of the group. In this

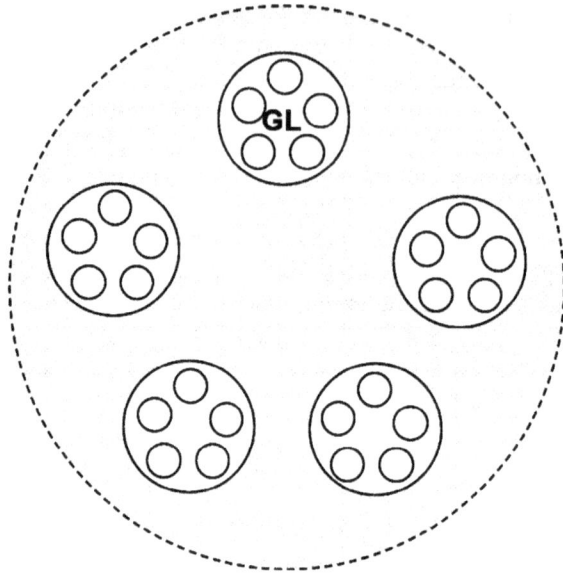

Figure 9.2 Group structure in the termination stage.

process, psychic energy is mobilized that supports coping with individual life – post therapy group. Figure 9.2 illustrates the group structure in the termination stage.

The group's therapeutic alliance in the termination stage

The realization and acceptance of group members' need to talk about the group separation are important features of the therapeutic alliance in the termination stage. The members now know each other and the group leader. As the group terminates, members are likely to experience a strong sense of loss. They need to talk with each other about their emotions and thoughts. In this process, the group leader should again take the initiative in directing the conversation.

It is possible, even at this late stage in group therapy, that the therapeutic alliance is in danger. The way in which the group members manage the separation depends in large part on the emotional "baggage", including loss and grief, that they brought to the group. Depending on individual sensitivities, some members will manage better than others. Members who experience strong separation anxiety may be late to the termination sessions, may forget meeting times, may send excuses, or may even leave the group prematurely. Group leaders may sometimes sense that the group has divided between members who can cope and want to work through the termination together and members who just want to escape. If a member simply "disappears", feelings of loss, grief, and abandonment may increase among the remaining members.

Group members who are apprehensive about the separation might sometimes "forget" the group discussion topic (i.e., the separation). They might talk about something else, simply ignoring the difficult task. The group leader needs to actively contribute to the termination work in the group. All conceivable aspects of the termination theme are reviewed (e.g., worries, frustrations, loneliness, abandonment, grief, gratitude, pride, and freedom). If the conversation is content-rich, group members may gain new knowledge in the termination stage – how they feel about the separation and how others feel about it.

Examples of group members' separation emotions include:

- Loss and sadness.
- Regret over something not expressed.
- Fear of abandonment; loneliness.
- Disappointment that there was not enough treatment time.
- Rejection and worthlessness.
- Appreciation of the treatment.
- Relief that the stress/tension experienced in the treatment is over.
- Longing to be free to live one's life post-treatment.

Group leaders are also affected by the group termination. Having experienced the members' relative independence, group leaders may be tempted to hand over the work of the termination stage to the members. However, the therapeutic work must continue to, and include, the final moment of the group therapy. Awareness of one's own feelings is an important part of the work as group leader, and in this stage, when the group leader also experiences loss it might influence his or her capacity to be present in the group's affective state. If the group leader is aware of his or her own issues regarding separation anxiety, it is recommended that he or she consult a senior colleague or request supervision in this stage.

The group leader's role in the termination stage

As in the previous stages, the group leader's responsibility in this stage is to guide the group members in conversations about their experiences and emotions.

It is important to draw group members' attention to the fact that the group therapy is nearing its end. Quite often a group member will ask: "How many meetings do we have left?" If the question is addressed to the group leader (as it usually is), the group leader can ask the members if they know the answer. If there is no response, the group leader should remind the members that the group therapy is nearing termination: "We have X sessions left." When no one asks how many sessions are left, the group leader should announce the number of remaining sessions.

If follow-up meetings are planned for patients, group leaders are advised not to mention this fact until the final session is nearing its end. If the announcement is made earlier, the termination activities may not be as effective as desired. Group members will think: *Well, this is not really the end.*

After the separation, the members will go their separate ways. As noted above, some members will find separation a very painful experience – almost like separating from a close friend or relative who will no longer be available to provide advice and comfort. The separation may remind some members of earlier losses in life when there was no way to change the situation. These memories can be explored and worked through at the same time as the termination of the group is discussed. The group leader might mention that it is understandable that some members may want to skip the last session. However, the group leader should discourage that action by explaining how important it is to talk about difficult feelings. The group leader can make the following point: "We started together, we worked together, we shared a lot together, and now we will end together."

In this stage, the group may revisit various difficult events (for both leaders and members) from previous stages. Some of these events may be the result of inadequate preparation work, such as the inclusion of members with severe personality problems who cannot deal with the difficult physical and mental responses associated with group therapy. Thus, the termination stage can be a discovery experience for both group leaders and group members.

Last, group leaders may feel somewhat discouraged when the group therapy ends. Despite their very high hopes for all members, they may feel in some cases they have not succeeded. Committed professionals, who often place very high demands and expectations on themselves, can easily become self-critical. We remind group leaders in group therapy that they are not miracle workers. Sometimes a group leader must be satisfied with a "good enough" outcome.

Group support around shared losses often increases members' capacity to cope with other losses that are part of life. In the following example, we see how the group members and the group leader talk about the end of group therapy. GL is the group leader; A, B, C, D, and E are group members.

Example:

A: I think this feels ridiculous [referring to the termination activities]. I am almost embarrassed that you [GL] talk so much about the group termination.

GL: 'Ridiculous' and 'embarrassing'. Why?

A: I have a hard time imagining I mean anything to all of you. I'm almost ashamed at the very idea. But you mean something to me. It's hard that we have to separate. Really, I have already left. I mean, I have just slipped away.

GL: Yes, it can be very demanding to be emotionally present at the last time we are together. Does anyone recognize anything in what A just said? Or do you feel differently?

B [to A]: Now that you mention it, I must admit that I have never thought it made much difference for you whether I was here or not. Actually, I have reduced the importance of my own and others' contributions to the conversations.

C: At the beginning, I thought it was a good idea not to get too involved with the rest of you. The group was going to end eventually. But now I am glad that we have talked so much about saying goodbye to each other. I hope I can keep what we experienced here. I feel others have seen and understood me.

D: At first, I was quite anxious about having to talk about the group termination. Now, it seems somewhat less impossible.

GL: Several of you say, quite bluntly, that the group is over. But what you have experienced here cannot be taken away from you. You will always carry these experiences with you.

A: I am afraid I will just forget about the group. In a way, that will be easier than remembering the group. If I think the group was rather unimportant, the separation will be less painful.

GL [to A]: You mention pain. It may be the case that our group termination reminds you of emotions experienced in previous separations. It may also be the case that you did not receive enough support that allowed you to manage those emotions.

D: It has always been hard for me. Do you remember that I said my parents never told me when they were going away or were going out for the evening? Suddenly, they were just gone. I was so sad and afraid they were not coming back. I was always neglected.

GL: You have all talked about that it is hard to leave – the pain, sadness, and fear. Perhaps there are other emotions provoked by terminations.

E: Yes, I actually think terminations can be positive. I have learned a lot here, but it has not been easy for me. I am looking forward to resting and taking a break from this treatment. I want to do something else with the time I have spent here.

C: Actually, I think I will take away something important from this treatment that I can retain.

Frequently, groups need to return to and process shared group experiences and memories. The group leader follows and supports the group members when they, with mixed feelings, talk about experiences and memories from "a long time ago" (which may only be from the sessions in the engagement stage). For example, group members may recall that some members left the group or at least threatened to leave the group. It is often astonishing that the "past" returns as important memories – the circle is closed as the beginning and the end meet. Distant events that have aroused strong feelings are now addressed. The members may now examine those events with respect to their responses then and now. If, however, the members do not initiate discussion of important events in the history of the group, the group leader may encourage them to return to them. This might offer members the opportunity to continue to work through these events. As a result, members may gain new perspectives.

Summation

What have we accomplished? Similar to the introductory "rounds" in the engagement stage, the group members individually summarize the group therapy experience in the termination stage. The group leader may prompt members by suggesting they ask themselves questions such as the following:

> Was this experience good, bad, or just so-so? What is helpful? What is difficult? Did anything surprise me? Did other members provide support? Or were they hindrances to my development? If we had had more time, would my impressions have been different? What makes me happy? What do I mourn? What do I need to say before we say goodbye? What will I retain from this experience?

Feedback

During the summation, the group leader might encourage members to talk directly to each other. For example, the group leader might suggest members begin their messages with the following statements: "This is how I have understood you. This is what you mean to me."

The future

The group leader can help the group members prepare for their post-group experience. Is there anything the members need to continue working on? The group leader may suggest members ask themselves questions such as the following: "How can I become my own source of comfort, my coach, or my therapist after I leave the group? Will I be able to continue my therapy by myself?" A group member might propose that the group continues to meet. Because such ex-group meetings take place outside the life of the therapy group, the decision to form such a group is best left to the members themselves. A group leader might say: "I have no opinion on what you decide to do. However, it is good to talk about it before we separate. You may want different things. Some people may want to meet; others not."

Important new information

Group members may reveal new information in the termination stage. This information may even suggest that additional therapeutic treatment is advisable. However, this is not the time or place for a group leader to follow-up on this suggestion.

A group leader must resist this temptation by focusing on the current task. A group leader might say: "Ellen, it seems that you have important things you need to talk about in the months ahead. Today, however, our task is to end this group."

Group leaders are also in the termination stage. They leave their leader role and return to their individual role outside the group. In the last few minutes of the final session, group leaders may encourage members to say a few words about how it was to be in this group with this group leader. It is also an opportunity to say a few words how it was to be a group leader in this group. Group leaders should choose their words carefully, because members will judge and listen attentively. It is not a good idea to address any member directly. General statements such as the following are appropriate: "We really did good work together. I also learned a lot. I am very grateful for our work together."

Next, we describe some more difficult situations in the termination stage.

When a group member is absent from the termination sessions

Some group members skip the termination sessions because they think they will find them very upsetting given their earlier separations in life. Because this feeling can be quite overwhelming, members may want to avoid its repetition. Nevertheless, the group leader needs to find ways to encourage members to attend these sessions. Group leaders can remind members to participate in the termination stage by texting, by letter, or by electronic message. A group leader might say or write: "The final meetings are very important. We will summarize our experiences and what we have learned. To part, maybe in a somewhat different way compared to before, is in itself a significant and worthwhile experience."

When there is not enough time in the termination sessions

New topics may appear near the end of the group therapy. Group members and group leaders realize there is not enough time to explore these new areas properly. Although there is no time at the present to address the topics that group members now raise, group leaders can assure members that they themselves have acquired sufficient self-knowledge to address these issues – independently, at a later time. This is a practical suggestion that has an additional benefit in that it indicates the group leader's confidence in the group members and the hope that the therapy has proven beneficial to them.

When interest in the activities in the termination sessions dwindles

Sometimes groups seem to lose interest near the end because they see no point in work that will soon end. Group members may just be marking time, waiting to leave. Some members are anxious about the separation; others look forward to life after the group therapy. One way to deal with this lack of interest might be to encourage discussions in sub-groups that take different positions on how to best use the remaining sessions. Whatever group leaders decide, it is essential that they help the members find a way to use these sessions constructively.

Summary of the termination stage

The main task during the termination stage is to explore what the break-up and the separation mean for all members. Each member will be confronted with personal reactions to the separation and loss. These reactions will vary from deep regret to a sense of liberation. The work during this stage can pave the path for increased member autonomy. Group leaders, who may also be affected emotionally by the termination stage, again play an important role in helping members navigate this final stage.

Chapter 10

Slow-open groups

A practical and commonly used solution to the burdensome and often time-consuming work of recruiting members to a new group is the slow-open group (Foulkes, 1984). The slow-open group therapy model allows new members to join groups that are presently meeting. New members may join the group when a member has left and an opening is available. Slow-open groups may exist for lengthy periods, even years, but each member's presence is time-limited (unless it is long-term, group analytic psychotherapy in which members leave the group on their own initiative). Typically, the same group leader leads a slow-open group during its entire existence, although leadership transfers can be made if needed or desired.

Occasionally, some members in a time-limited group would benefit from continued group therapy. A slow-open group, with the same therapeutic focus, content, and purpose, can develop from a concluding time-limited group. The slow-open group is composed of some members from the time-limited group plus some new members.

It may also be necessary and appropriate at times to form a slow-open group when a previous closed group has several unplanned member departures. There are now open places in the group, and several people are waiting to join a group. This situation may also occur when some members in a time-limited group would benefit from continued group therapy.

Advantages of the slow-open group

Compared to the closed group, the slow-open group has several advantages. Less time and energy are required to include new members in the flexible slow-open group than to start a closed group. Some burdensome, repetitive administrative tasks such as preparation work can be avoided. Not least, the time spent on the emotional work of planning a new group at the same time as termination work continues with another group is reduced.

The slow-open group, in theory, can continue for quite some time as its member composition changes. When the preparation work is completed, the slow-open group can begin with perhaps only four or five members. When the group has met for some time, additional members may join. It may also be easier and more efficient to organize slow-open groups in organization-sponsored group therapy where the professionals who make group therapy referrals know the focus and purpose of the various established groups. The waiting time is generally brief if slow-open groups are admitting new members. Because the flow of people who want to join group therapy is rarely a steady stream (in part, depending on the extent of member recruitment), it may be some time before a new closed group is formed.

Newcomers benefit from joining an established group like the slow-open group. It is a valuable experience to join, participate in, and end a group experience with people who have previously coalesced as a group. In many settings (work, school, teams, etc.), people often have to evaluate and manage new roles as they join groups in which they meet new people and learn new tasks. The learning process that is emphasized in slow-open group therapy can be useful in other life situations.

Boundaries, time limitations, and rules

The slow-open group has some of the same boundaries and rules as the time-limited, closed group. The most important difference between the two groups lies in the continuing need to establish boundaries and rules for the individual treatment of each new group member in the slow-open group. Group leaders decide on the group boundaries and rules and on the length of the treatment for each member in the slow-open group. They enter a kind of unofficial understanding with each member with respect to the treatment timeframe. In general, the sponsor organization exerts considerable influence in that decision.

Rules for member participation in slow-open groups are necessary. Among other things, the rules apply to each member's time commitment to the group therapy. Group members should know when their treatment is scheduled to begin and end. Apart from different times for members' admittance and departure, the work is the same as in closed groups. Group leaders have to prepare the group for the change in the group when new members join.

Starting and ending participation in a slow-open group

It is important that group members who join an ongoing group are involved early in their treatment. They need to be reassured that the participation of each and every one is essential for the success of the group as a whole. Attendance is a recurrent, emotionally loaded theme in the slow-open group as the group membership frequently changes. Absences, which are worrisome, distract the attention from the therapeutic work. In the slow-open group, it is important for the group leader to be very clear about changes in the group composition. The group leader should help the group welcome new members and bid farewell to those who are leaving. It may not be self-evident that a group wants to receive new members or wants to say goodbye to others.

In the following example, the group leader and several members talk about the addition of new members to their slow-open group.

Example:

A slow-open group consists of four members described as "adult children of addicted parents", which means they were raised by parents with substance abuse problems in some form. These group members have agreed to attend 18 meetings. If they wish to leave the group before its termination, they must give at least two weeks' notice. They met weekly. At the fifth meeting, the group leader informed the group that in two weeks two new members would join the group. The example takes place just after the group leader has made this announcement. In the example, GL is the group leader; A, B, C, and D are the original four group members.

A: But, hey, this is really difficult. I am just beginning to feel safe here. But now complete strangers will join and disturb us. No, I don't want that. [To GL] Do they have to come just now?

B: I agree. The group feels right just as it is.

GL: Yes, I understand that you are comfortable in the group and feel safe. I will answer your question, but first I would like to know if anyone else agrees with A and B. What do you think about adding two new members to the group?

D: I am comfortable with the group as it is now. Yet I also think it would be good for me to meet new people. [To GL] When you said this would happen, I thought it would be exciting. There are only four of us now.

C: I think two more members will be great. There's no special problem with that. Can't we just talk now in the way we do now and not waste time on members who aren't even here?

GL: I can see there are several different ideas in the group about the two new members. It's good that you are talking about your views. To answer A's question – yes, the two new members will be joining the group in two weeks' time. The plan is that the group will be open to more members. The maximum number of members scheduled for this group is seven, as I told you at the beginning. Do you have any thoughts about what makes you feel the way you do?

A: Yes. I think I have a hard time with any kind of change. Change makes me nervous. I become worried. Anxious feelings creep up on me. It just is very hard.

D: Yes. Actually, it is the same for me. But I really want to learn to manage change better. I want to find a way to cope with what I feel and with what I believe.

B: Now, when you say this, I recognize myself in what you say about change. It is rather good as it is. I don't want to feel anything else. That's how I always am. Yet maybe that is not so good. I become very passive and never take any initiative.

C [does not speak and looks at the floor]

GL [to C]:   I am thinking about your question – when you asked if we could talk about something other than the addition of the two new members. What were you getting at?

C [to GL]:   I am frustrated that we perhaps are talking about the wrong things. I want to get as much as possible from the group. But it seems we are using time poorly. There is so much I need to talk about. I wonder if that is possible in this group.

GL [to C]:   It is understandable that you want to get as much as possible from this group. Maybe there are others who feel the same way.

A: Yes, I am a little worried that the group will not help me. At the same time, I always feel at ease when I leave here. It's good to know I am not alone in thinking and feeling the way I do.

D: No, it feels right to be here. I feel better since I joined the group. I sleep better and I worry less. [To C] But I keep thinking about you. Has something happened to you since we last met? You started to talk last time about your relationship with your sister. I have been thinking about you all week.

C: Have you really? Yes, this was a very tough week for me. My sister and I quarrelled. We have very different ideas about what to do when Mom is drinking.

In the example, the group takes the opportunity to talk about the addition of new members. Some members are nervous about the change. They resist the change. This is a common reaction in any group that faces something new and unknown. When the group meets again, the group leader reminds the members about the impending arrival of the newcomers. The reaction this time will usually be different. The discussion at the previous session prepared the four members for the change in the group. Because they had the chance to voice their fears, they grew closer to the others. The group cohesion strengthened. When the four members felt more secure in the group, it was easier for them to welcome new members.

The example describes a group at the end of the engagement stage. They have had time to become acquainted. They are at ease with each other and are building a group alliance. It is important that the group has reached this stage – when group cohesion is established – before new members are introduced. If the announce-ment had been made at an earlier point, the group might not have coalesced. It would have taken longer for the group to feel safe. This group discovered enough similarities among the new and old members and began to look at differences. Although some ambivalence about the new group composition remained, the group members were looking forward to the stimulation that "fresh blood" would bring to the group.

The role of group leaders in slow-open groups

The group leader's role in slow-open groups differs somewhat from the group leader's role in time-limited, closed groups. The explanation lies in the cyclic (vs linear) nature of the slow-open group model. Both groups have similar develop-ment stages, but development in the slow-open group moves back and forth, up and down, among the four stages. The engagement and termination stages do not have fixed times. In fact, as members leave and other members join, the engage-ment and termination stages repeat. As in real life, different life themes run paral-lel and are mirrored in the group. Therefore, group leaders in slow-open groups must deal simultaneously with some members' attachment issues and other mem-bers' separation issues.

A significant factor is the group and its group climate. The group leader and the group members create a group climate that is built on boundaries, rules, coop-eration, and approaches. This climate becomes sustainable over time with, for example, routines for welcoming new members and ending their participation. In this cyclic and oscillating process, members make important contributions to the development of the group climate that will last long after the individual members have left the group.

In short, the group leader's role in the slow-open group is to some extent dif-ferent from the group leader's role in the time-limited, closed group. Slow-open group leaders must take into account, for example, the changing group composi-tion. Slow-open group members are often at different stages of development in the same group. In addition, new and evolving member interactions appear, and new leader–member relationships develop. Group leaders, who should be very attentive to members' emotions stemming from member arrivals and departures, should remain attuned to individual and group goals as the group composition changes. Group leaders should adapt their leadership style accordingly. As an example, member separation may be dealt with formally in one group but more informally in another group.

Summary of slow-open group therapy

The distinguishing features of slow-open groups are the changing membership composition and the absence of firm starting or ending dates. The development process in the slow-open group is cyclical as the group moves among its various stages. A positive aspect of slow-open groups for group leaders is that new members are successively admitted to groups already in progress. Thus, these leaders avoid the various complexities encountered in forming new groups "from scratch" (see Chapter 6). In that respect, the leader role is less demanding. In addition, slow-open groups have certain member benefits. With changes in membership, the members meet people with different life experiences and concerns. This situation provides members with opportunities to learn more about themselves and others.

Chapter 11

Group therapy with pre-planned content structure

In this chapter, we examine the role of group processes when the sessions are pre-planned such as in cognitive behavioural therapy (CBT) in groups and in psycho-education groups. We want to demonstrate how knowledge of group processes can inform CBT group therapy and psycho-education and contribute to the increased success of these treatment approaches. We will not describe the specific CBT or pedagogic methods involved, but we want to summarize some general group dynamic principles of importance in this context.

As mentioned in Chapter 4, most scientific studies on group therapy focus on the use of CBT. However, CBT is mainly practised as a treatment for individuals, which might explain why not until lately has there been an interest in developing a group theory for CBT (Bieling et al., 2006; Sochting, 2014).

CBT group therapy is described specifically for various patient conditions (e.g., panic disorder, agoraphobia, obsessive-compulsive disorder, post-traumatic stress, social anxiety disorder, generalized anxiety, depression, bipolar disorder, eating disorder, substance abuse, personality disorders, and schizophrenia) (Bieling et al., 2006; Sochting, 2014).

Psycho-education is offered to people who experience hardships due to illness, a relative's serious illness, or other challenging life situations (Brown, 2018).

People interact and develop in groups

Bieling et al. (2018) charge that CBT group manuals primarily view the use of CBT in groups as merely a way to teach practical CBT techniques. They claim that CBT group manuals are based in individual treatment strategies and emphasize specific teaching techniques adapted from individual application. The result is that these strategies and techniques seem to underestimate the fact that group CBT is used with people who interact and develop as a group.

We are convinced that typical group processes (see chapters 4, 5, 7, 8, and 9) are found in CBT groups. We arrived at this conviction from our leadership and supervision of CBT groups and from a research project that compared the use of group CBT with the use of focused group therapy (FGT). In this project, when we talked to the therapists who led the different sorts of groups, we were especially struck by the many similarities in the patients' stories, in the group discussion themes, in the spontaneous exchanges among patients, and in the group dynamics. The main dissimilarity was that the CBT groups had more structure than the FGT groups. The CBT therapists also had a more pedagogically oriented leadership style than the FGT therapists, who had a more dynamically oriented leadership style.

Nevertheless, there is an increasing interest among CBT therapists in the use of groups in therapeutic treatment. Therapy groups offer unique treatment opportunities. For example, in groups with people with depression or with social anxiety the group members may more easily detect their own and other group members' cognitive misinterpretations. In addition, group therapy can provide many more relationship examples (e.g., how thoughts and emotions are interconnected) than individual therapy can.

Structure and processes in pre-planned group therapy

Bieling et al. (2006) argue that CBT techniques cannot be separated from processes in either group therapy or individual therapy. They write that the use of CBT techniques alone in therapy is ineffective. In the clinical context, processes and techniques should always be used together. Bieling et al. argue that the group process in group therapy is a potentiating variable rather than an obstacle to treatment. Therefore, therapists who combine group processes with CBT or other techniques developed for individual therapy have a powerful tool to use in optimizing therapeutic treatment. The conclusion is that interactive group process thinking – as described in this book – is a very useful tool for CBT group leaders.

CBT groups and psycho-education groups use approaches that differ from psychodynamic approaches primarily because of their specific structure. CBT assumes that the therapy will only succeed if patients learn the techniques the therapists teach. Some structural techniques, especially homework assignments, are thought of as fundamental therapeutic ingredients because they are intended to be generalizable to everyday life.

In CBT groups and psycho-education groups, all sessions have a specific pre-planned structure. A group session (all sessions except the first session in the programme) usually has the following elements:

1   An overview of the latest homework assignment.
2   The presentation of new information.
3   An exercise, such as a discussion of examples, role play, or confrontation with anxiety-provoking situations.
4   The next homework assignment.

The CBT-oriented group leader's contributions to group processes

How can learning be facilitated in a group? From pedagogic research, we know that too much instructor control can be counterproductive. The same is true when the instructor exercises too little control. We also know that active participation and reflection facilitate learning much more effectively than teacher-centric instruction and passive listening instruction. One goal in CBT groups is that key skills and principles associated with the group members' problems are addressed while their actual problems are discussed and integrated following a flexible learning approach. The challenge for CBT group therapists is to encourage as much exchange of experience and reflection as possible at the same time that they address all agenda requirements specified in the CBT manual.

Bieling et al. (2008) list seven group process factors that are active in CBT groups and which therapists should support. These factors are the following:

1   Optimism.
2   Belonging.
3   Group learning.
4   Reduced self-focus.
5   Modification of non-functioning relationship patterns.
6   Group cohesion.
7   Group emotions processing.

In previous chapters of this book, notably chapters 4 and 5, we described the importance of the emphasis on emotions and on the modification of relationship patterns. We addressed the importance of optimism, hopefulness, belonging, and group cohesion. In CBT groups, typical CBT techniques are used, such as encouraging group members to offer advice to other members and recommending that therapists reinforce positive behaviours (e.g., when patients demonstrate group commitment). Our understanding is that therapists with a psychodynamic orientation also provide positive reinforcement without labelling it as reinforcement. They nod, smile, or make encouraging remarks when they observe a patient is making progress in some way or is contributing to the group effort. In a comparison of CBT and psychodynamic group psychotherapists' verbal interventions we found more similarities than differences (Sandahl et al., 2000).

Other similarities with the approach we advocate, i.e. emphasis on interaction, are the importance of the following:

1   Encouraging consistent group member attendance and group involvement.
2   Creating a safe group environment in which members can talk candidly about their thoughts and feelings.
3   Encouraging group members to make meaningful connections among their experiences, thoughts, and feelings.
4   Paying close attention to the group dynamics in a here-and-now context (see Bieling et al., 2008).

The CBT group should be a place where members can process their emotions and experiences.

In addition, Bieling et al. (2006) emphasize the importance of encouraging group members to share their problems with the group. Sharing facilitates the growth of group community and the sense of belonging. CBT group therapists contribute to this process by linking the members' emotions and experiences and by stimulating the members to talk about their specific problems and attempts to make behavioural changes.

In the instructional moments in CBT groups, therapists are advised to use the Socratic method of question and answer. This method provokes group members to think critically, to discover new knowledge, and (unique to group therapy) to facilitate the exchange of advice and feedback from other members.

The social aspect of group therapy is a repeated theme in this book. The members in CBT groups form a social community in which they learn that the best way to help oneself is, in part, to transfer the focus from their individual needs to a focus on the group's needs. The group becomes a mutually dependent system. CBT group therapists support this community by helping the group members to share information and action strategies with each other. The therapists also provide confirmation of positive group behaviour.

We offer the following advice for group therapists:

•   Encourage group members to observe interpersonal behaviour patterns, including the effects on other group members.
•   Focus on ongoing interactions in the group.

- Request feedback from members.
- Moderate members' comments on other members.
- Promote other ways of being in relationships.

The challenge for CBT group therapists is to focus on group processes at the same time that they adhere to a specific therapy agenda with its required techniques. It is a challenge that is both time-consuming and demanding. Consider, for example, the five-to ten-minute member rounds in conventional CBT therapy groups in which the therapist asks questions of each member – one by one. During these rounds, with their one-member focus, other members may look at their phones, read their notes, or simply pay no attention. When the focus is on one person, the other group members feel excluded. The effect is "dilution" of the group therapy experience. Some research even finds that the use of this practice in CBT groups produces worse results than the use of CBT in individual therapy (Burlingame et al., 2013). The one-member focus often results in dropouts and, in the worst case, the premature termination of the group. The message is that therapists must pay attention to the group as a whole even when a single member is in focus (e.g., in the presentation of a homework assignment, when the group leader can direct the attention to similarities and differences in how the tasks were solved).

The stages in a CBT group

According to Bieling et al. (2008), clinical use of CBT in group therapy shows that the groups pass through five relatively well-defined stages although scientific evidence is lacking for this claim. These authors list the following sequential stages (summarized):

Pre-group issues: formation of the group

Before the initial stage begins, the therapist, as the group leader, plans the group experience: the connection to the sponsor organization, the group member selection, the preparatory interviews, and other administrative matters.

Initial stage: orientation and exploration (cf. engagement stage)

In the initial stage, the group members meet each other at the initial group meetings, where they begin to create a foundation for mutual trust. As members begin to understand how the group will function and how they will contribute to the group, the identity of the group as a whole begins to emerge. The therapist, who is in charge of the therapy, works to create group cohesion and a group climate. Therapy guidelines and rules are reviewed. The therapist responds to members' questions and concerns about the goals and structure of the future therapy sessions.

Transition stage: dealing with resistance (cf. differentiation stage)

In the transition stage, after the group members have become more comfortable in the group and with their roles, the therapist must manage the occasional signs of member resistance to the therapy. Some members who guard their privacy decline to participate; others are afraid to reveal their vulnerability; still others are doubtful the therapy will be productive. Some members express their resistance quite openly by criticizing the therapist, the therapy structure and techniques, and even other members. Some members complain their symptoms have become worse during the programme since they examined their thoughts, feelings, and behaviours.

Confronted with this resistance, the therapist is advised to acknowledge group members' concerns directly and respectfully. The therapist should also remind the members of the goals of the therapy and review why the members joined the group. With experience, dealing with member resistance becomes less discouraging and difficult for the therapist.

Working stage: cohesion and productivity (cf. interpersonal stage)

In the working stage, group cohesion becomes well established. The group members are working more productively as they interact with each other. Their experiences between group sessions provide additional conversation topics. The CBT techniques used in individual therapy seem to be working in the group setting. The therapist encourages members to offer feedback and support (i.e., positive reinforcement) to other members in order to promote behavioural changes. The therapist tailors the homework assignments to the group as a whole.

The therapist now begins to address and support the seven group process factors (see above). The ambition is to help the group members analyse their problems from the here-and-now perspective as they learn and practice new behaviours that they can use outside the group. The therapist also reminds members that only a few sessions remain.

Final stage: consolidation and termination (cf. termination stage)

In the final stage, as the therapy nears its closure, the therapist focuses on reinforcing the members' behavioural changes and encourages them to evaluate the programme. For example, the therapist asks the group members if and how they have benefited from the therapy. The therapist also considers how additional post-group support can be provided to the members. For example, individual goals may require modification.

The therapist should reserve time in the final phase for discussions on how the members will adapt their new skills and behaviours to everyday life. Such discussions may be useful in preventing relapses to old habits and behaviours. Last, the therapist should encourage conversation on the group termination that is likely to produce a variety of member responses – from despair to relief.

Post-group issues: follow-up and evaluation

Therapists who use CBT in groups usually have one or more follow-up meetings after the final stage. In these meetings, the therapist reinforces the importance of the newly acquired skills and behaviours. It also gives an opportunity to address any difficulties that members have had in their post-group life resulting from the use of these skills and behaviours. The therapist also reviews the group's results. In some instances, the therapist may recommend additional group therapy or individual therapy for certain members. The follow-up meeting is a valuable opportunity to review and evaluate members' transition from group life to everyday life.

The CBT group as a learning environment

Techniques, which are also used in individual CBT therapy, can be powerful if used in a group learning environment. In such environments, group members are invited and encouraged to use these techniques in their various group interactions. The following example makes this point. T is the therapist; Lisa, Peter, and Ingrid are group members.

Example:

T: Today we are going to talk about catastrophic thinking and its effects. We have a catastrophic thought when we imagine the worst-case outcome of some potential event. Does anyone in the group have an example of a catastrophic thought?

Lisa: When I think about saying something in a meeting at work, I think I am going to blush and stutter. I imagine my colleagues will think I am an idiot.

T: Peter, I see you are nodding. Do you agree with Lisa? Do you recognize her catastrophic thought?

Peter: I think I do. Usually I just keep my thoughts to myself. I sometimes imagine I am going to lose my job and will have to apply for unemployment benefits. I then think I won't be able to make my loan payments and may have to sell my apartment.

Ingrid: I want to say something. [Turning to Lisa and Peter] I think both of you seem so confident and coherent when you talk in the group. I have actually been a bit envious. I was very surprised when I heard you describe these thoughts.

T [to Lisa and Peter]: How do you feel about what Ingrid has just said?

Lisa: It's rather strange. I don't feel confident and coherent at all. [Turning to Ingrid] It's nice to hear what you just said. Maybe my colleagues think the same.

As the conversation in this group continues, the group members explore situational factors that are likely to trigger catastrophic thinking. The therapist uses the group interaction to promote learning as the members share experiences and offer corrective feedback.

Therapists have to structure group conversations that, on the one hand, are easily understood, organized, and allow rational information exchanges. On the other hand, these group conversations should be reasonably flexible and spontaneous within a given structure. Striking this balance is a challenge for the CBT group leader. The practical advice to therapists is to make a time schedule for the four major group elements (overview of the latest homework assignment, presentation of new information, a group exercise, and the next homework assignment). A schedule with beginning/ending times for each element, which is either agreed on by the group or known only by the group leader, can keep the group on track.

Compared to the use of CBT in individual therapy, the use of CBT in group therapy has certain advantages. One of these advantages is the exercise (i.e., practice) activity. The group therapy model provides a rich opportunity to train for and test alternative behaviours. For example, in the form of CBT known as exposure therapy, group members practice dealing with frightening situations. The group therapy model facilitates practice with several such situations whereas the individual therapy model likely only deals with one such situation. Furthermore, the group therapy model encourages members' exchanges on how this training can be used outside the group.

Another advantage stems from the use of role play. In the group therapy model, various group members are available to take different roles in imaginary situations. Role play, which is intended to suggest behavioural alternatives in other contexts, is especially effective for group members who suffer from social anxiety disorder (i.e., social phobia). For example, a group member who fears public speaking can role play by pretending to speak publicly before the entire group. The group setting is safe, controlled, and relatively relaxed. Furthermore, as always, group members can offer support and feedback. These possibilities are unavailable in individual therapy.

Psycho-educational groups

Many psychiatric and somatic illnesses cause severe stress. Stress is a natural reaction to worry and fear when, for example, people learn they have a serious illness. They may find themselves in a crisis situation if the illness is life-changing or life-threatening. Friends and relatives may also be affected by the crisis.

In such crises, complications such as depression, panic attacks, and anxiety pose a risk to people's mental health. They require support in processing their reactions. Friends, relatives, and work colleagues often provide physical care as well as emotional support. For some people, this care and support may be sufficient. For people who need additional support, professional individual or group counselling may be required. Often a patient's relatives also need such professional support.

People in these circumstances search for all kinds of information about their condition. They want to know if their condition will improve or deteriorate, the available treatment options, which treatment is best, and if lifestyle changes are recommended. Such information is a self-evident part of conversations with physicians or other healthcare personnel during diagnosis and treatment. It is often difficult for patients to understand and grasp all aspects of this information when they are sad or worried. In health care, as Dr Joseph Pratt discovered at the beginning of the twentieth century (see Chapter 4), the group experience encourages the repetition of information among members, increasing their knowledge. Groups also provide opportunities for members to offer advice and to work through the emotional reactions associated with particular conditions. The psycho-educational group is designed to provide such information and learning in combination with emotional and social support. The special characteristic of a typical psychotherapeutic group is that members have not, in the main, joined the group seeking help for psychological/psychiatric problems. Rather, they usually seek help in coping with a current and demanding life challenge.

Knowledge, reflection, and exchange

Psycho-educational group support, which may complement other mental health care support, focuses on three areas: (1) knowledge – educating group members on their condition; (2) reflection – offering group members the opportunity to reflect on their condition; and (3) exchange – helping group members talk with others who share the same condition.

The psycho-educational group therapy, which is of brief duration, is designed specifically for people with a difficult life crisis or life challenge. Groups meet with a group leader approximately four to eight times in 90-minute sessions. The length of the programmes varies. The therapy takes a learning perspective in providing both educational and psychological support that is offered to patients, relatives, or other key persons in the patient's life.

Types of psycho-educational groups

Psycho-educational groups are appropriate in numerous situations. These situations include patient rehabilitation after myocardial infarctions or strokes or treatment for patients with severe medical conditions such as ALS (amyotrophic lateral sclerosis), eating disorders, bipolar disorders, and even mild forms of schizophrenia. Other potential group members may be recovering from a serious accident or extended medical treatment, undergoing treatment for cancer, or relatives with secondary trauma. Psycho-educational groups may be formed for many different kinds of people. Examples are grief support groups, body awareness groups, affect groups, and insomnia and stress groups.

Life itself can pose critical challenges for people as they pass through their life stages: childhood, adolescence, adulthood, parenthood, mid-life, old age. Each stage has challenges that can pose risks to mental health. However, most people manage minor life crises without medical or psychiatric intervention. They rely on their own resources and on the support of friends and relatives. For other people, these challenges may lead to anxiety or depression. Psycho-educational group therapy is an option worthy of consideration as a preventive measure for young adults, young parents, or the elderly at risk of depression. A Swedish project for retired people who meet in so called life-story groups recently gained attention because of its appeal to lonely people and the improvements it made in their life satisfaction (Pettersson, 2019).

Generally, people with one of these conditions or in one of these situations are receptive to group meetings. They usually think it is a good idea to meet with others in the same situation or with the same condition. They think they can learn from others as they ask questions and share experiences. Perhaps another member will ask a question they are too embarrassed to ask themselves. In the same way that people react to other kinds of group therapy, people in psycho-educational groups are relieved when they can share their situation or condition. They can also contribute methods or coping strategies that have worked. As a result, group members learn from each other.

Preparations for psycho-educational groups

Various pedagogic activities are used in psycho-educational groups. These activities include lectures, homework assignments, role play, and group conversation. Group leaders must spend considerable time and effort preparing these activities. For each activity, they need to think about its suitability for the group, how much explanation it requires, how much time it takes, and how it will be received and evaluated. It is easy to overestimate people's ability to absorb and use new knowledge, their willingness to participate, and their receptivity to constructive criticism.

There are other preparation considerations for psycho-educational groups besides the group leader–group member preparation. Organizational support is necessary. The target group must be identified. Administrative matters such as meeting locations, times, and dates must be confirmed. Programme frameworks, guidelines, and rules must be prepared. Chapter 6, "Starting a therapy group", describes these preparation activities. Group leaders are advised to follow-up on these activities so that they are completed in a timely and competent way.

Programme frameworks for psycho-educational groups differ somewhat from frameworks for other kinds of therapy groups. While the requirements of confidentiality, attendance, and punctuality are no different, the rule that prohibits outside contact is irrelevant in psycho-educational groups. In fact, members in psycho-educational groups are sometimes encouraged to meet each other away from the group.

After the group type is chosen and a list of potential groups members is prepared, the group leader may invite these people to an information meeting. A useful practice is to send them an information sheet in advance. The group leader or care centres can provide registration information.

Although a psycho-educational group has a therapeutic goal, its primary goal is learning. Therefore, unlike other therapy groups, it is not necessary for the group leader to conduct extensive preparatory interviews with group members. Typically, the first encounter of group leaders and group members is at the introductory meeting.

The information sheets should describe the psycho-educational group very clearly and in some detail. Group members will want to know, for example, the group's themes or topics, its goals and structure, and their own roles. Different groups will have different concerns. If the group consists of people who have a serious illness, apart from sharing experiences related to their condition they will probably be interested in learning more about their condition. If the group consists of people who suffer from depression or stress, the focus will be less on information and education and more on reflection, sharing of experiences, and, for example, relaxation and mindfulness exercises. Group leaders consider all these concerns when they prepare the information sheets.

Because psycho-educational groups meet only four to eight times, each meeting should be thoughtfully planned so that the three areas (knowledge, reflection, and exchange) are in focus in each meeting. Sometimes it is tempting for group leaders to prioritize knowledge over reflection and exchange. The explanation may be that group leaders find giving a lecture less demanding than leading and monitoring group activities and conversations. For group members, sitting and listening require less effort than contributing and participating. However, as we have previously argued, teacher-centric instruction and passive listening instruction are not necessarily the most effective ways to learn. Such instruction ignores the fundamental principle of group therapy: people learn from each other as they exchange information, especially when they have very pertinent information. The group leader's employer, however, sometimes exerts considerable influence when it requires reports on the factual data communicated. It may be quite challenging for a group leader to explain to administrative officials how this kind of learning works. Nevertheless, it is important to inform the employer about the prerequisites for group therapy to work. One is that groups need support from its organization. Another is that confidentiality must be respected.

Content, arrangements, and structure

Nina W. Brown's work provides much of the inspiration for this section, especially with respect to its practical recommendations. Brown is a professor and psychologist at Old Dominion University in Norfolk, Virginia. We recommend her book titled *Psychoeducational Groups, Process and Practice*, now in its 4th edition (2018).

The group leader presents the general outline of the group's content, arrangements, and structure at the first group meeting. In this meeting, the group members learn how the programme will function – from introduction to termination. As noted above, arrangement details are tailored to the group members' specific conditions and situations. The suggestions that follow are intended to help group leaders structure the group meetings.

First group meeting

- Welcome everyone. Introduce yourself as the group leader. Ask the members to introduce themselves and to state their expectations from the programme. (This information is also useful for planning purposes.)
- Describe the group purpose and the content of future sessions.
- Emphasize the importance of attendance and punctuality for group cohesion and mutual trust.
- Explain the group structure: the number of meetings and the location, times, and dates of meetings. Explain that each meeting begins with a short introductory lecture by the group leader, which is followed by examples, discussions, and possibly group activities (e.g., role play and other exercises).
- Emphasize the nature of the group. As a pedagogical group, explain that in-depth responses to members' questions and needs are not possible.
- Use a flip chart/whiteboard to list important points in this short introduction (and in future meetings). As needed, distribute paper for notetaking.
- Encourage members to ask questions and to share their thoughts (now and in future meetings).
- End with a homework assignment that is linked to the group theme or topic. Ask members to prepare the assignment in writing.

Subsequent group meetings and follow-up on previous meetings

- Begin with a short summary of the previous meeting.
- Ask about the last homework assignment – if and how it was completed.
- Ask if anything discussed so far is unclear.
- Be attentive to the meeting's dynamics. Intervene if necessary (e.g., when a member takes too much time or a member is reluctant to speak).
- Continue with a theme for the lecture, discussions, and exercises as in the previous meeting. Encourage members to ask questions and to share experiences.
- Introduce the new homework assignment and encourage members to think more about the meeting's themes or topics.
- Be prepared to adapt the meeting structure and content to the group. Changes in the teaching activities, the discussions, the exchange of experiences, and so on may be needed.
- Remind members at the next-to-last meeting that the next meeting is the final meeting.

Final group meeting

- Begin with a short summary of the previous meeting.
- Mention that this meeting is the last meeting. Return to themes or topics that need further attention.
- If time permits, ask members if they want to know more about any topic or theme.
- Summarize the main points from the previous meetings. Reflect on the degree of cohesion that the group has achieved, and on how various individuals have experienced the work. Encourage the members to reflect on what they have learned.
- About 20 minutes before the end of the meeting, ask the members for key words related to, for example, a discussion, a homework assignment, or an event that expressed their most important learning from the programme.
- Ask for suggestions on how the programme can be improved.
- Summarize the learning in key words, acknowledge suggestions for improvements, thank all members, and wish them well.

There is always a special mood among the members when a group terminates. In the best circumstances, members leave the programme with new knowledge of their condition or situation and feel more confident and hopeful about handling it in the future.

The group leader roles in psycho-educational groups

The three roles: teacher, manager, and counsellor

Group leaders in psycho-educational groups have several roles. As teachers, they must have a comprehensive understanding of the knowledge they teach. (On occasion, group leaders may wish to invite an expert to talk to the group about a particular topic.) Usually group leaders are staff members of organizations that offer general medical care or support to target groups. Therefore, group leaders are therefore expected to demonstrate enthusiasm and curiosity about the themes or topics they teach. As teachers, they need pedagogic skills for making assignments, lecturing, using multimedia applications, leading activities, and supervising role play.

Group leaders in psycho-educational groups must also be competent managers who can structure a series of meetings for a number of people in a group setting. Although psycho-educational groups are short-term, their group leaders must be comfortable with group relationships, communications, and interactions. While the group members share some commonality, they nevertheless have unique personalities with their individual needs and problems. Experience and skill are required to manage the group meetings. Group leaders plan and monitor the meetings, oversee the activities, and guide the members' conversations. We offer the following "classroom tip" to group leaders for the first meeting. A group leader might say:

I will begin each meeting with a review of the previous meeting. I will then lecture on some topic or theme of interest and relevance to the group. Next, you will have an opportunity to talk about that topic or theme. You can emphasize what is important to you. At the end of our meetings, I will summarize what you have learned and describe the homework assignment.

Group leaders in psycho-educational groups, however, must be more than teachers and managers. Unlike the group leaders described in other chapters of this book, the role of the group leaders in this chapter is not primarily a therapeutic one. Nevertheless, group leaders in psycho-educational groups must show warmth, interest, and support in their interactions with the group members. In this capacity, group leaders are counsellors. They must create an open and trusting group climate. This is a complex task. However, group leaders also lead by example. If they are respectful and trustful, group members will be inclined to imitate this behaviour.

Communication in a psycho-educational group

The discussion to this point focuses on the conversation and discussion among group members as overseen by the group leaders. In a psycho-educational group, in which the goal is to teach a skill or just increase knowledge, the group leaders have a different role. They take the role of teachers with the group members as students. Yet even in such groups, avoidance of "red light communication" and "noise" is applicable. (See Chapter 4.) Furthermore, it is essential that group leaders in psycho-educational groups communicate in ways closely connected to the group members' reality. If group leaders use obscure language or professional jargon, they are unlikely to be effective teachers.

Group leaders should pay close attention to the group members, watching for signs of boredom or inattention (e.g., yawning or texting). These signs are often indications that the instruction has strayed too far from the group members' experiences. They are thinking about other things. Therefore, in psycho-educational groups, it is usually a good idea to initiate a discussion among the members. For example, group leaders can encourage members to ask questions and to offer examples. A fundamental pedagogic principle is that learning increases with participation and active engagement in sessions. Long episodes of one-way communication by the group leader should be avoided.

Recommendations for psycho-educational group leaders

Nina Brown (2018) prepared a list of recommendations for leaders in psycho-educational groups. We summarize her recommendations next.

- Direct members' individual learning.
- Show members how they can interact in ways that reduce isolation and that support each other.
- Create a trusting climate that provides opportunities for members to express their emotions.
- Build and support hope among the members.
- Help members learn useful techniques and attitudes.
- Teach strategies that members can use to build self-confidence and increase self-knowledge.
- Create possibilities to use and practice new learning.

These recommendations seem as appropriate for leaders of other therapeutic groups as for leaders of psycho-educational groups. Yet there is one important difference: the first recommendation in the list. People who join therapeutic groups are motivated to seek help for a mental disturbance of some kind. People who join psycho-educational groups are motivated to learn about a condition or situation that creates worry or stress. They want knowledge that can give them more control and provide relief from such worry or stress.

Balancing the psycho-educational group leader roles

Group leaders have to balance these three roles. The roles have different priorities at different times. For example, while the group may be focused on a theme or a topic (requiring the teacher role), at some point members' concerns and worries mean the group leader must provide comfort (requiring the counsellor role). When members' emotions seem to steer the group away from its main focus, the group leader has to redirect the group to its learning task (requiring the manager role). In the following example, which illustrates this kind of role shift, GL is the group leader and Elena is a group member.

Example:

Members in a psycho-educational group are very interested in learning more about their grief reactions. They want to learn how to manage their grief and anxiety and to hear other members' experiences with grief. During the conversation, members describe some very private and painful experiences. The conversation becomes increasingly personal in a way that is typical for a psychotherapeutic group. Elena in particular is very disturbed by a memory of a violent episode from her past. She turns to the group leader for help. The group leader realizes that Elena has crossed a boundary into an area outside the scope of the group. The group leader wants to return the conversation to a more general and objective discussion of grief.

GL [to the group]: I am not surprised that the conversation has brought back some very painful memories. I know that many of you have had terrible incidents in your life. [To Elena] Do you think the group benefits from hearing these memories?

Elena: No. But I just had to relieve some pressure on myself. These memories really don't fit this conversation.

This example show how group members in a psycho-educational group can be tempted to talk about painful memories. When this happens, the group risks becoming a psychotherapy group. A group leader of a psycho-educational group must be careful to avoid "the deep water" when members want to talk about past and current experiences that may have caused them harm. It is all too easy for a group leader to unintentionally shift roles: from teacher to therapist. Given Elena's ready admission that her outburst was disruptive, the group leader was able to steer the conversation easily back to the grief discussion. The situation would have been more challenging for the group leader if Elena had not agreed. Then the group leader would have to remind the group of its guiding framework and the responsibility of the group members to work within that framework.

Group leaders may have to balance their roles as teachers and counsellors. For example, consider the following scenario when the group members disagree on the primary group focus. Recall the goals of psycho-educational groups: knowledge, reflection, and exchange. Sometimes some group members prioritize knowledge while other members prioritize reflection and exchange. The group leader is caught in the middle. In the following example, we see how a group leader solves this problem.

Example:

A psycho-educational group for patients who were in recovery following their heart attacks began in the usual way with individual presentations and a review of the programme. The group leader described the group themes, topics, and framework. The group members said they were very interested in others' experiences.

Following a brief lecture by the group leader, several group members asked questions about the lecture content and offered their opinions on the group leader's remarks. These members seemed to monopolize the conversation. They wanted to focus on the lecture content. Others, who wanted to focus on their worries and insecurities, found it difficult to say anything.

The group leader then decided to alter the regular meeting agenda by adding a new element. After each lecture, the group leader invited all group members to describe their current worries as well as their responses to the lecture. Using these descriptions, the group leader directed the subsequent group conversation so that reflection and exchange as well as knowledge were in focus. As a result, the group members acquired knowledge at the same time they learned coping strategies for everyday living.

The example shows that a willingness to be flexible is a commendable leadership characteristic. Group leaders of psycho-educational groups who sometimes make minor changes in meeting agendas need not fear loss of control if the changes are reasonable. However, a word of caution: such changes are allowed, but programmes and frameworks must be retained. They are the foundation of the leader–member–group agreement.

Dual group leadership

Some psycho-educational groups have two group leaders. The leaders may divide their leadership responsibilities in various ways depending on their knowledge and interests. (See Chapter 7 for a discussion of dual leadership.) In the following example, we see how two group leaders share the group leader role.

Example:

The theme for a primary care patient group was diabetes and diet. The patients, who had recently been diagnosed with diabetes, had been advised to consider making certain lifestyle changes. The group leaders were a nurse and a dietician. Both were well qualified in their fields by their professional education, training, and experience. Although both leaders presented brief lectures at the group meetings, the nurse was more experienced in leading groups. Therefore, she assumed greater leadership responsibility in the group.

Outside experts

At times, group leaders may invite an outside expert to present a lecture at a group meeting. Outside experts should be scheduled well in advance of the group's first meeting. In the group's first meeting it is advisable to inform group members if outside experts will be part of the programme. A delicate situation may arise when the outside expert joins the group, even if only for one meeting, not least when the expert has a higher position in the organization than the group leader. The mere presence of the outside expert changes the group dynamics. Who is in charge now? Has the group leader surrendered the leadership role? Despite the members' possible confusion, we emphasize that the group leader is the host; the outside expert is the guest. The group leader unquestionably remains in charge of the agenda, the time schedule, and the activities. The outside expert is someone whose special expertise is a welcome source of supplementary knowledge. When the group leader takes the in-charge role, the members feel safe. They can focus on the expert's lecture.

Summary

In groups with a pre-planned content structure, group processes provide the structure that advances the treatment. In these kinds of group therapy, the group leader has a challenging role in balancing the use of cognitive interventions with the required group processes. Both must be in harmony to achieve the best outcome. In this chapter, CBT groups are described as learning environments with stage-specific development and a group leader who has responsibility for the various stages. The purpose of psycho-educational groups is to provide people with knowledge about their condition or situation, and to facilitate reflection and exchange among people in similar circumstances. The psycho-educational group leader is a teacher, manager, and counsellor. The teacher role distinguishes the psycho-educational group leader role from the group leader role in other therapy groups. Each of the four to eight group meetings in psycho-educational groups focuses on some theme or topic. These meetings help group members learn more about their condition and about more effective management of their situation.

Chapter 12

Focused group therapy (FGT)

Since the early 2000s, the authors of this book have been deeply involved in developing a group therapy method for exhaustion syndrome based on the general principles of group therapy. In our development of the method, which we call focused group therapy (FGT) and which is based on the principles of group therapy described in this book, we found that it is particularly helpful to identify an individual focus for the treatment.

We describe this method in our manual *Time-Limited and Focused Group Therapy* (in the original Swedish: *Tidsbegränsad och fokuserad gruppterapi: manual*; Sandahl et al., 2012). In recent years, we have had success with the use of FGT with groups other than those we worked with in the beginning. (We note the scientific literature regarding this treatment model currently addresses only individuals with work-related stress and fatigue; Lindgren et al., 2008; Sandahl & Lindgren, 2006; Sandahl et al., 2011).

The many psychotherapists we have trained over the years have become enthusiastic supporters and users of FGT. Therefore, in this chapter, as we describe the method, we also want to emphasize that training and supervision in its use are required.

FGT is characterized by the time-limited format (we recommend 18 sessions), its intensity (two meetings in each of the first five weeks of treatment), and the focus on the individual and on the group as a whole. The purpose of this focus is to give the therapy a clear direction. Together, the client and the therapist carefully formulate the focus before treatment begins. If the chosen focus reflects the reality of the client's struggles, it can be worked with at different levels. This focus, which can produce coping strategies for various situations, is thus generalizable to other areas of the client's life.

This book frequently observes that group therapy is particularly well suited for people who have difficulty with personal relationships. These difficulties (found among many group member categories) include an inability to express emotions and needs, hesitant self-assertion, lack of empathy, and an inability to control impulsive outbursts. Sometimes these relationship difficulties mask other difficulties, such as depression and anxiety; sometimes they are the consequences of the other difficulties. Regardless of whether relationship difficulties are a symptom or a cause, people who experience such difficulties often have a reduced ability to cope with everyday life.

Self-confidence and self-esteem in life experiences

Self-confidence and self-esteem derive from how people feel about their abilities and themselves. People with high self-confidence know they are competent and can accomplish certain things. It is even possible to have high self-confidence in specific situations ("self-efficacy") despite generally low self-esteem. People with high self-esteem have a positive regard for themselves in general. They think they have value as human beings, irrespective of how their life seems at the moment. Of course, an attitude of self-confidence and self-admiration is sometimes a narcissistic defence against the self-perception that one has very little value. A combination of heredity and early life experiences is influential in how this attitude develops.

Michael Basch (1995) created a "developmental model" for individual "brief" (i.e., short-term) therapy based on his work with the concept of competence. Broadly speaking, he defines competence as the power to cope with life's normal challenges. He describes the group members who are well suited to this therapy as people who have previously considered themselves generally competent and functioning well, for example, in professional positions or in social contexts.

Basch's fundamental premise in his analysis of competence is that depression and other non-psychotic psychological conditions are natural outcomes when people find they are unable to deal with everyday life in their usual and familiar way. Sometimes they make this discovery when they fail to respond effectively to a crisis or to an extraordinary challenge. They find the actions, analyses, and mechanisms they used previously to handle crises are now ineffective. According to Basch, people's personal characteristics and past experiences influence how they respond to a crisis. Another influential factor is whether they had some role in, or responsibility for, the situation that later presented coping difficulties. A sense of helplessness only exacerbates their inability to manage the crisis.

When people feel incompetent in some situation, their self-esteem is undermined. Here we understand self-esteem in a broader sense than is often used in psychotherapy. We refer to the belief, according to the theory of *self-efficacy*, that people have in their capacity to manage and control their behaviour, motivations, and social environment in a way that accomplishes a certain action *in a particular situation* (Bandura, 1977). When we refer to self-esteem, we mean the mainly positive feeling people have about their value as a person or in a specific role.

According to Basch (1995), striving for *competence* – that is, the effort to demonstrate a capability for accomplishing something that you are reasonably well adapted for and which satisfies some personal need – is a fundamental driving force for most people. Incompetence can result in anxiety disorder, fear of failure, and the associated shame. Competence then is an important factor in the quest to build self-esteem. In positive circumstances, when the individual feels competent, self-esteem can develop and strengthen. Basch uses a spiral image to depict the striving for competence as a positive upward development. The movement may also spiral downward. This happens when decisions do not produce the desired results. People do not usually feel incompetent when this outcome occurs just one or two times, but with repeated occurrences self-esteem suffers (see Figure 12.1).

As mentioned, it is possible to have strong self-confidence in a specific situation in spite of a low degree of self-esteem. However, the opposite relation is probably more common – a low degree of self-esteem that generalizes to several situations. Basch's theories place him in the psychoanalytic tradition known as self-psychology in which affects are viewed as the fundamental psychological forces of change. More recent research in affect and attachment psychology

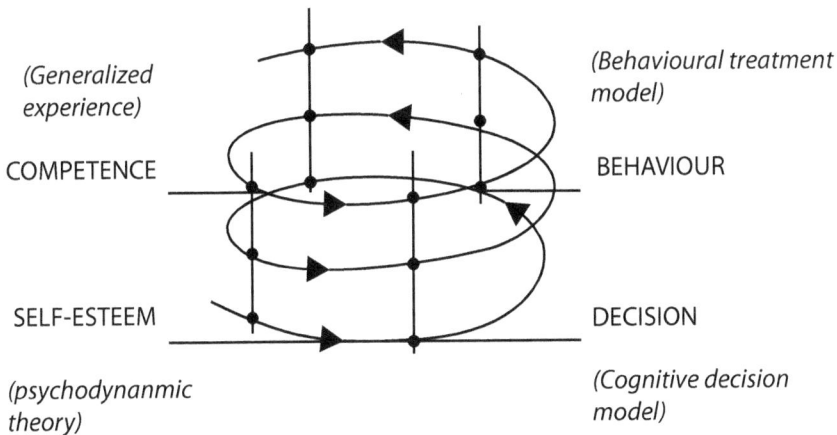

Figure 12.1 The relation between experienced competence in coping with life, self-esteem, thoughts, and behaviours.

(adapted from Basch, 1995)

supports Basch's ideas (Bråten, 1998; 2007; McClusky, 2005; Schore & Schore, 2008). Therefore, we believe it is essential that the point of departure for FGT is to begin with group members' self-esteem with a focus on affectively charged situations and generalizable outcomes.

The FGT framework and guidelines

The FGT framework

The core of FGT is the communication between group members and the conscious use of the group process. It is a here-and-now approach to therapy. FGT is time-limited with two meetings a week during the first half of the treatment and one meeting a week during the second half.

In FGT, the starting point is what functions well in a person's life, not "what is wrong with the patient". The focus is on experienced obstacles to coping and solving problems. The client is not regarded as a victim. Instead, attention is directed towards current experiences rather than possible trauma from early childhood. People have a tendency to activate negative feelings quite easily if they are stuck in such narratives. By repeating old stories about difficulties and injuries, the risk is that the therapy will strengthen old, non-adaptive patterns rather than open new doors.

The FGT guidelines

The main task of the group leader is to facilitate the group's development (see chapters 8 and 9) and to help members talk openly with each other about their shared conditions and situations, including their experiences and feelings in the group. FGT follows certain guidelines, as described next.

- Before starting an FGT group, the group leader meets the potential group members two or three times, gives them information about FGT, and works on a focus formulation. The group leader and each group member decide on a specific focus that will set the direction for that member's therapy during the group programme. A specific and sustained focus can lead to a solution for each group member's specific problem and perhaps for other life problems. The group leader takes the instructor role in these preparatory interviews, which include a careful explanation of group processes as well as what each may expect from the therapy.
- FGT groups consist of five to eight members. As it is closed group therapy, new members are not admitted to the group after it begins.
- FGT groups meet 18 times. Each session lasts 90 minutes. For the first four to five weeks, the group meets twice a week. After that, the group meets weekly. The concentration of meetings in the first five weeks is to facilitate the group cohesion and to accelerate the process of alliance with the group. Reducing

the twice-weekly meetings to weekly meetings gives group members more time for the subsequent emphasis on individual psychotherapeutic work.

- FGT tries to create a group climate in which group members honestly and freely express their feelings. Therefore, group members must be assured that the group setting is secure and supportive. They must also be assured that confidentiality of what is said and done in the group is fully respected.
- Because of FGT's here-and-now emphasis, group members are encouraged to concentrate on current emotions and recent experiences rather than on external or past events and relationships. FGT views the group as a social "laboratory" in which the group members can practice new ways of being. Although the group leader sometimes suggests "homework" for an individual member (e.g., relationship exercises for use at home or work), we are convinced the most important learning occurs in the group meetings. Other process-oriented therapy models are based on the same conviction (e.g., group analysis and systems-oriented group therapy).
- Group members in FGT sometimes discuss events that are external to the group. In these discussions, the group leader encourages the members to examine the emotions these events aroused and to relate those emotions to other themes under discussion. The focus in FGT is always on the emotions and experiences in group members' present lives with special attention paid to group members' interactions and group processes.

Group members in FGT join a group with high expectations of an engaging and interesting experience that will prove beneficial. However, group members are also likely to have some concerns and doubts about the therapy. Given such ambivalence about the benefits of FGT, the group leader must provide group structure and security. Group members should be assured of confidentiality and privacy when they share very personal emotions or recount embarrassing or painful experiences.

Who is well suited for FGT?

Time-limited treatment interventions generally offer effective treatment for people with circumscribed psychological problems or for people who have experienced recent troubles of some kind. One would expect that potential group members could express their clear wish to change. Because much of FGT involves inner relationships, group members should be motivated to reflect on these relationships. In addition, FGT most benefits group members who can process and make changes in the short term. The goal of FGT is that when future problematic situations occur, group members will not only be able to manage them on their own but will also be able to prevent at least some reoccurrence of these situations.

Clinical experience and some empirical research (Sandahl et al., 2011) have shown positive results from the use of FGT with a variety of conditions and in a variety of situations. We list some of these conditions and situations next.

(Note: we recognize that positive clinical experience is not equivalent to scientific evidence).

Examples of conditions and situations suitable for FGT

- Exhaustion syndrome.
- Chronic pain.
- Moderate anxiety or depression.
- Young adults with identity problems.
- Complicated grief.
- Women at risk of abuse.
- Male loneliness.
- Eating disorders.
- Stress-related disorders.

For FGT to work as intended, the group members should have the same or similar condition or be in the same or similar situation (see below: "The group focus in FGT"). This commonality is the foundation of group cohesion and inclusivity.

Group member exclusion criteria for FGT

People with serious attachment problems that prevent them from relating to others in a group situation cannot benefit in any meaningful way from time-limited group therapy. Patients with schizoid, paranoid, or narcissistic personality problems are therefore not suitable for FGT. Generally, patients who fear group situations or are deeply uncomfortable in such situations are unsuitable for time-limited group therapy. Such patients need longer periods in a group in order to develop the trust needed to begin relating to other group members.

People who lack sufficient impulse control are also unsuitable for FGT because they are unable to process and reflect on ideas and emotions in a group. People with borderline personality disorder, or with exclusionary or psychotic problems, require long-term treatment. People who suffer from ongoing alcohol or drug abuse issues are unsuitable for FGT because of their need for hands-on support. However, after a period of abstinence (individually determined), patients with a low or a moderate degree of dependency are well suited for FGT. People with severe social problems will not benefit from FGT because they will be preoccupied with coping with daily life and will lack the energy and motivation needed to focus on relations and processes in group therapy. Last, people who have recently experienced some kind of trauma and are still in shock require individual care rather than group therapy.

Preparatory interviews in FGT

In the preparatory interviews in FGT, group leaders talk with the potential group members about their needs and motives for seeking group therapy. They also explore the potential group members' expectations and fears related to group therapy. Taking part in group therapy is unfamiliar to most people; they really do not know what group therapy is. These interviews also give group leaders the opportunity to learn about members' current and past life experiences and their current and past relationships. Besides acquiring this information, group leaders establish an alliance with each individual that leads to the joint formulation of a purpose, goals, and a specific focus for the therapeutic treatment. In some respects, the therapeutic treatment begins in these interviews. In addition to an agreement about *which* outcomes to expect from the therapy in forming the working alliance, the patient needs to understand how the group will function. The patient acquires trust and confidence in the group leader when all these matters are openly discussed.

Group members who are new to group psychotherapy will have many questions. Group leaders can provide a good deal of information in the preparatory interviews. A general introduction to group psychotherapy can be given to potential group members as verbal information or as printed leaflets at the first interview so that patients can ask questions at the next individual session. This information, which should be of a general character, should include boundaries and rules for the group work. An example of such written information is given in Chapter 6.

Although people seek group therapy, such as FGT, for many reasons, nearly all struggle with their relationships with other people. It is often very difficult for them to talk about these problematic relationships. In the preparatory interviews, group leaders should emphasize that group members will need to be as open and honest as possible in talking in the group about their relationships. This is the essence of group therapy. Group leaders can explain that when group members become more comfortable in the group, they will be less inclined to hide their emotions and more willing to try new behaviours.

The preparatory interviews should be prepared and conducted carefully and thoroughly. In the preparatory interviews, group leaders gain a preliminary understanding of the group and its members. Group leaders assure potential group members that they will be less anxious and afraid once group cohesion is established. It may take two to three preparatory interviews to reach this understanding. If a group leader senses that a patient has not had enough time for preparation, we recommend that the group leader schedule another interview with the patient.

The focus of FGT

Successful short-term therapy, regardless of its theoretical basis, is characterized by clear boundaries and a therapeutic focus. The description of the focus of therapy as simply general relationship problems is too broad and theoretical.

In working with a relational focus in FGT, the problems should be described in everyday behavioural terms. Group leaders and group members should be able to recognize a problem when it surfaces in the interaction in the group therapy setting. Therefore, FGT requires a group focus and an individual member focus that must be clearly stated, clearly understood, and evident in the therapeutic process.

FGT has this dual focus: the group focus and the individual focus. The focus of the group is the commonality that unites the group members – the reason they sought out therapy because of their condition or their situation (as listed above). The individual focus speaks directly to the client and reflects the unique condition or situation of the group member. The paradox is that while group members have something in common, each member is different from all other members. The individual focus respects this individuality.

The dual focus in FGT – the difficulties and relationship problems that unite the group members – specifies a clear purpose and sets a clear direction for the therapeutic treatment for the group as a whole and for the individual patient With the individual focus, FGT helps group members understand how their problems have lowered their self-esteem and how their previous ways of managing these problems have failed. Thus, even as FGT identifies negative, limiting behaviour patterns, it should also identify resources that can counteract and change these behaviour patterns. These new patterns, once established, can be generalized to other areas of group members' lives.

The work of formulating an individual focus helps group members to:

- Become directly involved in their therapy.
- Understand how therapy works by provoking inward analysis instead of attributing causes of problems to external factors.
- Feel less influenced by uncontrollable powers.
- Be more hopeful.
- Be more motivated.
- Be more curious and self-reflective.
- Understand their behaviour patterns, limitations, and resources.

The FGT focus benefits the group by:

- Contributing to building a therapeutic group alliance.
- Guiding group leaders in the therapeutic treatment.

The group focus in FGT

Group leaders develop the FGT group focus – its overall theme – and explain it to the group members at the beginning of the therapy in the preparatory interviews and at the first group meeting. The group focus describes what the group as a whole will work with in the 18 meetings. For example, a group focus might be the condition of exhaustion syndrome that the group members share. The task of the group members is to explore feelings and thoughts regarding what has happened, to observe and share with others how they have handled stressful situations, and to test new ways of dealing with such situations.

The individual focus in FGT

The individual focus in FGT is formulated in cooperation with the patient during the preparatory interviews. This focus reflects each member's personal background, current problems, relationship difficulties, hindering limitations, and supportive resources. The group leader should be able to determine from the individual focus what the members need to develop or change so they can better manage a specific difficulty and similar difficulties in the future. It is easy for patients to assume that their lives are completely consumed by such difficulties. Indeed, a concentrated focus on such problems can undermine self-esteem. Therefore, identifying the hidden strengths and resources in patients' lives is an essential part of the individual focus formulation.

The individual focus is a very delicate matter because it involves goals related to patients' emotions, personal characteristics, and fears. The work involved in the formulation of the focus thus implies that patients must lower their emotional defences and become more vulnerable. It is essential that group leaders act respectfully and sensitively in this work.

Formulating an individual focus for as many as six to eight group members is an arduous and time-consuming task for group leaders. It also requires group leaders to have considerable knowledge, empathy, and tact. Therefore, we recommend group leaders meet individually with group members at least two to three times before the first group session. The learning acquired in these preparatory interviews will help group leaders formulate a suitable individual focus for each member.

Formulating the individual focus in the preparatory interviews

Concurrently with formulation of the individual focus in the preparatory interviews, group leaders and groups members begin to develop their therapeutic alliance. In the interviews, group leaders identify each member's strengths and weaknesses and acquire information on their life history, interpersonal relationships, and present difficulties. During this interaction, group members can decide whether they and their group leader are a good fit and whether they can function in a group situation.

We advise group leaders, when working with patients' interpersonal relationships, to ask each potential group member to complete a self-assessment questionnaire on such relationships. If available, we recommend the use of the Inventory of Interpersonal Problems (Horowitz et al., 1988). The responses to each item are the main interest, not the scores on the sub-scales. An item-by-item analysis with the patient will provide the information needed to identifying specific inter-personal situations that the patient finds challenging. The clients complete the questionnaires at the first preparatory interview. After reviewing the questionnaire responses, group leaders can use these responses in discussions and decisions in the second (and/or third) preparatory interview. If a group leader decides that FGT is a suitable therapeutic approach for a patient, an individual focus is formulated for that person. When a group leader and a potential group member agree on the individual focus, the client is ready to decide to start therapy or not.

Helping group members become active agents in their therapy is an important task for group leaders. This can be a difficult and sensitive task in the preparatory interviews. The therapist may take a positive, hopeful approach with a client who may have a victim-mentality mindset or who feels shame or guilt about a particu-lar condition or situation. It may be useful to encourage clients to express their feelings about the trauma behind their sense of victimhood.

When FGT sheds light on the causes of group members' condition or situation (e.g., fear of rejection, inability to express anger, or lack of assertiveness), the members are in a better position to understand their problems and can imagine that change is possible.

The Basch competence model in the individual focus

FGT uses Basch's (1995) competence model. (See Figure 12.1.) As described above, the model requires analysis of thought processes and behaviour patterns that either increase or decrease self-esteem related to emotional competence. These are the processes and behaviours that have a positive or negative effect on the indi-vidual's self-esteem and feelings of competence in specific situations. The theoreti-cal structure of Basch's model consists of the following areas:

- *Affect/Thought* – this area deals with the interaction between individual affect differentiation and intellectual capability and quality. Are emotions and thoughts integrated? Or is behaviour controlled at times by some emotions/ thoughts and at other times by other emotions?
- *Attachment* – this area refers to the quality of relationships with others. Can the client establish close and mutual relationships with others? Do rela-tionship difficulties result in isolation, self-sufficiency, or clingy emotional attachment?
- *Autonomy* – this area deals with integrity and the ability to be independ-ent and to demand respect. Can the client pursue interests that are to his/her benefit?
- *Creativity* – this area is broader than artistic creativity. Can the client create enjoyable activities and experiences (e.g., the satisfaction from problem-solving)?

- *Psychosexuality* – this area refers to sexual arousal and sensual desire. Do the client's relationships satisfy these needs? How is he or she dealing with conflicting feelings related to sexual needs?
- *Other* – any other areas of importance for the client not included in the above factors.

Before FGT begins, it is helpful for group leaders to identify the area(s) where group members have low self-esteem. The purpose of evaluating the psychological resources and limitations that group members use to increase or decrease their self-esteem is to identify which resources are available that can restore self-esteem.

Having evaluated the potential group members' personal resources in terms of affect/thoughts, attachment, autonomy, creativity, and psychosexuality, group leaders in cooperation with clients can better develop the formulation of the individual focus. This focus should be expressed in layman's terms (vs professional jargon) that members can understand and that is specific to their personal situation or condition. The goal is that a member will respond: "Yes, precisely. That is exactly my problem!"

Categories of FGT focus expressions

In this section we describe seven categories of FGT focus expressions. For these descriptions, we use our experience from around 200 focus discussions with our patients and with FGT groups in which we were group leaders.

- Identify needs.
- Show vulnerability.
- Express negative feelings.
- Be assertive.
- Define and defend boundaries.
- Manage performance anxiety.
- Take time for reflection.

The categories, which may overlap, can be used in the preparatory interviews to identify a core focus. Each group member's focus should be specifically framed for that individual in a personal way. The focus should also use simplified behavioural language that can be understood as something the client needs to do in the group (e.g., expressing needs or negative feelings). The focus is a self-command. In some instances, more than one focus may be suitable for a group member, although usually choosing a core focus is recommended.

Examples of FGT focus expressions

Identify needs

This focus expression stems from a relationship difficulty that results from the uncertainty evoked in others when two messages are sent: one message on personal responsibility (a resource); another message on over-adaptation to others' needs and their associated sense of victimhood (a limitation). We think it is important to identify the resources and limitations in group members' behavioural patterns. If these resources and limitations are not identified, members may think the therapy deprives them of something that actually increases their self-esteem:

> Just as I show respect to others, I must also respect myself. I have to identify and state my needs. I also have to learn to accept that others may not respond to, appreciate, or agree with my needs
>
> I am quite energetic in many situations. I need to use that energy to express my own wishes and needs, even at the risk of being misunderstood and rejected.

Show vulnerability

If people feel a strong urge to support others (a resource), they may experience an imbalance (a limitation) in relationships if others are unaware of the vulnerability that might be a prerequisite for empathy and care. The limitation in these cases is an inability to reveal doubts and to express vulnerability (in most cases, this is actually another resource):

> I want to show more of my social awareness and responsibility in the group. I want to show who I am and how I feel. I will practice identifying situations when it is helpful for me to be more open in revealing my insecurities and my fears about being an outsider.
>
> I want to use my power to support and encourage others as well as to care for myself. Even when I am worried and guilt-ridden, I will be open about myself.

Express negative feelings

Task commitment and loyalty to others are resources that advance work, community, and creativity in any group. However, space is needed in groups for the expression of negative feelings, such as disappointment and unhappiness when members feel betrayed, frustrated, or angry. If people do not know how to express such feelings, they might indirectly communicate them in bitter comments, unjust accusations, or impulsive attacks on others. These responses are damaging to group community and creativity:

I will use my commitment to identify and express my unpleasant feelings. I will say what I need and want even when I worry about other people's reactions.

I wish everyone well. Therefore, I need to control my responses instead of reacting impulsively. I need to become aware of my feelings (e.g., anger and fear) and express them even when I am afraid of what others think of me.

Be assertive

People refrain from asserting their opinions or making demands (a limitation) for various reasons. It may be rather easy to step into someone else's shoes, so to speak (a resource), but this may increase others' feelings of guilty and anxiety in addition to increasing one's own dissatisfaction and the suspicion that one is being exploited:

> I understand others and listen to their needs. In the same way, I want to assert my own wishes and ask for what I want – even if it gives me a bad conscience.
>
> By using my energy and creativity, I will have the courage to act assertively by stating what I want. I do not need to take responsibility for other people's needs – even if I risk disappointment or rejection.

Define and defend boundaries

Sometimes people need to protect their privacy in ways other than by openly expressing emotions or asserting themselves. In some contexts, the use of good judgment, sensitivity, and perseverance (a resource) is needed so that privacy boundaries do not lead to isolation, exclusion, or condemnation. Group members who extend these boundaries too far may carry a burden that is too heavy for them. Alternatively, they may impulsively narrow these boundaries (a limitation):

> I want to use my purposefulness to establish appropriate boundaries in my relationships with others. When I feel unsure of myself and just want to escape, I will try to take a stand and speak up for myself.
>
> I need to use determination in my quest to establish appropriate relationship boundaries. I do not want to react impulsively when I find myself in an unpleasant situation.

Manage performance anxiety

Various powerful motivations lie behind people's will to perform. These motivations can be problematic if they serve self-esteem – the need to look important to others (a limitation). To balance these motivations, people need to identify valuable aspects of themselves (a resource):

I listen to and engage with others. In the same way, I want to accept myself. I want to express who I am and how I want to change. I want to be less self-critical. I want to decrease my demands on myself. I want to learn to take criticism less personally.

As I am a good listener in my relations with others, I want to be as responsive to myself and to accept my abilities and strength as well as my limitations. In that way, I will feel I am good enough without having to perform at a level of 150 percent.

Take time for reflection

People with a high degree of energy and commitment (a resource) risk developing a fixation on immediate results. This often leads to unreflective reactions and responses. Then they may lose contact with the nuances of their own and others' reactions (a limitation):

I need to focus my high energy and commitment on taking myself more seriously. I need to pause, examine my feelings, and then express myself honestly. I should not use the humour and sarcasm that are my usual defences – even when I feel uncomfortable.

I will use my energy and commitment to give myself time for reflection, to listen carefully, and then to express my own feelings and needs. I will practice "being" rather than "doing" even if others are disappointed with my actions.

These seven focus expression categories are generalizations and, as mentioned above, sometimes overlap in the same individual. In our experience, despite the obvious limitations it is still possible to identify the core focus of people's problematic conditions or situations. This core focus identification can be useful for increasing the clients' engagement with their feelings and for examining their motivations in group relationships. Group leaders and group members who succeed in identifying that focus will observe, however, that concerns about privacy, vulnerability, and control soon arise. For this reason, group leaders should *not* begin the first group meeting with a review of each member's core focus. Cohesion and trust must be developed before it is useful to share these foci, including sensitive personal matters related to resources and limitations.

Three stages in FGT

In FGT, group leaders, who are expected to be engaged and active in the group, sit attentively on chair edges (so to speak). This posture contrasts with that of group leaders in other group therapies who lean back in their chairs and are somewhat less directive. FGT is a structured form of therapy. Our experience – consistent with the research on structured work groups (e.g., Wheelan, 2005; Hackman,

2002) – is that the differentiation stage is relatively brief and unproblematic in FGT. In Chapter 8, we described four therapy stages in our adaptation of Mac-Kenzie's (1990) interactive group model. In this chapter, we combine MacKenzie's second and third stages (the differentiation stage and the interpersonal stage) as the "interaction stage". Thus, in this section, we describe the following three stages in FGT: (1) the engagement stage, (2) the interaction stage, and (3) the termination stage.

The engagement stage in FGT

The goal of the engagement stage in FGT is to create a degree of group cohesion that is sufficient to facilitate the transition from a group of unique individuals to a group of individuals united around some shared condition or situation. The transition will occur if group members are comfortable with each other and if the group leader takes a supportive role as instructor and facilitator.

In the engagement stage (sessions 1–4), the group members become acquainted and observe how the group will function. As the members begin to talk about themselves, they soon realize they have something in common as indicated by the group focus. A sense of community begins to develop along with the hope that the group therapy will prove valuable. The group leader's leadership style is influential in this development. It is essential to understand and agree on the significance of the boundaries. The group leader's main task in this period is to support the development of group trust and cohesion that are essential for productive therapeutic treatment.

For much of the engagement stage, the group climate (i.e., shared mood) is one of insecurity and uncertainty. This mood is a sign that group members' attachment problems are activated when they start creating relationships with each other, with the group leader, and with the group as a whole. The group leader works to quell these concerns by guaranteeing the group security (i.e., privacy and confidentiality) in various ways, such as linking members' stories to other members' stories. The group leader may suggest that the members introduce themselves, and provide examples of how to respond, such as actively asking for reactions, thoughts, and feelings, etc.

The first session

When the group members first meet as a group, they have already met individually with the group leader in the preparatory interviews. The group leader has a good grasp of their conditions or situations and of their expectations from FGT. However, no member has met any other member. The joint journey is about to begin.

At the first meeting, the group leader should welcome the group members, ask them to introduce themselves, briefly review the group's purpose and goals, and describe the members' commonality (i.e., the reason they are members in this particular group). The group leader should review the various group guidelines and rules and the responsibilities of group members. The group leader may also describe the leadership role in the group.

The group leader should review the group focus by reading it aloud and by recalling that it was discussed in the preparatory interviews as an expression of the group's purpose and possibilities. The group leader should re-emphasize the importance of the group focus. It is also advisable in this presentation that the group leader informs members of the importance of their participation in the group conversations even though it may require them to break certain social norms (e.g., speaking openly about private thoughts and emotions). The group leader should stress that the purpose of group conversations is to share and empathize with each other.

Throughout the engagement stage, the group leader encourages discussion and often asks group members for their opinions and ideas. For example, the group leader might ask at the first meeting: "Do you have any ideas about the kind of ground rules you would prefer for the group?" In response, members usually offer practical suggestions. For example, they might suggest cell phones be turned off and that food and drinks not be allowed in the meetings. Then the group leader should stress the importance of group openness, sincerity, and spontaneity. Members should feel free "to think out loud" in the group. In this way, the group leader confirms the contract with the group as a whole.

With such actions, the sessions in the engagement stage establish a structure that is conducive to group members' sharing of reflections and emotions. As the first session concludes, the group leader may ask members to talk about their reactions to the group's conversations. Usually members react positively. They may feel relieved that they have been able to talk openly about their difficulties and to learn that others have similar problems. Often, the first session ends on a hopeful note as members feel that they might get help with their difficulties.

The interaction stage in FGT

The goal of the interaction stage at the group level is to create the conditions required for successful therapeutic treatment. On the individual level, the goal is to create interpersonal learning and to describe affective experiences, which can lead to new ways of being with others.

In the interaction stage (the number of meetings can vary, but can be as many as 12), the individual focus is emphasized. When the group leader is convinced that sufficient trust and acceptance have been established, group members are given a memorandum of their individual focus agreed to in the preparatory interviews. The group leader asks the members to read their focus to the group. As they listen, the members recognize these descriptions of their individual focus. This procedure generally leads to a spirited conversation in which members offer comments and reflections on each focus. The members are engaged, thoughtful, and committed.

The interaction stage (as noted above, a combination of a brief differentiation stage and the interpersonal stage) begins after group cohesion has been established in the engagement stage. This is typically in session 5 but may be one session earlier or one or two sessions later. This is a group leader decision. The interaction stage continues until the termination stage begins (sessions 16–17). The interaction stage is the stage in which the group's conversations turn to action as group members exchange experiences, share emotions, and respond to each other. Mostly the therapy is based on the members' spontaneous communication among themselves. Sometimes, when the group leader is engaged with one member, the others become observers. After this dialogue, the group leader can turn to the members and ask for their comments. Throughout, members are expected to work conscientiously to communicate in an emotionally meaningful way.

The group leader in this stage is responsible for supporting the group climate that provides assurance that group members will benefit from:

- Group cohesion and security that allow members to express emotions and thoughts they would hesitate to express in other settings.
- A here-and-now group focus that encourages self-reflection on present emotions.
- Acceptance of members' differences.
- Exploration of alternative ways of coping with conflict.
- Respectful exploration and support of members' personal experiences in the group, including personal styles, emotional defences, and reactions.
- Exploration of new and more rewarding ways of relating to others.

The best learning situations occur when the group members experiment with new ways of being in their relationships with other members. When members have managed a difficult situation, they receive positive reinforcement from the others. In this way, members share their success with other members. They also begin to understand that their behavioural change is generalizable to situations outside the group. In other contexts, this process is usually described as "action learning" or "learning by doing".

The termination stage in FGT

The goal of the termination stage in FGT is to summarize the group members' learning. Termination in FGT, as separation is in most important human events, is a purposeful experience. To be effective, the group leader and the group members must maintain the group commitment and climate created in the previous stages. The group leader reviews the positive results related to each member's therapeutic focus as well as the negative results when certain ambitions were not achieved. In this review, the group leader takes a forward-looking approach even when addressing possible separation anxiety in some group members.

Separation is not a discussion topic that should be avoided until the last meeting. Group members often ask questions about the end of the FGT throughout the entire process. For some members, the impending group separation may cause them to begin distancing themselves from the group rather early in the scheduled meetings. For other members, the impending group separation is a cause for alarm. Because of the strong attachments they have formed with their group leader and the other group members, they worry about loneliness after the separation. They do not want the group to end.

At the group level, the termination stage simply ends the group experience. At the individual group member level, the termination stage is in some sense a new beginning. The members take their learning from the group to their lives outside the group setting. If, in rather unusual circumstances, group members do not take the initiative to talk about what termination means to them, the group leader should raise the issue no later than session 15 or 16.

The connections among group members end in the termination stage. As noted, responses to the separation vary among group members. Usually, these responses are most emotional in the next-to-last and last meetings. For example, some members are very relieved; some members are depressed; some members are angry. There may even be members who hope to continue the group experience with the same members in some formal or informal way. Group leaders need to be prepared for this variety of responses so that they can support members through what is, for many, a stressful, painful experience. It can be quite supportive for members if the group leader describes the group termination as the connecting link between "the now" and "the future".

Suggestions for group leader interventions in the termination stage

- *Review the group's development and critical events* – this intervention helps the group leader and the group members recall and share the entire group experience including their most important memories.
- *Summarize the behavioural changes in the group members* – this intervention allows the group to return to each member's focus and to comment on the behavioural changes observed in each other. The intervention also allows the members to explore how the new interpersonal knowledge will be of use in post-group life.
- *Examine group members' feelings about the group termination (in terms of separation and loss)* – this gives group members the opportunity to talk about the end of the group experience. As explained above, group members will have mixed feelings in the termination stage. Typically, not all problems are solved in the group. If this is the case, some members might feel disappointed and sad. On the other hand, they now have a more realistic inner picture of themselves. They may have raised their self-esteem and become more independent.

- *Talk about how group members are ready to take on new challenges* – this intervention allows group members to think about how they will manage without the group given what they have learned about relationships. *What can be transferred to life outside the group?*
- *Give feedback and allow feedback from the group* – this intervention allows the group leader to talk about the importance of the group: what it has meant to be part of this group in its search for answers to questions (some of which may not have been answered). The group leader also invites group members to evaluate the leader's role and contribution.
- *Reflect on the entire group experience* – group leaders and the group members may ask themselves at the end of the termination stage: *What can I take from the group and this experience? What have I learned about myself? What do I want to work on next? Would I do anything differently?*

Summary

FGT is suitable for people with circumscribed psychological problems. These are people who, for example, have mild or moderate symptoms of depression or anxiety. Some of them have difficulty coping with the stress of everyday life even though they were once able to manage life tasks and commitments. They seek group therapy in the expectation and hope that they will regain their self-esteem and restore their sense of competence. They often want to improve their ability to communicate and interact with other people such that their relationships with others will improve. The emphasis in FGT is on the here-and-now emotions rather than on past emotions. Therefore, people in FGT formulate an individual focus for their therapy that they can express in everyday language and which they can work on in the group.

FGT requires 18 meetings. Two meetings a week are held in the first five weeks of treatment. The entire programme lasts three to four months. The group therapist conducts the meetings through three stages (engagement, interaction, and termination). Each stage has specific goals and activities. The ultimate aim of FGT is that the group will help group members, through conversations and interactions about shared emotions and experiences, to change their ways of being with others.

Concluding remarks

Group therapy has a greater potential than is realized. This was the starting point for this book. Our experience is that professionals in health care and social care are hesitant to recommend group therapy and that it is very seldom the client's first choice. We believe that most people have experienced painful feelings in groups, either in their family of origin, at school, or at work. Groups can sometimes be scary and dangerous places. They can generate intense feelings of shame, sometimes scapegoats are created, and bullying can be reinforced. Most people have had a taste of this, either as victims, perpetrators, or observers. It is obviously one of the primary tasks of a group leader to prevent such things from happening in group therapy. However, when somebody is troubled by difficulties in their life it is safer to turn to one person rather than a group of strangers. Group leaders must understand this fact and have a strategy to deal with it. Affects and attachment behaviour play a dominant role in the biology of human beings. This is our point of departure.

When a person suffering from psychological or medical problems seeks help, an attachment behaviour described as care-seeking (McClusky, 2005) is often activated (sometimes described in terms of regression) and is normally met with care-giving behaviours by the helper. This is very human and normal, and creates the desired feeling of being safe and protected. However, it also creates a problem in psychological treatment in that the outcome is a relationship characterized by dependency and inequality. Usually both client and helper are ambivalent to this position. There are some advantages in the position, both in being taken care of and in being the strong and caring part in the relation. In medical treatment such a solution can be acceptable and sometimes even desirable. However, in the long run it hampers the work that must be done by the client in psychological treatment and psychotherapy.

It is an intricate task to find a balance that creates the psychological safety which is needed for the cognitive and emotional work required. The client needs to trust the authority of the helper, and the therapist needs to accept the position of being in authority. In the psychotherapy literature this work is often described in terms of building a therapeutic alliance; i.e., agreeing on goals of the treatment and procedures used and creating a relationship of trust. One might say that such a relationship reflects a mature dependency in which both parties accept that they need each other to be able to use their full potential. Such bonding behaviours between client and therapist have been found in psychotherapy research to be one of the most important therapeutic factors related to the outcome of the treatment. Therapeutic alliance can fluctuate during treatment. Even ruptures in the alliance have an implicit meaning and can be used therapeutically in the treatment. In individual therapy, alliance is normally established quickly after one or two sessions.

Reaching a stage of mature dependency is somewhat more complex in group therapy. As we have described in detail, there are three main steps before the members can feel the degree of safety that is needed to be open with one's feelings and thoughts. It is essential that there is a working alliance with the group leader. This work usually begins during the preparatory interviews. However, that is not enough for the trust needed for interpersonal work. The group members need to develop a sense of belonging to the group, a wish to be part of it and a feeling of being accepted and supported by the other members, i.e. group cohesion. The alliance with the group is not established until there is group cohesion and a joint understanding of the goals of treatment and how to work together to achieve them. This can take three to five sessions.

There is a consensus among group therapists that time-limited group therapy needs a focus to build this alliance with the group, sometimes also including individual foci (see, for example, Lorentzen, 2020). However, based on research on group therapy in general, group development, and how to start and conduct a group, we have taken this principle further.

The essence of focused group therapy

The book culminates in the final chapter on focused group therapy (FGT). There we describe a way of working in groups that is based on current knowledge about the social character of human beings and research on group therapy. As we see it, it provides an understanding of the kind of interpersonal problems, threats to inclusion, and struggle for sense of meaning that many people face today. The main features of FGT are:

1   *The individual focus should represent a deeply personal aspect of the client.*
    As a group leader one must always take the presenting problem seriously. At the same time, the task is to redefine the problem in such a way as to capture the core of the problem and how it is manifested in relations to others. If this is done skilfully it will express some of the client's inner working models and therefore be a personal, and in a sense private, matter that one is not prepared to share with just anyone who happens to be around. When the work with the client during the preparatory interviews has been done carefully and resulted in a focus that reflects an essential relational problem for the client, one can also be sure that it will present itself in the here and now of the group therapy, and therefore be possible to work with in interaction with the other clients.

2   *In FGT, the starting point is what functions well in a person's life, not what is wrong with the patient.*

The reason behind this is that we want the clients to be able to start building relationships with the other members of the group early on in treatment. If they are too much in a state of care-seeking (and regression), exploration and curiosity will be prevented. Problematic behaviours including care-seeking and regression will certainly appear in the therapy, but preferably later, when the climate is safe enough to allow vulnerability and neediness to be expressed.

3   *The focus must build on a strength.*

When a person seeks treatment, it is common to focus on the problem. However, the problem is typically a consequence of something that is in fact a strength. In such cases clients are often recommended to do less of what is experienced as possibly one of the few things he or she is proud of, something that is a basis for a feeling of competence and self-esteem. Diminishing a strength should not be a therapy goal. On the contrary, a goal of therapy is to build on those aspects and focus on obstacles for the client to use his or her competence to solve problems. This approach to focus formulations allows each member of the group to start treatment with a sense of dignity and individuality.

4   *The individual focus cannot be introduced in the group until the alliance to the group is established.*

In time-limited group therapy in general it is common that the individual foci will be presented to the group during the first session as part of the introduction. Due to the private and personal character of a well-formulated focus, we recommend not introducing the foci in FGT until the alliance to the group is established, and when members feel sufficiently safe with one another. This requires another three or four sessions.

5   *In the beginning of the group therapy twice-weekly sessions are recommended.*

It is hard work for members of a new group to get to know each other. Such a simple thing as remembering the names can be difficult, not to mention the different stories told. It is our experience that a week is too long an interval between the first sessions. For the members to be able to internalize the group, we recommend twice-weekly sessions during the first four to five weeks. This will speed up the process and facilitate the development of group cohesion and a climate of psychological safety.

Learning to be a group leader

For somebody who has worked mainly with one person at a time in treatment, it is a challenge to develop the skills needed to work with group therapy. The reward, however, is great. Working with individuals in group therapy is varied, stimulating, and can be less tiring. Quite simply, it makes work more fun!

An individual who aspires to be a group leader requires the kind of formal theoretical knowledge that this book highlights. However, theoretical knowledge alone is not enough.

People who want to be group leaders would do well to begin their journey as a member of a therapy group. They will learn a great deal about groups when they "step into the shoes" of a group member.

Recommendations for new group leaders

- Take advantage of the guidance an experienced colleague can provide, or speak with a knowledgeable person (perhaps a supervisor or mentor) before and after each group meeting. Reflection and evaluation are essential for good leadership.
- Co-lead with someone with experience in group leadership. Leading a cognitive behavioural therapy group or some other structured and manual-based-method group might be a good start. Obviously, you must have a good understanding of such methods before you can use them in the group setting.
- For relationship-intensive and interaction-focused groups, such as FGT groups, update your training. You need to get acquainted with the theoretical principles and the group management advice before commencing.
- Develop your therapeutic and pedagogic skills by attending workshops and conferences. Group therapy conferences differ from many traditional conferences in that they provide self-experience groups. Therapeutic associations worldwide organize such conferences. Lectures and seminars also provide theoretical knowledge and practical examples.

Group therapy networks

Many countries have group therapy networks. Two international organizations are the International Association for Group Psychotherapy and Group Processes (IAGP; www.iagp.com/), and the Group Analytic Society (International) (http://groupanalyticsociety.co.uk/). Both groups sponsor conferences every third year.

The American Group Psychotherapy Association (AGPA; www.agpa.org) holds an annual conference that focuses on training in group methods. The Systems-Centered Training & Research Institute (www.systemscentered.com/) offers seminars, workshops, and conferences in various parts of the world.

References

Agazarian, Y.M. (2006). *Systems-centered practice: Selected papers on group psychotherapy*. London: Karnac Books.

Agazarian, Y.M. (2010). *Systems-centered theory and practice: The contribution of Yvonne Agazarian* (Edited by SCTRI.) Livermore, CA: WingSpan Press. Reprint (2011). London, UK: Karnac Books.

Agazarian, Y., Gantt, S. & Carter, F. (2020). *Systems-Centered Theory, Therapy and Training: An Illustrated Guide for Applying a Theory of Living Human Systems*. London: Taylor and Francis.

Ahlin, G. (1996). *Exploring psychotherapy group cultures: Essays on group theory and the development of the Matrix Representation Grid. An observation method for studying therapeutic group processes*. Doctoral dissertation. Stockholm: Karolinska Institutet.

Ahlin, G., Sandahl, C., Herlitz, K. & Brimberg, I. (1996). Developing the Matrix Representation Grid (MRG): A method for observing group processes. Findings from time limited group psychotherapy for alcohol dependent patients. *Group*, 20(2), 145–173.

Allen, J.G., Fonagy, P. & Bateman, A.W. (2008). *Mentalizing in clinical practice*. Washington, DC: American Psychiatric Publishing.

Arn, I., Theorell, T., Uvnäs-Moberg, K. & Jonsson, C.O. (1989). Psychodrama group therapy for patients with functional gastrointestinal disorders–a controlled long-term follow-up study. *Psychother Psychosom*, 51(3), 113–119.

Arnold, J. red (2010). *Work psychology: Understanding human behaviour in the workplace* (5th ed.). Upper Saddle River, NJ: Pearson Education/Prentice Hall.

Asch, S.E. (1956). Studies of independence and conformity: A minority of one against a unanimous majority. *Psychological Monographs*, 70(9), 1–70.

Bakali, J.V., Wilberg, T., Hagtvet, K.A. & Lorentzen, S. (2010). Sources accounting for alliance and cohesion at three stages in group psychotherapy: Variance component analyses. *Group Dynamics: Theory, Research, and Practice*, 14(4), 368–383.

Bandura, A. (1977). *Social learning theory*. New York: General Learning Press.

Barwick, N. & Weegmann, M. (2017). *Group Therapy. A group analytic approach*. London: Routledge.

Basch, M.F. (1995). *Doing brief psychotherapy*. New York: Basic Books.

Bateman, A. & Fonagy, P. (2009). Randomized controlled trial of outpatient mentalization-based treatment versus structured clinical management for borderline personality disorders. *American Journal of Psychiatry*, 166, 1355–1364.

Battle, M. (2009). *Reconciliation: The Ubuntu theology of Desmond tutu*. New York: Seabury Books.

Benjamin, B., Yeager, A. & Simon, A. (2012). *Conversation transformation.* New York: McGraw-Hill.

Berg Nesset, M., Lara-Cabrera, M.L., Dalsbö, T.K., Pedersen, S.A., Björngaard, J.H. & Palmstierna, T. (2019). Cognitive behavioural group therapy for male perpetrators of intimate partner violence: A systematic review. *BMC Psychiatry.* doi:10.1186/s12888-019-2010-1

Bieling, P.J., McCabe, R.E. & Antony, M. (2006). *Cognitive-behavioral therapy in groups.* New York: The Guilford Press.

Bion, W.R. (1961). *Experiences in groups.* London: Tavistock.

Bowlby, J. (1988). *A secure base: Clinical applications of attachment theory.* London: Routledge, Swedish edition: *En trygg bas i kliniska tillämpningar av anknytningsteorin.* Stockholm: Natur & Kultur, 2010.

Bowlby, J. (1999/1969). *Attachment: Attachment and loss* (vol. 1, 2nd ed.). New York: Basic Books.

Bråten, S. (ed.) (1998). *Intersubjective communication and emotion in early ontogeny.* Cambridge: Cambridge University Press.

Bråten, S. (ed.) (2007). *On being moved: From mirror neurons to empathy.* Amsterdam: John Benjamins Publishing Company.

Bridges, K.M.B. (1932). Emotional development in early infancy. *Child Development,* 3(4), 324ff.

Brown, N. (2018).*Psychoeducational groups: Process and practice* (4th ed.). New York: Routledge.

Burlingame, G.M., Fuhriman, A. & Mosier, J. (2003). The differential effectiveness of group psychotherapy: A meta- analytic perspective. *Group Dynamics: Theory, Research, and Practice,* 7(1), 3–12.

Burlingame, G.M., MacKenzie, K.R. & Strauss, B. (2004). Small-group treatment: Evidence for effectiveness and mechanisms of change. In M.J. Lambert (ed.), *Bergin and Garfield's handbook of psychotherapy and behavior change* (pp. 647–696). New York: John Wiley & Sons.

Burlingame, G.M., Strauss, B. & Joyce, A.S. (2013). Change mechanisms and effectiveness of small group treatment. In M.J. Lambert (ed.), *Bergin and Garfield's handbook of psychotherapy and behavior change* (pp. 640–689). New York: John Wiley & Sons.

Cambell, A. (2009). Oxytocin and social human behavior. *Personality and Social Psychological Review,* 14(3), 281–95.

Conyne, R.K. (ed.) (2011). *The Oxford handbook of group counselling.* Oxford: Oxford University Press.

Delafield-Butt, J. & Trevarthen, C. (2013). Theories of the development of human communication. In P. Cobley & P.J. Schulz (eds.), *Theories and models of communication: Handbooks of communication science* (pp. 199–222). Berlin: De Gruyter Mouton.

Erickson, R.C. (1987). The question of causalities in inpatient small group psychotherapy. *Small Group Behavior,* 18, 443–458.

Fiamenghi, G.A. (1997). *Intersubjectivity in infant–infant interaction: Imitation as a way of making contact: Research and clinical center for child development.* Annual Report. Hokkaido: Faculty of Education, Hokkaido University.

Fonagy, P., Jurist, E. & Gyorgy, G. (ed.) (2005). *Affect regulation, mentalization, and the development of the self.* London: Other Press.

Fonagy, P., Steel, H. & Steel, M. (1991). Maternal representations of attachment during pregnancy predict the organization of infant–mother attachment at one year of age. *Child Development,* 62, 891–905.

Foulkes, S.H. (1983). *Introduction to group-analytic psychotherapy: Studies in the social integration of individuals and groups*. London: Karnac.

Foulkes, S.H. (1984). *Therapeutic group analysis*. London: Karnac.

Foulkes, S.H. & Anthony, E.J. (1957/2014). *Group psychotherapy: The psycho-analytic approach*. London: Karnac.

Fraiberg, S., Adelson, E. & Shapiro, V. (1975). Ghosts in the nursery: Psychoanalytic approach to the problem of impaired infant–mother relationships. *Journal of the American Academy of Child Psychiatry*, 14, 387–421.

Fuhriman, A. & Burlingame, G.M. (ed.) (1994). *Handbook of group psychotherapy: An empirical and clinical synthesis*. New York: John Wiley & Sons.

Gantt, S.P. & Agazarian, Y.M. (2010). Developing the group mind through functional subgrouping: Linking Systems-Centered Training (SCT) and interpersonal neurobiology. *International Journal of Group Psychotherapy*, 60, 515–544. doi:10.1521/ijgp.2010.60.4.515

Goffman, E. (1959). *The presentation of self in everyday life*. New York: Doubleday.

Hackman, J.R. (2002*), Leading Teams: Setting the Stage for Great Performances*. Boston, MA: Harvard Business School Press.

Horowitz, L.M., Rosenberg, S.E., Baer, B.A., Ureño, G. & Villaseñor, V.S. (1988). Inventory of interpersonal problems: Psychometric properties and clinical applications. *Journal of Consulting and Clinical Psychology*, 56(6), 885–892.

Kadden, R.M., Cooney, N.L., Getter, H. & Litt, M.D. (1989). Matching alcoholics to coping skills or interactional therapies: Post treatment results. *Journal of Consulting and Clinical Psychology*, 57, 698–704.

Kennard, D., Roberts, J. & Winther, D.A. (1993). *A work book of group-analytic interventions*. London: Routledge.

Keysers, C. (2012). *The empathic brain: How the discovery of mirror neurons changes our understanding of human nature*. London: The Social Brain Press.

Kipper, D.A. & Ritchie, T.D. (2003). The effectiveness of psychodramtic techniques: A meta-analysis. *Group Dynamics: Theory, Research and Practice*, 7(1), 13–25.

Knauss, W. (2005). Group psychotherapy. In G.O. Gabbard, J.S. Beck & J. Holmes (eds.), *Oxford textbook of psychotherapy* (p. 3543). Oxford: Oxford University Press.

Kolb, D.A. (2015). *Experiential learning. Experience as the source of learning and development*. New Jersey: Pearson.

Korda, L.J. & Pancrazio, J.J. (1989). Limiting negative outcome in group practice. *The Journal for Specialists in Group Work*, 14, 112–120.

Laland, K., Wilkins, C. & Clayton, N. (2016). The evolution of dance. *Current Biology*, 26(1), R5–R9. doi:10.1016/j.cub.2015.11.031

Lambert, M.J. & Bergin, A.E. (1994). The effectiveness of psychotherapy. In S.L. Garfield & A.E. Bergin (eds.), *Handbook of psychotherapy and behavior change* (pp. 143–189). New York: John Wiley & Sons.

Leman, P., Bremner, A., Parke, R.D. & Guavain, M. (2019). *Developmental psychology*. New York: Mc Graw Hill Education.

Lewin, K. (1935). *A dynamic theory of personality*. New York: McGraw-Hill.

Lewin, K. (1936). *Principles of topological psychology*. New York: McGraw-Hill.

Lewin, K. (1948). *Resolving social conflicts: Selected papers on group dynamics*. G.W. Lewin (ed.). New York: Harper & Row.

Lewin, K. (1951). *Field theory in social science: Selected theoretical papers* (Edited by D. Cartwright). New York: Harper & Row.

Lindgren, A., Barber, J.P. & Sandahl, C. (2008). Alliance to the group-as-a-whole as predictor of outcome in psychodynamic group therapy. *The International Journal of Group Psychotherapy*, 58, 163–184.

Lo Coco, G., Melchiori, F., Oieni, V., Infurna, R.R., Strauss, B., Schwartze, D., Rosendahl, J. & Gullo, S. (2019). Group treatment for substance use disorder in adults: A systematic review and meta-analysis of RCTs. *Journal of Substance Abuse Treatment*, 99, 104–116. doi:10.1016/j.jsat.2019.01.016

Lorentzen, S. (2013). *Group analytic psychotherapy: Working with affective, anxiety and personality disorders*. London: Routledge.

Lorentzen, S. (2020). Short-term Focused Group-Analytic Psychotherapy (SFGAP): An integrative approach to change based on research. *Group Analysis*, 53, 2. doi:10.1177/0533316420901433

Lorentzen, S., Bögwald, K.-P. & Höglend, P. (2002). Change during and after long-term analytic group psychotherapy. *International Journal of Group Psychotherapy*, 61(3), 367–395.

Lorentzen, S., Ruud, T., Fjeldstad, A. & Høglend, P.A. (2015a). Comparing short- and long-term group therapy: Seven-year follow-up of a randomized clinical trial. *Psychotherapy and Psychosomatics*, 84(5), 320–321. doi:10.1159/000381751

Lorentzen, S., Ruud, T., Fjeldstad, A. & Höglend, P. (2013). Comparison of short- and long-term dynamic group psychotherapy: Randomised clinical trial. *British Journal of Psychiatry*, 203, 280–287.

Lorentzen, S., Ruud, T., Fjeldstad, A. & Höglend, P. (2015b). Personality disorder moderates outcome in short- and long-term group analytic psychotherapy: A randomized clinical trial. *British Journal of Clinical Psychology*, 54, 129–146.

Lyons-Ruth, K. & Jacobvitz, D. (2008). Attachment disorganization: Genetic factors, parenting contexts, and developmental transformation from infancy to adulthood. In J. Cassidy & P.R. Shaver (eds.), *Handbook of attachment: Theory, research, and clinical applications* (2nd ed., pp. 666–697). New York: The Guilford Press.

MacKenzie, K.R. (1990). *Introduction to time limited group psychotherapy*. Washington, DC: American Psychiatric Press.

MacKenzie, K.R. (1997). *Time-managed group psychotherapy: Effective clinical applications*. Washington, DC: American Psychiatric Press.

Mahoney, A., Karatzias, T. & Hutton, P. (2019). A systematic review and meta-analysis of group treatments for adults with symptoms associated with complex post-traumatic stress disorder. *Journal of Affective Disorders*, 243, 305–321. doi:10.1016/j.jad.2018.09.059

Main, M., Hesse, E. & Kaplan, N. (2005). Predictability of Attachment Behavior and Representational Processes at 1, 6, and 19 Years of Age: The Berkeley Longitudinal Study In K.E. Grossmann, K. Grossmann & E. Waters (eds.), *Attachment from infancy to adulthood: The major longitudinal studies* (pp. 245–304). Guilford Publications.

Main, M., Kaplan, N. & Cassidy, J. (2005). Predictability of attachment behaviour and representational models at 1, 6 and 19 years of age: The Berkeley longitudinal study. In K.E. Grossman & E. Waters (eds.), *Attachment from infancy to adulthood* (pp. 245–304). New York: Guildford Press.

Hollon, S.D., Shaw, B.F. (1979). Group cognitive therapy with depressed patients. In A.T. Beck, A.J. Rush, B.F. Shaw, G. Emery (eds.), *Cognitive therapy of depression: A treatment manual* (p. 326–351). New York: Guilford.

Malmquist Saracino, A. (2011). *Spädbarn vill ha kul med jämnåriga: Uppmärksammar, benämner och använder sig terapeuter av kraften i spädbarnens inbördes interaktion i gruppbaserad psykoterapeutisk relationsbehandling?* Stockholm: Barn- och ungdomspsykiatri, Verksamhetsområde Sydost, Stockholms läns landsting.

Mandela, N.R. (1994). *Long walk to freedom: The autobiography of Nelson Mandela.* London: Little, Brown and Company.

Marziali, E. & Munroe-Blum, H. (1994). *Interpersonal group psychotherapy for borderline personality disorder.* New York: Basic Books.

McClusky, U. (2005). *To be met as a person. The dynamics of attachment in professional encounters.* London: Karnac.

McLaughlin, S.P.B., Barkowski, S., Burlingame, G.M., Strauss, B. & Rosendahl, J. (2019). Group psychotherapy for borderline personality disorder: A meta-analysis of RCTs. *Psychotherapy*, 56(2), 260–273. doi:10.1037/pst0000211

McMain, S.F., Links, P.S., Gnam, W.H., Guimond, T., Cardish, R.J., Korman, L., David, L. & Streiner, D.L. (2009). A randomized trial of dialectical behavior therapy versus general psychiatric management for borderline personality disorder. *American Journal of Psychiatry*, 166, 1365–1374.

McRoberts, C., Burlingame, G.M. & Hoag, M.J. (1998). Comparative efficacy of individual and group psychotherapy: A meta-analytic perspective. *Group Dynamics*, 2(2), 101–117.

Michélsen, E. (2004). *Kamratsamspel på småbarnsavdelningar.* Doktorsavhandling. Stockholm: Pedagogiska institutionen, Stockholms universitet.

Milgram, S. (1975). *Lydnad och auktoritet: Experimentsituationer, resultat och utvärdering.* Stockholm: Wahlström & Widstrand.

Nitsun, M. (1996). *The anti-group: Destructive forces in the group and their creative potential.* London and New York: Routledge.

Norcross, J.C. & Lambert, M.J. (Eds.) (2019). *Psychotherapy relationships that work. Vol 1. Evidence-based therapist contributions* (3rd ed.). New York: Oxford University Press.

Orkibi, H. & Feniger-Schaal, R. (2019). Integrative systematic review of psychodrama psychotherapy research: Trends and methodological implications. *PLoS ONE*, 14(2), e0212575. doi:10.1371/journal. pone.0212575

Parten, M.B. (1932). Social participation among pre-school children. *The Journal of Abnormal and Social Psychology*, 27(3), 243–269.

Pettersson, U. (2019). *Livsberättargrupper. Ett samarbetsprojekt mellan Sveriges stadsmissioner och Linnéuniversitetet. Slutrapport.* 2019-05-09. Kalmar/Växjö: Linnéuniversitetet.

Piper, W.E. (2006). Short-term group therapy for complicated grief. *Direction in Psychiatry*, 26, 69–78.

Piper, W.E. (2008). Underutilization of short-term group therapy: Enigmatic or understandable. *Psychotherapy Research*, 18, 127–138.

Piper, W.E., Debbane, E.G., Bienvenue, J.P. & Garant, J. (1984). A comparative study of four forms of psychotherapy. *Journal of Consultant and Clinical Psychology*, 52, 268–279.

Piper, W.E. & Joyce, A.S. (1996). A consideration of factors influencing the utilization of time-limited, short-term group therapy. *International Journal of Group Psychotherapy*, 46, 311–328.

Piper, W.E., McCallum, M., Joyce, A.S., Rosie, J.S. & Ogrodniczuk, J.S. (2001). Patient personality and time-limited group psychotherapy for complicated grief. *International Journal of Group Psychotherapy*, 51(4), 525–552.

Piper, W.E., Ogrodniczuk, J.S., Lamarche, C., Hilscher, T. & Joyce, A.S. (2005). Level of Alliance, Pattern of Alliance, and Outcome in Short–term Group Therapy. *International Journal of Group Psychotherapy*, 55, (4), 527–550. https://doi.org/10.1521/ijgp.2005.55.4.527

Punter, J. (2009). Not group analysis as we know it: Response to Mohammed Taha, Refaat Mahfouz and Magdy Arafa's "Socio- cultural influences on group therapy leadership styles". *Group Analysis*, 41(4) 42(1), 80–87.

Romanowska, J., Nyberg, A. & Theorell, T. (2018). *Developing leadership and employee health through the arts. Improving leader-employee relationships*. New York: Springer.

Rutan, J.S., Stone, W.N. & Shay, J.J. (2007). *Psychodynamic group psychotherapy* (5th ed.). New York: Guilford Press.

Sandahl, C., Gerge, A. & Herlitz, K. (2004). Does treatment focus on self-efficacy result in better coping? Paradoxical findings from psychodynamic and cognitive behavioural group treatment of moderately alcohol dependent patients. *Psychotherapy Research*, 14(3), 388–397.

Sandahl, C., Herlitz, K., Ahlin, G. & Rönnberg, S. (1998). Time-limited group psychotherapy for moderately alcohol dependent patients: A randomized controlled clinical trial. *Psychotherapy Research*, 8, 361–378.

Sandahl, C. & Lindgren, A. (2006). Integrative focused group psychotherapy. *Journal of Contemporary Psychotherapy*, 36, 113–119.

Sandahl, C., Lindgren, A., Asklin-Westerdahl, C., Björling, M., Nilsson-Ahlin, H., Wennlund, L., Åkerström, U. & Örhammar, A. (2012). *Tidsbegränsad och fokuserad gruppterapi: Manual*. Stockholm: Medical Management Centrum, Karolinska Institutet.

Sandahl, C., Lindgren, A. & Herlitz, K. (2000). Does the group conductor make a difference? Communication patterns in group-analytically and cognitive-behaviourally oriented therapy groups. *Group Analysis*, 33(3), 333–351. doi:10.1177/05333160022077380

Sandahl, C., Lundberg, U., Lindgren, A., Rylander, G., Herlofsson, J., Nygren, Å. & Åsberg, M. (2011). Two forms of group therapy and individual treatment for work-related depression: A one-year follow-up study. *International Journal of Group Psychotherapy*, 61(4), 539–555.

Schlapobersky, J. (2016). *From the couch to the circle. Group-analytic psychotherapy in practice*. London: Routledge.

Schore, A. (2003). *Affect regulation and the repair of the self*. New York: Norton.

Schore, J. & Schore, A. (2008). Modern attachment theory: The central role of affect regulation in development and treatment. *Clinical Social Work Journal*, 36, 9–20.

Selby, J. & Bradley, B. (2003). A paradigm for the study of early social experience. *Human Development*, 46, 197–221.

Shannon, C.E. & Weaver, W. (1949). *The mathematic theory of communication*. Urbana, IL: University of Illinois Press.

Simon, A. & Agazarian, Y.M. (1967). *SAVI: Sequential analysis of verbal interaction*. Philadelphia, PA: Research for Better Schools.

Simon, A. & Agazarian, Y.M. (2000). SAVI – The system for analyzing verbal interaction. In A. Beck & C. Lewis (eds.), *The process of group psychotherapy: Systems for analyzing change* (pp. 357–380). Washington, DC: American Psychological Association.

Sloan Wilson, D. (2015). *Does altruism exist: Culture, genes and the welfare of others*. New York: Yale University Press.

Smith, D.J. (2011). *Young Mandela*. London: Phoenix.

Smith, M.L., Glass, G.V. & Miller, T.L. (1980). *The benefits of psychotherapy*. Baltimore, MD: Johns Hopkins University Press.

Sochting, I. (2014). *Cognitive behavioral group therapy. Challenges and Opportunities*. New York: John Wiley & Sons.

Stern, D.N. (1985). *The interpersonal world of the infant*. New York: Basic Books, Swedish edition: *Spädbarnets interpersonella värld*. Stockholm: Natur & Kultur, 1991.

Stern, D.N. (1995). *The motherhood constellation*. New York: Basic Books.

Strauss, B., Burlingame, G.M. & Bormann, B. (2008). Using the CORE-R battery in group psychotherapy. *Journal of Clinical Psychology*, 64(11), 1225–1237.

Tillitski, L. (1990). A meta-analysis of estimated effect sizes for group versus control treatments. *International Journal of Group Psychotherapy*, 40(2), 215–224.

Trevarthen, C. (2003). *Infant psychology is an evolving culture: Commentary on "Infants in groups: A paradigm for the study of early social experience"*. Edinburgh: Human Development. Department of Psychology, University of Edinburgh.

Trevarthen, C. (2006). *Paper presentation at the WAIMH Conference*, Paris. Primary human intersubjectivity, development of sympathetic action and self conscious appreciation of others' meaning. Supplement to *The Mental Health Journal*, vol. 27, abstract 25.

Trevarthen, C., Kokkinaki, T. & Fiamenghi, G. (1999). What infants' imitations communicate: With mothers, with fathers and with peers. In J. Nadel & G. Butterworth (eds.), *Imitation in infancy* (pp. 127–185). Cambridge: Cambridge University Press.

Tschuschke, V. (1996). Gruppentherapie versus Einzeltherapie – gleich wirksam? *Gruppenpsychotherapie und Gruppendynamik*, 35, 257–274.

Tschuschke, V. & Anbeh, T. (2000). Early treatment effects of long-term out-patient group therapies: Preliminary results. *Group Analysis*, 33, 397–412.

Tschuschke, V., Anbeh, T. & Kiencke, P. (2007). Evaluation of Long-term Analytic Outpatient Group Therapies, *Group Analysis*, 40 (1), 140–159.

Tubert-Oklander, J. & De Tubert, R.H. (2003). *Operative groups: The Latin-American approach to group analysis*. London: Jessica Kingsley Publishers.

Tutu, D. (1999). *No future without forgiveness*. London: Rider Random House.

Uvnäs Moberg, K. (2003). *The Oxytocin factor; Tapping the hormone of calm, love and healing*. New York: Perseus.

Uvnäs Moberg, K. (2005). The psychobiology of emotion: The role of oxytocinergic system. *International Journal of Behavioral Medicine*, 12(2), 59–65.

van Ijzendoorn, M.H. (1995). Adult attachment representations, parental responsiveness and infant attachment: A meta-analysis on the predictive validity of the attachment interview. *Psychological Bulletin*, 117, 387–403.

van Ijzendoorn, M.H., Schuengel, C. & Bakermans-Kranenburg, M.J. (1999). Disorganized attachment in early childhood: Meta-analysis of precursors, concomitants and sequalae. *Development and Psychopathology*, 11, 225–249.

Wampold, B.E. & Imel, Z.E. (2015). *The great psychotherapy debate. The evidence for what makes psychotherapy work* (2nd ed.). New York: Routledge. doi:10.4324/9780203582015

Wheelan, S.A. (2005). *The handbook of group research and practice*. New York: Sage.

Whitaker, D.S. (2001). *Using groups to help people* (2nd ed.). Hove: Brunner & Routledge.

Whitaker, D.S. & Lieberman, M.A. (1964). *Psychotherapy through the group process*. Oxford: Atherton Press.

Widlund, I. (ed.) (1995). *Den analytiska gruppen: Gruppanalys i teori och praktik*. Stockholm: Natur & Kultur.

Yalom, I.D. & Leszcz, M. (2005). *The theory and practice of group psychotherapy* (5th ed.). New York: Basic Books.
Yalom, I.D. & Leszcz, M. (2020). *The theory and practice of group psychotherapy* (6th ed.). New York: Basic Books.
Zimbardo, P. (2007). *The Lucifer effect*. New York: Random House.

Index

chain analysis 60

change: resistance to 115, 138; strategies for 1

children: attachment behaviours 9, 11–12; emotions 39; parent groups 59, 60; social learning 13

climate 21, 29–30, 56; CBT groups 145; commonality 71; differentiation stage 112; engagement stage 101, 103, 109, 173; feedback from group members 81; focused group therapy 163, 175, 180; interpersonal stage 123; interventions 93, 95; leader role 83, 84, 87, 97; negative 79; practical preparations 70; psycho-educational groups 154, 155; safe 51, 53; slow-open groups 139; therapeutic group process 51; of trust 40

closeness 8–9, 14, 113

cognitive behavioural therapy (CBT) 6, 28, 29–31, 51, 110, 141–148, 158, 181

cohesion 9, 18, 29–30, 73; as active therapeutic factor 32, 33; belonging 36; CBT groups 143, 145, 146; commonality 164; differentiation stage 113, 114, 115; engagement stage 99–101, 108, 109, 114, 173; exclusion of leaders 96; focused group therapy 172, 173, 175, 180; interpersonal stage 122; interventions 92; practical preparations 70; psycho-educational groups 152, 153; research 31; slow-open groups 138–139; support 34; termination stage 127; therapeutic alliance 36, 88, 89, 179; therapeutic group process 51

collaboration 34, 65

commonality 71, 77, 106, 164, 166, 173–174

communication 9–10, 16, 21, 38, 42–46, 71; action 35; differentiation stage 114; direct 54; engagement stage 108; focused group therapy 175; interpersonal stage 99, 120; interventions 93, 120; leader's style 104; Matrix Representation Grid 53; noise 44–45; psycho-educational groups 154; therapeutic group process 49–50; traffic light metaphor 43–44

competence 160–161, 168–169, 177, 180

conductor metaphor 4, 51, 84, 97

confidentiality 65, 66, 67–68, 97; engagement stage 109, 173; focused group therapy 163; group boundaries 20; preparatory interviews 76, 77, 102; psycho-educational groups 150, 151; therapeutic alliance 89

conflicts 20, 45, 51, 64; differentiation stage 109–110, 112, 114–115, 119, 121; focused group therapy 175; interventions 94; leader's own 96

conformity 19, 22, 51

confrontation 126

contact outside the group 47, 68, 69; contact with leader 125; ex-group meetings 132; preparatory interviews 76, 77; psycho-educational groups 150

contagion effect 75

contradictions 45

control 56–57, 76, 115, 172

conversational flexibility 126–127

conversational impasses 94

Cooley, Charles Horton 16

cooperation 9, 10, 85–86, 139

costs 2

creativity 168, 169, 170

criticism 106, 110, 112, 116, 117, 126, 146

Cuban missile crisis 19

culture 19

DBT see dialectical behaviour therapy

decision making 51

dependency 54, 178–179

depression 27, 49, 57, 59–60, 71, 148, 160; CBT 141–142; focused group therapy 6–7, 164, 177; psycho-educational groups 150, 151; relationship difficulties 160; termination stage 176

destructive processes 20, 84–85, 93, 113

developmental psychology 13

dialectical behaviour therapy (DBT) 29, 60, 65

dialogue 45–46, 65, 83, 89

differentiation stage 6, 57, 86, 91, 99–100, 109–119, 120, 172–173

direct instructions 96

direct intervention 56

disruptions 79, 84, 85

diversity 72, 79

drop-outs 32, 56, 118–119, 145

drug use 59, 73, 141–142, 164

dual leadership 74–75, 83, 85–87, 118, 157, 181

Durkheim, Émile 16

early departures 77

eating disorders 27, 57, 65; CBT 141–142; focused group therapy 6–7, 164; psycho-educational groups 149

Taylor & Francis Group
an **informa** business

Taylor & Francis eBooks

www.taylorfrancis.com

A single destination for eBooks from Taylor & Francis
with increased functionality and an improved user
experience to meet the needs of our customers.

90,000+ eBooks of award-winning academic content in
Humanities, Social Science, Science, Technology, Engineering,
and Medical written by a global network of editors and authors.

TAYLOR & FRANCIS EBOOKS OFFERS:

A streamlined
experience for
our library
customers

A single point
of discovery
for all of our
eBook content

Improved
search and
discovery of
content at both
book and
chapter level

REQUEST A FREE TRIAL
support@taylorfrancis.com

Routledge
Taylor & Francis Group

CRC CRC Press
Taylor & Francis Group

For Product Safety Concerns and Information please contact our EU
representative GPSR@taylorandfrancis.com
Taylor & Francis Verlag GmbH, Kaufingerstraße 24, 80331 München, Germany

www.ingramcontent.com/pod-product-compliance
Lightning Source LLC
Chambersburg PA
CBHW070326270326
41926CB00017B/3780

* 9 7 8 0 3 6 7 4 3 9 6 8 2 *